I0027798

Intelligently

Emotional

Ray W. Lincoln

Intelligently Emotional

Copyright © 2012 by Ray W. Lincoln
All rights reserved.

No part of this book may be reproduced or transmitted in
any form or by any means, electronic or mechanical,
including photocopying, recording, or by any information
storage and retrieval system, without the written
permission from the author, except for the inclusion of
brief quotations in a review.

International Standard Book Numbers
Hardcover: 978-0-9835718-7-2
Paperback: 978-0-9835718-5-8

Library of Congress Control Number: 2012940203

Printed in the United States of America

Apex Publications
Littleton, CO, USA

Dedication

*To Del Rand, a never-ending source of emotional stability
and intelligence to many.*

Contents

Preface

I have heard it so often, "Why don't you write it down for me?" So I have. Struggling with our emotions is a challenge, and this book is my response to all those in my seminars, workshops, and coaching/counseling sessions over the years who wanted a better understanding of their emotions and how to manage them and put them to good use. The lessons were, of course, learned by teacher and student alike.

We are often seemingly at the mercy of feelings that plunge us quickly into negativity. How can we control these runaway, impulsive invaders of the mind? Can we be taught to use emotions positively? The urgency for a book that seeks to help us according to our own temperament (not someone else's) to manage and develop our emotions also led me to attempt this needed goal.

The coaching or counseling room can be where people reveal their most perplexing problems. It is a place where angst, hurt, anger, and all the emotions can express themselves unhindered by conventionality, embarrassment or judgment. "How do I control my emotions?" was for most an agonizing plea. These strange urges we call emotions sometimes turn on at will and are a challenge to almost everyone.

Less common but also vented was the question "Can I learn to use my emotions for better things?" Relationships were being torn apart by emotions, but emotions were also lifting people who were finding the secrets to managing them and who felt, some for the first time, what it was like to be on a natural exhilarating high. It's our emotions we must control.

The familiar instructions my clients expected to hear and that had failed so often — the ones that said, "stuff it," "hold the feeling in," "use your willpower," "you'll just have to try harder," or "breathe." They wanted more. "Tell me something that works" was their plea. Give me understanding and tools to use beyond those familiar instructions that admittedly worked for some but failed for so many others.

So, combining the knowledge of temperament with the findings of research into the field of emotional behavior, plus listening to the invaluable wisdom of the ages, offered knowledge and an answer that they found made sense. It was also successful. The real test always is: does it work?

The wisdom of the ages that I mentioned is preserved in philosophies, ethical systems and, not least, in religions. Some "wisdom" turns out to be less than wise and not to be loved as the Greek word *sophia* suggests it should be. You will have your beliefs, but an open-minded person will seek to find the best jewels of wisdom wherever they appear, even if they surface in what is to them an unpopular source. Some of those great sources, popular or not, will be cited and used when appropriate to the subject of emotion.

With children to raise and teach, parents and teachers also wanted some help to develop the strengths of their children and understand how to respond effectively to tantrums and moods along with all the other problematic emotions. Children, because of their struggle to develop quickly and discover their world, pose a special urgency in understanding their emotions and finding successful ways to manage them.

Because temperament brings an understanding of ourselves, it is a key to finding motivation and using emotions intelligently. So, by using innerkinetics (my term for the inner powers and drives that form our temperament) we can gain invaluable help to meet the needs of all who want to be intelligently emotional. There is no one way for every person to manage and develop emotions. People are best helped by applying methods that are consistent with the urges of their temperament.

I am indebted to many authors who have gone before me in the fields of temperament, emotion, and ethical studies. David Keirsey and his studious contributions to temperament psychology, Stephen Montgomery and his literary masterpieces on the same subject, along with Linda Berens and many others who have added so insightfully to the field of human understanding, are some. Many philosophers have also been my sources, with special mention of Robert Solomon. Daniel Goleman and his masterpiece, *Emotional Intelligence*, has not been overlooked, and Sacred texts have featured as well.

My respect and thanks to my editor, Dr. Marian Bland, whose knowledge of literature and vibrant personality have been a great help, and to the many I have had the privilege of coaching and who have struggled with me through the vagaries of emotional trauma. I could not forget my wife who has labored skillfully, lovingly, and tirelessly over the manuscript ,often adding her insights. I owe to her more than I can explain.

My hope is that this book will lead you, as its content has led many others, to be intelligently emotional. If it helps you to develop the intelligent use of your emotions and a rewarding lifestyle, my labor will not have been in vain.

Intelligently Emotional

Introduction

It is with the heart that one sees rightly; what is essential is invisible to the eye.
~ Antoine De Saint-Exupery, *The Little Prince*

Is This What You Want?

Have your emotions puzzled you, driven you almost to insanity, or at times transported you to the heights of ecstasy? Have you asked, "Why do they both help me and hurt me?" Perhaps you have been ashamed of them at times and proud of them at other times? Do you want to be in charge of these emotions, a good manager and controller of these powerful surges that live and pulse inside of you?

There's more. Do you want your child to grow up to be intelligently emotional, handling their feelings wisely? Of course you do. We all want this for both our children and ourselves. So, how can we harness the power and energy of our emotions and have them lead us to be our best? Emotions are the key to reaching our potential.

In these pages you will come to an intimate knowledge of your emotions (don't be scared), understand why you (or your child) act the way you do, and learn how to manage and maximize the power of your emotions in your life. Wouldn't it be great to know how to make the emotions you love stronger and more intelligent, and learn how to control and manage the pesky ones? You'll also be better able to teach your child and yourself with the tools this book offers.

Emotions and Temperament

How you are designed to think and feel will be part of our journey together and a guiding factor in our understanding of ourselves. Temperament, how we are made on the inside, has been talked about in literature for 2,500 years and because it is such a user-friendly and accurate tool for self-understanding, we will press it into service and let the understanding of it do its magic.

You may want to go to the Appendix, entitled "The Temperament Key," now and determine your temperament before you read any further. Knowing your temperament will make the book understandable and, therefore, much more helpful. You'll need to know what the letters SP, SJ, NT, NF and others signify. It's a quick exercise, so do it now. If you want a more complete understanding of temperament you will find one in my book, *INNERKINETICS*.

This is a very different book on emotional intelligence; it's what I will call being *intelligently emotional*. It's not going to be a book on the operations of the brain or the philosophical formation of a school of thought, although we may discuss these things in brief. Rather, it is a practical tool, an examination of the struggle the temperaments have with emotion and how they can do something about it.

How emotions play their powerful role in our temperament and how temperament helps us understand emotion is what you will find here. All of human history has witnessed the connection between the two, along with the dramatic results of management and mismanagement. Temperament profoundly affects emotional control and even how the emotions are expressed. It guides our understanding and is our greatest tool in becoming intelligently emotional. As a parent, you may be longing to discover why your children act and feel the way they do and what to do about it, but you and your emotions must come first.

Emotion is not to be despised, rather to be appreciated, understood, and directed. Those who are supersensitive are also highly emotional. We call them the NF temperament. If you are one, you will probably recognize the struggle you have with your emotions and their seemingly uncontrollable nature. This book is certainly for you and for those who are training an NF child.

Others who insist on not making their decisions without consult ing their feelings are also prone to emotional trauma and will benefit from the help it offers. Some (the Ts, who are approximately 50 percent of the population) have difficulty being sensitive to the emotions of others. Some of them even prefer to keep their own emotions under lock and key. They can sometimes see little benefit in emotional drives but, as a result, miss the riches of emotion and need to be introduced to its logic — yes, logic; emotions have logic. This book will help the Ts too.

Whatever temperament you are and whether you are a T (one who downplays emotion) or an F (one who lives in emotion's riches), emotions are an issue in your life and an understanding of them will enrich your thinking and your living.

This enriched life is called a life of intelligent emotions. Once we thought of intelligence in terms of IQ only and revered those who had a high score, but now we are beginning to understand the importance of having a high EQ — emotional quotient — as well. We also know that no decision we make is truly devoid of emotional content and, therefore, we must see the sense of paying more attention to our emotions. As we learn more about how we are made, we will find even greater help with living a full and complete life. I will be using an expression, "living in your strengths," as the fullest expression of our potential as humans.

The teenage years are the emotional and social testing ground where maturity in emotional development is won or postponed to be painfully struggled with in adulthood. We have more trouble with our emotions than we do with our analytical thinking, probably because emotions are such slippery, abstract elements that we often don't even identify, let alone grasp, them long enough to direct or manage them. They present a totally different challenge for teenagers than the acquiring of physical skills, and they test teens more severely.

Emotional intelligence or the lack of it fashions our social lives, of course. All relationships could do with an emotional tune-up at times. The help to treating your partner with intelligent and loving emotions lies ahead.

Our Journey

Now let's take a quick tour of the book as it leads us through the amazing world of human emotions and how it will teach us the skills for being intelligently emotional.

The first part of the book begins with the chapter, *My Emotions and Me*, and it will explore the mystery and power of emotions and how they shape our lives. Relationships and how they are affected by emotion, together with an introduction to being intelligently emotional, starts here.

On to chapter two, *What is Emotion"* Here, we'll try to define emotions, which is important if we are going to understand them. Then we discover their real purposes in our lives, how temperament really helps us understand our emotions, and how we can develop and control them with the understanding of our temperament. Among other sundry questions, we will learn how emotions have a habit of mutating.

Did you know your emotional brain operates at ultrasonic speed? The implications of that and how the emotional mind sees reality will open up more questions in chapter three, *The Emotional Mind*, and you will gain deep insight into how you have been designed.

In Part Two and Part Three, the remaining chapters that form the major practical message of the book, you will be taken to the actual steps of how to manage, control, and develop your emotions according to your temperament, producing a lifestyle of intelligent emotional behavior. To do this, we will first examine the emotions that drive each of the eight letters, or energy centers (four of which you will have identified as your *type* in the temperament key). Then the chapter, *How the Four Temperaments See Emotion and Use It*, makes it easy to know what generates our temperament (the two letters are the core of our temperament) giving us a fast, user-friendly way of understanding the infinite mutations of our emotional urges.

Part Three, "Surefire Emotional Intelligence," plunges into the steps to intelligent emotional behavior that we all must master. It's here the practice of controlling our emotions begins in earnest. We will now understand how to manage emotion's slippery urges.

Intelligent emotions do not live in our weaknesses but in our strengths. Twelve easy-to-follow pointers to the intelligent use of our strengths are included. The real, powerful secret to the intelligent emotional lifestyle we all want is then revealed as living in our strengths, while appropriately developing the emotions that power them. The next four chapters take us on a tour of each temperament's strengths and their emotions.

A final chapter, which is a step-by-step guide to being and teaching intelligent emotions, completes the book. This last chapter will hopefully be your practical worksheet for personal improvement and mastery of your emotions.

The appendices offer a temperament key with instructions and a score sheet that will provide a needed tool to determining your temperament. A short summary of each temperament, followed by a list of their strengths, round out the tools for self-discovery. Helpful material in understanding the letters used in this book and the categories for the determination of temperament are in the last appendix.

All you need to know to manage and live with intelligent emotions is at your fingertips. You do not need to read all the book if you don't want to: just the chapters that help you understand emotions and the chapters or parts of chapters that feature your temperament.

Let's begin.

Part 1

1 - My Emotions and Me

Men must live and create. Live to the point of tears.
~ Albert Camus

I don't want to be at the mercy of my emotions. I want to use them, to enjoy them, and to dominate them.
~ Oscar Wilde, *The Picture of Dorian Gray*

Scenery is fine — but human nature is finer.
~ John Keats

To increase your understanding of what this book discusses, please complete the Adult Temperament Key located in the Appendix and score it to determine your temperament. Please follow the instructions carefully in completing the key. Then read the short description of each temperament.

Travel with me through the intriguing land of our emotions to familiarize ourselves with its landscape. Later we will examine more thoroughly its landmarks and hidden details.

Intelligent emotions, the subject of this book, are no more and no less than living in the strengths we are given, while expressing care and consideration for others by our intelligent emotional choices. Emotions power those strengths and we function at our best when we understand ourselves and are aware of how our emotions function.

The Mystery of Emotions

Our limbic system reveals an amazing complexity in the processing of our emotions. Emotions can be convulsive, expressing a volatility that can scare us. We also know our emotions operate mysteriously, without warning at times, and seem to have a will of their own. We live with them and wrestle with them every day but don't really know them. The detailed, though limited, understanding that scientific studies have given us of our emotions is, however, another shot across the bow to remind us of the ability of our emotions to control us. It also reminds us of how we must use them with care and wisely manage their contribution to our lives.

I will use the word "wise" and its derivatives frequently, even though it is not in vogue today. The current street philosophy is "Do your own thing," not "Seek wisdom." The Greeks sought wisdom; the Chinese (think of Confucius) thought wisdom governed life; the Hebrew wisdom literature contains some of the greatest philosophical literature of all time, and Solomon is still the recognized proverbial King of Wisdom. Wisdom comes from the Greek word *sophia*. Read this reminder and see if you don't agree with me that it is still a much needed concept today. It is the opposite of foolish, stupid, and all inappropriate and damaging behavior. Foolish behavior has never benefited our race or advanced such things as science. Therefore, I will define intelligent emotions, in part, as "wise" emotions. Wisdom and emotions are both in the business of making judgments, and the quality of their judgments surely concern those who seek the best in life.

Sitting in front of us, as though only his body was present, sat a male in his late teens, the "cool" advocate of opposition to all those who were, in his mind, stupid enough to work hard — those elite bigots of society, he called them. He had no bank account and choked at the thought. He favored apathy and long days of laziness, promoting a life of ease for which he had to depend on the support of others. A "do-nothingness" and a sour dislike of success under-girded his beliefs and his habits. It was no surprise that he was about to enter a place that matched his lifestyle — a place of free board and lodging.

4

He confessed that his disappointment over the unfortunate turn of events hid a suppressed anger that he did not know how to mange and ate at him constantly.

Unintelligent choices followed him into incarceration, and he came out years later, still devoid of an intelligence that acted in even his own best interests.   The best in life is often most clearly seen against the backdrop of such dismal and unfortunate emotional disasters.

Emotions have fascinated all of us.   Interest in them dates back to the earliest of Greek philosophers and writers such as Homer, followed notably by Socrates, Plato, Aristotle and the Stoics.   No one has been able to write without revealing his own emotions or, for that matter, his temperament.   All religions are replete with their acknowledgement and use of emotion, from the earliest Bible records about life in the Middle East to the Upanishads of Hinduism and the Analects of Confucius.   Philosophers have not avoided the subject either. The interest of Robert C. Solomon, Professor of Business and Philosophy at the University of Texas, in his scholarly book, *The Passions*, testifies to our continued modern philosophic fascination with emotions.

Perhaps, you are among those who wonder at their usefulness or struggle with their power, still trying in the twenty-first century to understand emotions and control them.   Why have we not learned in millenniums of history to master the way we function and act as though we are informed about our emotions' vagaries?   Our children, at least, will soon convince their parents of the need to understand the basics of emotion's mysterious powers.

Emotions are the down-to-earth, "nitty gritty" of life.   They devastate us when not controlled and drain our lives of meaning when not appreciated.   Life without them would be unromantic to say the least. And with them, well, who knows?

As mentioned, neurology has entered the field of emotional understanding and its helpful contributions should be viewed with caution, not worshipped.   Science is an ever-changing, ongoing field of knowledge. At the moment no one theory dominates the understanding of emotions and no scientific data fully explains them. They still stand above explanation, controlled and channeled beneficially by wisdom (there's that word again) alone. Approach them humbly or they will make a fool of you and advertise your immaturity.

Emotions provide a full range of feelings from pleasure to pain. They are involved in ecstasy and depression, dreams and defeat — dashing endlessly, it seems, from one end of the spectrum of life to the other. They vary in nature and constantly change their intensity, rising to a crest and falling away again like the waves of the ocean. Our lives will always be molded by their surges and their temporary absences.

The strongest urges and motivations in our nature derive their potency from emotion. Our temperament's drives, with which we are born and which fashion our lives like nothing else, are not without emotional energy. Neither are our plainest thoughts. When I say of the sunset that it is red or crimson, my simple use of a noun harbors a feeling, an emotion.

Emotions work as a team, giving birth to other emotions, educating and empowering each other. Like can be transformed into love, and love can mate with passion to form another expression of love, while envy and jealousy wait in the wings of love's theater to change the feelings yet again. Their interrelatedness is too complex to document or at times predict; yet emotions come and go with a predictability that belies their complications.

Little Shane was needled by his playmates because he was so nice to everyone. Strange how being nice attracts the vultures. He was a very sensitive, introverted NF. His mother said the transformation, on retrospect, was fast. First, he got angry and lashed out verbally against his foes, quickly becoming the opposite of who he really was. His emotions soon morphed into a team of ugly actions driven by feelings too strong for his seven years to control. Hate and a poisonous revenge took over. He spat, kicked, fought with an emotionally powered ferocity that frightened his peers and resulted in his violently beating one of his critics. Consequences followed, and so did a self-hatred that quickly changed his emotions yet again.

Depressed and de-motivated, he was persuaded in his bewilderment to be who he was: a loving, tender boy who felt good when he accessed those intelligent emotions that his anger had persuaded him to discard. Again, his emotions changed. Change is one of their properties, and with each change they attracted other emotions of like sort. Shane, via his emotions, had emerged as three persons: angry, sad, and happy. Such is the changeableness of human life that emotions mysteriously produce. Yes, they are complex, but without them we would not recognize life.

When seeking to help a child to emotional intelligence, the task may seem overwhelming. However, as profound as emotions are, they often yield to simple measures and reward with unexpected pleasures. Develop the strengths of temperament that they fuel and most of the goals of emotional intelligence will be achieved.

The history of emotions is the history of sex, love, fear, hate, courage, and an unnamed myriad of other feelings. Each emotion can and has stamped its potent effects on our lives and that of our race. As we ponder the mystery of emotions, let's remember that they give us the "good life" and the "bad life," but not without the freedom to choose. They have handles, although ethereal and slippery to grasp, and a logic of cause and effect to follow. Learning these relationships is what this book will help you master.

The Power of Emotions

Out of the heart, the mouth speaks.
~ Luke 6:45

Emotions are not just mysterious; they are the most potent expressions of our mental system. They can literally drive you to drink or transport you to nirvana. One moment you are living in heaven and the next in hell, or so it seems. What gives emotion this astounding power for both good and harm? We will find the answer in our beliefs and in the degree of focus we decide to give those beliefs — two compelling seductive tools hidden in our minds. Have you noticed how adults can cave before the power of their own emotions, and we can only imagine the leverage they exert on children. Thankfully, we can control them, even if they seem to control us most of the time.

Dale Evans Rogers wrote a book called *Angel Unaware* that I read many years ago. It is the story of her handicapped child who lived only a few years but who she saw as their "God-sent angel." Her emotions went through a buzz-saw as a parent, she recalls. However, even though they brought moments of agony and suffering to all the family, she could also see what others could not in the gift of this child. Emotions of thankfulness and love swept in with the grief and she interpreted the experience as a wonderful blessing. It's part of the power of emotions that they can transform experiences and events from devastating to delightful or vice versa with only the believing eyes of the soul.

Humans often speak of this metamorphosis that emotions take us through, from pain to confessed joy in the matter of a second. Perhaps all of us have observed how emotions can put life's sad events into a simple positive perspective or, by contrast, distort positive, neutral events so they destroy both our confidence and hope immediately and with a vengeance.

Emotions can lock us up for life in a prison of fear or free us, even when our faces are pressed hard against the bars of a jail cell. What is the purpose of a power that shapes our realities, surging relentlessly in us and carrying us to the extremes of mental joy or pain? In a word: meaning. In another two words: personal significance — making the cowards brave, creating impossible dreams, shaping the self-images of the down-and-out, forcing the explorer to venture into the jaws of death, making a child stand toe-to-toe with a towering adult while fused in a fearless battle of egos. This is the mighty power we simply call *emotion*. But this is not all emotions are famous for.

Emotions actually power our temperaments, a thing you will hear often in this book because this is life-changing news of which I don't want you to be ignorant. Each strength in our innerkinetics (temperament) is coerced or powered by some form of emotion that endlessly exerts its energy to direct our preferences and, ultimately, our lives. Even when we misuse our emotions by either ignorance or ill-purposed design, they still mold us. We are what we direct our emotions to do.

Misty was imprisoned in her home. Extroverted and empathetic, she was created to be a people-person and, in her case, that meant engaging particularly with adults. Strong emotions fueled her temperament's strengths. Three kids milled around her all day long and she felt guilty that they did not bring her the pleasure she felt they should bring a mother who had the liberty of being a full-time mom. Her friends had chided her with statements like, "You should be happy; any mother would give their right arm to be able to be with their children like you can." Her guilt increased. What was wrong with her, she asked me.

Nothing to feel guilty about, I suggested. The unfulfilled drives of her temperament were not satisfied, and the emotions that she was deprived of by the nonuse of her strengths completely overwhelmed the pleasures that a mother can feel. She needed opportunities to be the adult teacher she was. It all changed for Misty when she realized that the unfulfilled drives of temperament don't lie down peaceably. Only when she acted in accordance with the powerful emotions of her temperament did love for her children return, and happiness then drove out her despair. Everything bows to the power of our temperament's emotions.

That mighty force called "reason" can cower in the face of emotion too. Aristotle was wrong when he said that we are primarily rational creatures. We are not; we are emotional beings. Driven by emotion, people kill each other and engage in blood-drenched war, yet also die for those they don't even know and love the enemy that seeks to destroy them. Logic bows, albeit with reluctance, in abject obedience to emotion's wishes. Common sense succumbs to its governance. What clout!

Mount Everest was conquered by the sheer grit of unrelenting emotions, and we wonder if there is nothing emotion cannot do. Here's another example: To crown its achievements, love (one of emotion's most potent agents) has claimed billions of hearts and motivated them to follow the loving example of Jesus as he sacrificed himself for others. The result was the formation of the world's largest religion. Emotion has done it all.

Let's return our thoughts to what I will call the miracle that can be enacted in each of us. We can control our emotions and use them as we choose, even if they seem to control us most of the time.

Memories Are Strengthened by Emotion

These powerful emotions have purchased their own real estate in our memories as well. My first memories are loaded with emotion. I can remember as a child in New Zealand, when what we called the Japanese scare in World War II had forced the government to seize my father's farm and turn it into an airport in preparation for the defense of the country. I was a toddler, and the memory of the thunderous bulldozers working all night has never left me. My head was on a pillow that shook with the pounding of the giant machines, and the feeling of fear mixed with curiosity is still a very vivid recollection. I still have the vague feeling that I wanted to go out into the dark and watch the monstrous shadows heave and roar as the earth gave way to their might; yet at the same time I wanted to escape to some quiet and safe place.

Why have such memories lasted and remained so vivid? Because they were packed with such strong emotions. Each memory of the ranch where we relocated is also emotionally rich and has lasted in my memory, most of them pleasant but some, like when the neighbor shot our dog, unsettling.

Therefore, the past is influenced by emotion just like the present. Emotions, not just facts, shape our past. In *A Journey Through Fear to Confidence*, I tell how we can rewrite these emotion-packed memories, if need be, changing fear into confidence.

Emotions Shape Our Whole Lives

Even in my childhood, I somehow knew that emotion would be the player in the greatest battles of my life. These struggles with my feelings have made me who I am, giving motivation and direction to my life. That direction inevitably shapes us; it shapes everything about us.

As we have indicated, our temperament's drives, or strengths, only appeal to us and motivate us because of the emotions they contain. One of the NT's drives — logic — will motivate the NT because the emotion that accompanies its use makes them feel, in a sense, superior and in control of their world. However, it may leave an SP in the same circumstances unmoved, because it lacks a compelling, in-the-moment challenge. Logic appeals to the NT as essential simply and only because of the feelings it produces in them. Each temperament dances to its own emotive music.

We have all walked long journeys with emotion. I feel I know some of its subtleties and, although it has tested me more than I would like to remember, in moments of calm refection, I treasure how its intelligent judgments have shaped my life more than anything else.

Have I mastered emotional intelligence? No, I can't say that I have, and because there is still so much to learn, the shaping is not over yet either. Each new adventure into the land of feeling and emotion introduces me to yet another interpretation of its vagaries and schemes, some delightful and some still testing me to make better and wiser choices.

I have listened to many stories and over most of them could be written the title "Emotion Shapes My Life." We could also entitle them "My Choices of Emotion Have Formed My Future." Emotion impacts us, and then we rationalize our response which, if unintelligent, creates a kind of internal Hell.

One promising couple is an example. Falling in love, they peered through their hopes and saw the possibilities of a wonderful match, so they married. Happiness reigned for a while, and then they discovered that they were both sensitive and, even though they didn't want to, they hurt one another with their criticisms of each other's imperfections. Strange how we don't "get it" that a successful marriage is, to a large degree, learning to be happy with an imperfect partner.

After the hurts, they would withdraw within hearing distance and hurl angry words at each other. The anger comforted them in a kind of distorted way. They felt secure behind their defensive accusations and their rationalizations. (As long as we feel we are right, we gain confidence and a sense of moral justification emboldens us.)

Soon their battles created an ugly reality — bitterness and strife bred the inevitable divisiveness. They would find ways to be apart more and more. Sleeping together only amplified the pain, so they chose the solution of separate bedrooms. The sorrow had to be mitigated, so drinking became the norm for both, and then excessive drinking until one night he came home drunk and picked a routine fight, which escalated as usual. They verbally battled, charging time and again into each other's bedroom with another barrage of poisonous words. The wife became fearful and called the police, which led to her claiming the bruise on her leg was inflicted by her husband, and he was dragged off to jail. That began a court battle.

The wife then filed for divorce, which the husband, with equal emotional heat, countered with an attempt to gain custody of their children. A bitter divorce and years of anger and hate only escalated their emotional battle, and joint custody with the manipulation of an emotionally unstable child added to the mess of their lives. Finally, he left for another country, but the baggage he took with him has never let him find relief. His wife now controls him without doing anything as he nurses his bitterness each day.

What a catastrophe. Of course, there were more details than I have told, but the reality remains the same. Emotions shape our lives and the mess can be tragic.

We only have one life, so determine to walk the path making intelligent emotional decisions. In future chapters, we will examine the turns in the road and how they shape us, while learning to use the tools of self-management and personal development.

Emotions — The Speedsters of the Mind

Basic to the understanding of the role of emotion in our lives is its speed. Emotions present themselves to our consciousness at the speed of light and often catch us unaware of their presence before we can fasten our safety belt for the ride. Any NF adult or parent of an NF child can vouch for this.

The development of an emotion is faster, by far, than the processing of reason. Emotion, as we will see in more detail later, warns of danger even before our senses have completely identified the source of danger. Data from within us and from without our body reaches the amygdala (the emotional hot spot of the brain) before it reaches the cortex, which I suggest we may have mistakenly called the higher order of intelligence in the brain. Both the emotional and analytical functions of the brain, in my humble opinion, should be given the title "executive functions" because of their decision-making powers.

The speed of our emotions can prematurely force a decision if we don't learn to slow them down by the use of reason and the process we call thinking. We want to be in control of our emotions and thinking is one way to gain control. How often have you observed someone flare with anger at some remark and spiral out of control? How often have you seen it result in fights and the severance of relationships, all because emotion ruled their minds and was not halted and subjected to reason's examination?

How fast can a person fall in love? We all know the answer to that. Emotions can be lightning fast and catch us off guard so easily that we succumb to their influences, and we think later. Understanding how to catch them in flight and take a mental timeout to think can be our deliverance. Coping skills are helpful but are not the long-term answer. Hidden in the design of our innerkinetics are the answers we are looking for.

For the NF temperament, halting the powerful surge of emotion can call for a struggle that takes time and effort to win. Often, an SJ will criticize the NF for not instantly pulling out of their "funk" or their mood. The NF must process the emotions because they know from repeated experience the value and the wisdom of deep-seated emotions and are wired to proceed only after the emotional issues have been sorted out. The SJ, without using any particular coping skill, is suspicious of emotion, naturally cautious, and not impacted by the emotion or even valuing it to the same degree. Precisely for the above reasons, it is easier to teach an SJ to question their emotions and take time out to think before they commit. One temperament should not criticize the other in whose shoes they have not walked.

Emotional intelligence is not denying your emotions the right to speak, but making them pause and enter a debate with reason, whatever it takes. Trying to eliminate these speedsters of the mind is futile. They will always out-pace the fastest thought. Whatever their task or accomplishment, they do so in a flash so fast our consciousness of them lags behind their development. As a result, a person *feels* depressed only after they *are* depressed, and is elated after the feeling of joy (already present) is perceived.

I have spoken as though emotions are not always right in their judgments, and that is true. We should also keep in mind that sometimes they will prove logic to be wrong. This is another reason to evaluate our emotions with care and not summarily dismiss them.

Relationships With and Without Emotion

As we have found, cognition is not enough in this life. This is especially true in the sensitive world of relationships. Emotional intelligence is not limited to the ability to control our own emotions. It is also the understanding of our world. The challenge to understand the emotions of others and respond to them appropriately and successfully means we will become intelligent in our relationships. Only the knowledgeable use of emotion will achieve this goal.

We need also to develop the positive emotions that drive our strengths so that we can improve our relationships. For example, if you are an NF you will want to develop your love and empathy, which will help you strengthen many beneficial relationships. The emotions that drive your passion may need to be held in check or given their full rein.

Wouldn't you expect that by the end of our teenage years we would have sorted out how to handle our emotions intelligently in our relationships? The coaching room says this is not so. Few adults have learned the intricacies of emotional engagement. In fact, few want to. Ego and selfish goals dominate the desires of most people when it comes to relationships. All they want is to get what they want. That spells disaster. I heard of a marriage that ended in 72 days! For love to be lost and emotional intelligence voided in such a short time is an amazing feat but is, unfortunately, all too well known. For children, maybe, we can understand their ignorance; but for adults, what happened to the learned skill of blending one person's emotional agenda with another? Was understanding and respect of another's needs and personal worth not considered to result in an end to a relationship in 72 days? One wonders at the pervasive lack of emotional skills in our society.

Terri was enamored with her date. Something attracted her and she soon felt she was in love. The vibrations of love were present and she could see herself giving her whole life to make her prince happy. The more time she spent with him, the more she felt a growing commitment to the relationship. Her emotions were alive and, apparently, healthy. Were they intelligent? By that I mean, were they making sound judgments? She was convinced enough to tie the knot. Her emotions would not seem to let her question them without condemning her motives.

Within a few months, the love had faded amidst angry disputes by both of them over their own selfish wants. She allowed her grievances to find a welcome in her mind, and emotions that she never felt before about this relationship began to grow. Did she stop to think about what was going on with her feelings? No. She simply let them direct her life, unexamined. Soon she told her friends of how inconsiderate he was and railed on his failures and faults. That sped the growth of her negative feelings toward her husband and soon she admitted she had lost all love for him. Feeling she had moved on in her mind, he tried to make up and get her back. He wanted the relationship to heal, but she did not feel the motivation any longer. They split in an ugly divorce, and the blood of hurt was spilled everywhere. Can you trace the lack of intelligence in both their actions and non-actions?

All relationships would be non-engagements without emotion, and the lasting quality of the relationship depends on the intelligent use of emotions. What becomes of love and care if emotions are not wisely and considerately handled? What becomes of the motivation to please your spouse without the encouragement of love for each other? If we are going to have good relationships, we need to be emotionally aware of the emotions of others, manage successfully our own, and use all emotions intelligently. Emotion fuels all factors in a relationship. Emotions have to be fed, and not the least, love. One of our most unintelligent actions is to expect positive emotions to last without being nurtured and given the nutrition they need.

Think of the occupations where emotional intelligence is obviously needed, such as receptionists, salespeople, teachers, clergy, counseling, politicians, personal relations, coaching, and all leadership positions. The list never seems to end because most occupations require interaction with people where emotions are always in play. Imagine a doctor with no bedside manner, a salesperson who cannot assess the emotions of their prospect, clergy that are remote and distant, counselors who have no feeling. Interpersonal intelligence demands emotional intelligence.

We need to know what other people are feeling in order to be thoughtful, considerate and successful in our behavior toward them. It is basic emotional intelligence. Emotions can tell, even to those with no intuition, most of what is going on in others. Our world — not just individuals — stumble when we fail to heed the importance of all the emotional interactions that fill our personal encounters. You often hear statements like "It's surely a matter of just doing what is right" or "why should we have to consider their emotions?" Such emotional ignorance is the cause of many of our failures in life. The wise consider the emotions of others; the fools think only with their heads.

Nor is it just the feelings of others that we must consider. It's their inner moods, their hidden desires, their motivations, and their all-important temperament, together with the presence or absence of a host of emotional influences like love, hate, dislike, distrust, reserve, withdrawal — the list that matters is endless. Emotional intelligence is not a matter of a few limp rules of behavior. Such is the teaching you receive in the kindergarten of emotional wisdom. Consider this: intelligent emotions are ones that achieve the needed goals and hold everyone to responsible behavior, while seeking to do so diplomatically.

To discern when others are turned on or off, or when and they are interested or not, or if they are halfway round the world in their thoughts strongly affects all purposeful communications. Without exception, emotions are woven into the fabric of all relationships, and human interactions and cannot be removed

17

without destroying the intricate patterns of human experience and the meaning of life itself. Those who try to understand intelligence in the hard terms of reason and logic alone, repudiating the soft facts of emotion, become ignorant of life's heartbeat.

Admittedly some relationships exist as platonic partnerships, near to emotionless. But even these are guided by emotions of a protective sort. Emotions penetrate all meaningful relationships. Don't try to get rid of your emotions or sideline them when interacting on any level with others. If you choose to disregard the importance of emotions in human interchanges, then concede to the destruction of your relationships.

Emotions Make Us Smart

Without emotions, the smartest among us would be dumb. Surprised? The thought turns all our thinking about our intelligence upside down. Consider: without emotion, the charging tiger might look to us like a soft harmless, oversized house cat. Dangerous places could seem safe. A description of a sunset could sound like intellectual snobbery or the trickery of "word-smithing" and nothing more. Imagine making a choice of a mate without the use of emotion? Emotions must be intelligent and smart because of the way they penetrate our lives and make sense of them. Do those who are traditionally called "smart" possess the high IQs; and are those who seek to eliminate emotion from their thinking more intelligent? Or could they be more intelligent with the use of emotion? The later, of course.

In his eye-opening book, *Emotional Intelligence*, Daniel Goleman addresses the question "Are the smart dumb?" Compiling considerable evidence, he concludes that a person's IQ is a poor indicator of intelligence. Success in life is not a matter of IQ, he argues, but EQ (our emotional quotient). To be the smartest we can be, we must use both reason and emotion and realize the wise use of emotion is the determining factor in success. Emotion is simply a different kind of intelligence, one that sees what reason does not, and one that evaluates all issues from the point of view of the meaning of life.

So it follows, logic without emotion, we might say, discovers only half the world. Logic is limited. It deals with the relationship of thoughts and their accurate usage or the correct use of mathematical units. What does logic know of love or hate, for example? Aren't love and hate some of this world's most potent intelligent realities? Some people have never considered the limitations of reason, nor have they put the two worlds of logic and emotion effectively together. They have not learned to be what we are referring to as emotionally intelligent.

People are different and the way they use emotions intelligently will differ with each of the temperaments. This should be a warning not to generalize and suggest that all people must learn emotional intelligence the same way or with the same set of rules.

For example, the quick-acting SP is driven to respond quickly to the data their senses gather, often before they have time to think about all the factors involved. That speed is their asset.

The cautious SJ temperament, the one Galen called "Melancholic," prefers to treat their emotions with a more somber, cautious concern, questioning their usefulness. Their approach to emotion is more pedantic.

The NTs, on the other hand, feel emotions detract from and destroy the efficiency of their world of analytical thought, which they treasure. This attitude can cause them rarely to be conscious of their own emotions and not favorably disposed to the emotions of others.

Conversely, many NFs living in the brilliant display of their emotional intensity, are often unable to harness their emotional powers or control their explosions. Favoring emotions can, for them, become a dangerous invitation for their emotions to strengthen and dominate.

Both the NT and the NF, for different reasons, may wonder at times at the usefulness of emotion. It's the overuse or uncontrolled use of emotion that has given it its questionable name. Once emotion is seen to be an indispensable part of our thinking, giving meaning and instilling value to all that we think and do, it will take its rightful place in our lives.

All temperaments can be smart and all can be emotionally dumb. Emotional intelligence is not found in one temperament. So how do you teach the temperaments to be emotionally intelligent? Differently, and according to how they see and use their emotions. This is the path to the greatest emotional intelligence.

Introducing Emotion's Intelligence

How can emotions be thought of as irrational when all the meaning we have in life is a result of our emotions? As I will say repeatedly in this book, emotions are facts, and all facts are to be considered and taken into account whenever we interact with or engage our world. Any intelligent exercise that dismisses half of the facts is surely not intelligent.

Clyde was fed up with his wife's emotional outbursts, and she was growing tired of him too. He thought of her as immature and mentally inferior to him because, in his opinion, she couldn't control her emotions. He was indeed intelligent, though not emotionally so, and would make a thoughtless (at best) remark directed at her. She would then go silent while anger and hurt exploded inside her, sometimes hurled at him in a flood of angry words, but more often just bottled up somewhere inside as a nagging ache. From her point of view, why couldn't he control his tongue or at least be motivated by love not condemnation or thoughtlessness toward her. Didn't she mean anything to him? He was unemotional and inconsiderate of her feelings, as she told her closest friends.

On the other hand, he felt she was oversensitive and, yes, he was bearing a grudge for the way she seemed to blame him for things he felt were simply little inescapable errors natural to all humans. The relationship was poisoned by unintelligent emotions on both sides.

This couple needed to learn that:

- The unintelligent emotions both of them displayed were red flags seeking to call their attention to the damage that was being inflicted. Flagging us is an intelligent act on the part of our emotions.

- The wrong emotions, when replaced with intelligent emotions that build intimacy, trust, and love would create a motivation to heal the hurt and make their dreams for a great relationship a real possibility. We need emotion to achieve any dream and, of course, much of it to succeed in our challenging trials. Emotions refuse to be responsible for our responses to them or decisions about them. They insist we are responsible for choosing and backing an emotion, even when we choose the wrong one. Emotions won't make the right choice for us. Choice is the field in which our lives are played.

- Each needed to address his or her own emotions and think of what the logical results would be if the emotions were not changed. Emotions are smart enough to disclaim any responsibilities to change someone else's emotions.

- Each would have to recognize the need to get out of the business of trying to blame the other person. We need big shoulders to carry our own mistakes. Blame leads to grudges that we must also carry on those shoulders, making our load too heavy for happiness.

- Emotional intelligence wants us to react to the other person in terms of his or her needs, not our own. The use of these intelligent emotions not only calms our mind, but positively affects the other person's mind. When we choose an emotion that is considerate of who the other person is, it influences them to change their attitude towards us... "A soft answer turns away wrath." We can change others, but an unintelligent emotion won't do the trick.

The path to self-correction is never easy when it involves our emotions and usually needs help in understanding what to do and how to do it. Clyde and his wife got help and gained respect for each other as they sympathetically watched each other struggle with choosing intelligent feelings.

Emotion drives everything. The most fact-driven, calm, logical scientist or cold, aloof professor must acknowledge the presence of feelings which drive their professional pride, marital relationships, and their convictions, or they must settle for displaying a debilitating ignorance. In all these personal and professional experiences, emotion shows a penetrating, smart intelligence, offering both helpful and unhelpful feelings from which we make our personal and professional images.

This intelligence is, in part, the wisdom of first impressions. With a speed we will examine later, our emotions see, sense, and react to their first readings of a circumstance for good reason. Our safety, respect for our values and preferences, and the protection of our beliefs drive our feelings into the role of protective agents. First impressions may not always be accurate, but neither are the calculated conclusions of logic. Thank God that first impressions can contain great wisdom. When faced with that proverbial tiger, we are grateful.

The self-understanding that we are preeminently emotional beings is another intelligent conclusion of our emotions. Awareness precedes decisions and life is all about making the right choices. Therefore, it follows that emotions play an intelligent role in preparing us for our choices. Perhaps it will help us to realize that the emotional facts of life are not half of life's facts but the majority of what makes up our intelligent consciousness and our existential world.

Another example of emotion's intelligence is the discernment that all of our decisions are somehow infused with the emotions of our personal history. We are who we have emotionally become and all our decisions reflect this. Unraveling our emotions from who we are would be impossible and, if possible, destructive. We would become another individual and lose all of our "color."

Every sports coach knows that motivation is the key to success, and motivation is best achieved with the skillful use of emotions — emotions that operate with a positive purpose. Are we ever motivated in sports if we have no feelings? The pep talk before and during the game has claimed its rightful place as necessary, stirring the all-important emotions. When we are in love, don't we reasonably attribute our motivation to our feelings? Desire itself is another form of intelligent emotional motivation. Feelings purposefully move us, indicating that they are intelligent.

Do you remember the saying "We are a bundle of nerves?" Our nerves relay messages from their terminals to the brain as they react to stimuli and, as a result, set off an emotional response. It is not a false understanding that, when our emotions are on edge, we also say our nerves are on edge. The two are connected in the same way that cause and effect are related. A "nervous breakdown" is an emotional experience: nerves and emotions acting in response to stresses. When we feel nervous, we set off emotions that judge the information the nerves are reading. In what seems like an automatic experience, intelligence is present. We are wired so that our emotions warn us of extremes and dangers, pleasures and possibilities, whether physical or nonphysical, all with the help of an amazing communication system: our nervous system.

Social intelligence is also emotional intelligence. All our observations of how emotion is part of the structure of personal relationships should convince us of this. Mr Spock (of Star Trek fame) finds relationships difficult, to say the least, precisely because he lacks an understanding of the importance of emotion because he is governed by pure logic and misses the part emotion plays in every moment of our human existence.

Emotions add a richness or color to our thinking and imagination. This contribution adds meaning to life. We do not live our lives or process things mentally in colorless images. Emotion projects everything in rich color. Emotion also reads the temperature of our words and our thoughts, adding emotional elements to all our communications with ourselves and with others. Should we choose to ignore this emotional dimension and all it can tell us, we would become unintelligent. Hopefully, gone is the day of equating reason and logic with intelligence and emotion with unintelligence. Welcome the new day where reason and logic take their place as equals alongside of emotion's brilliant intelligence.

Are you by now convinced that emotions are intelligent, not least because they help us know ourselves and become aware of the quality and shape of what we are doing and becoming?

What Will Emotional Intelligence Do for Me?

The Stoics thought that *apatheia* (apathy or the absence of feeling to the Stoics) was the aim of all goodness and, therefore, we must constantly struggle to rid ourselves of all feeling and emotion. Emotion was the cause of all sin and failure. Without emotion we are true and better creatures, or so they thought. Incidentally, some parents of emotionally sensitive children might agree passionately, and some readers may harbor that belief even today. The Stoics failed to understand that an emotional void is an unbearable hole in the heart.

Emotional intelligence will not make me into a non-feeler, but into a more sensitive, responsive person. It will offer me:

- Control of my emotions
- Enjoyment of my emotions
- The freedom to use emotional power wisely
- Better relationships
- Insightful, sensitive, and purpose-driven leadership
- The advantage of emotionally sensitive decision-making
- A meaningful view of my world
- A better understanding of others

- Maximization of my temperament's drives
- An inner comfort and heightened confidence
- And more, much more

Emotional Intelligence in My Child

It's a parent's prayer. "Tell me how to teach my child emotional intelligence," a wise parent asks. So what will the understanding of emotions in this book teach a parent so they can better train their child?

First, that a child must learn to recognize and become aware of his emotions and the impact they are having on his world. Understanding of ourselves is the first step to managing ourselves.

Second, emotional intelligence is a long process, never complete. There are no shortcuts. Emotional intelligence will be the hardest lesson in life for any of us to learn. However, we will learn the ways we can manage and develop our emotions and we'll be able to note the improvement.

Third, teaching emotional intelligence to a child is the same as for an adult, except for dealing with a brain that is in the process of development, which flags the need for more incremental learning and patient teaching.

Fourth, understanding the child's temperament and teaching emotional control with an understanding of that temperament's drives is the road to faster learning. We will have a hard or impossible task if we neglect understanding temperament — very frustrating too.

Fifth, focusing on developing the strengths of the child's temperament and teaching them to do the same will rob the unintelligent behaviors of their energy and give the parent the most effective path to teaching emotional intelligence.

Sixth, modeling the learning of emotional intelligence for them. and showing them what to do when we fail or when we are mentally under the influence of damaging emotions cannot be overemphasized. Children want models.

Now, from my emotions and me to a more technical question that will hold some important answers. What is Emotion?

2 - What Is Emotion?

An emotion is a transformation of the world.
~ Jean Paul Sartre

*What everyone forgets is that passion is not merely a
heightened sensual fusion but a way of life which produces, as
in the mystics, an ecstatic awareness of the whole of life.*
~ Anais Nin, *Diary*, Vol. 5

I don't think anyone has defined emotion to our satisfaction
yet, but their attempt helps us grasp its meaning and get a
glimpse of how complex it is. Emotion doesn't give up its
secrets or its design easily so, hopefully, this chapter will make
us think more deeply and profitably about what constitutes it.

We will discuss twelve characteristics surrounding emotion,
especially its relationship and role in our temperaments, how
emotions mutate, and the role of emotion in ethics. If you are
on a fast track to finding out how to be intelligently emotional,
you may want to skip this chapter and come back to it later to
fill in some of these illuminating and instructive details.

This chapter will seek to throw some light on such questions
as:

- How should we define emotion?
- Why try to understand our emotions? What purpose is there
  in doing so?
- Why do we have emotions?
- How do they play out their role in our temperaments?
- Why do some feelings last a lifetime?

- Do emotions mutate and change?
- How does emotion affect the building of our values?
- Are emotions ethically neutral, since they seem to energize both good and bad decisions equally?

Lately, emotions seem to have attracted a great deal of criticism and, with it, much attention lately. Why are they being given such a bad rap? Is it because their negative effects can be so destructive? People come to fear them and, as a result, want to get rid of them altogether. Well, let's find out more about them.

Hard to Define

What is emotion? Wow! That's a difficult question. Even psychologists and philosophers can't agree on emotion's basic definition. Religions don't define it either. We just live with how we have been designed. Is that a bad thing? Not really, because it forces us to examine and discover at least a part of the meaning and purpose of our design. That is, if we are concerned enough to understand ourselves better and the way we have been made. That understanding is the beginning of self-discovery and self-management, two tools used in becoming intelligently emotional.

Perhaps this will help: if we are to make progress with managing and developing our emotions, a detailed definition will not be necessary. What will be needed is a defining battle as we personally struggle with the power and intricacies of emotion while all the time trying to make beneficial choices. It is in the struggle with our emotions that we come to our best understanding of them.

After decades of fighting his emotions, Jamie became discouraged with ever finding out how to mange them successfully. "The older I get, the less I understand and the more I am baffled by my own feelings," he complained. I encouraged him to keep struggling but not to approach the battle with the belief that he was making no progress. "Open your mind to the possibility that you can understand them, and be their master," I suggested.

Some months later, he reported first to himself and then to me that he felt he was making progress because he could select the emotion he wanted more easily and end the unwanted emotions more quickly. Jamie was discovering what his emotions were and how they could be used for good rather than allowing them to control him.

One of his success factors seemed to be identifying his emotion more precisely. Instead of just saying "I am angry," he would ask, "What kind of anger is this? For what purpose should I use it? How intense is it? And will it serve the purpose that I want?" His answer would be something like this:

> *I am hurt; that's why I am angry. I am trying not to get hurt anymore. I am very hurt because... [he would name the reason],* and then he would ask, *"Is it going to help or hurt me more to remain hurt and angry?"*

It was in his struggle that he discovered the meaning of his emotions and gained the upper hand. Try it.

Since this is not a book on the neurological pathways in the brain or the formation of a philosophical school of thought, we will not attempt to define emotion scientifically or philosophically. Rather, we will aim at a practical understanding of emotion, an examination of the struggle each temperament has with emotion, and how they can do something about it. We will begin with why an understanding of our emotions is necessary.

Should We Attempt to Understand Emotion?

We think we understand our emotions because we can recognize what love, fear, anger and the other common emotions are. But emotions are more complex than that and need a more elaborate knowledge. Anger, for example, is not just an emotion; it is a decision, an action, and an emotion, as well as being anger of a more specific nature (as Jamie found out). How many different descriptions of our anger are there? As many as the various circumstances of our lives will demand, as various as our inner responses to those circumstances could be.

To complicate matters further, understanding our individual emotions is not the same as understanding emotion. Emotions are the individual expressions of a felt judgment of what is happening to us, in us, and around us. They motivate, inform, and challenge us for some reason or purpose. From all we said in chapter one, this should now make sense. On the other hand, understanding emotion will be a real brain teaser for all of us. Only as we examine what our emotions do to us and what we can do with them will we begin to have a real sense of what the strange, intelligent force we call emotion is all about.

We need to understand our emotions so we can detect the direction our lives are going and the purposes for which we are using our emotions. We may well discover that those purposes are selfish or unfair to others or bent on creating us further harm. Understanding our emotions and why we welcome them or reject them can be our best guide to understanding ourselves. "Discretion will protect you, and understanding will guide you," says the writer of Proverbs, and life tells us he is absolutely right.

Perhaps a different question is better: not why do we need to understand emotions, but why do we need to understand anything? We could almost say it is human to want to know. Such is the fire that burns in our curious minds. And then again, how can we manage or control what we can't understand? And how do we make wise choices without understanding. Understanding has been said by inspired writers of old to be the beginning of wisdom. And who would seriously doubt that? Once children know they have emotions, they must be helped to understand them or they will be, unfortunately, controlled by them. They will grow up to be adults who others say can't control themselves. People who can't control themselves certainly don't understand themselves.

Every temperament understands emotions in a different way. The SP welcomes them; the SJ seeks to control them; the NT buries them, and the NF both welcomes and fears them. Even educated people cannot claim to be without bias or agenda in their understanding of their emotions. Therefore, all of us see our emotions through our temperament and its preferences and through our beliefs. Explaining emotion through the lens of our own emotions further colors our understanding of them. So, can we know anything for sure about our emotions? Yes!

Emotions are universal and, for the most part, what we experience, others do also. Love is one thing to one person and something else to another, but love is generally understood by all. We can detect each other's biases, however, and know an individual interpretation when we see one. We try to be fair and balanced and, in large part, we achieve it. Therefore, although we are all influenced by our own emotions when we think, or even when we write about emotion, we can be believable and helpful. If we did not have a common understanding of the emotions that are common to all of us, we could not communicate with any positive result.

Another's emotional bent can illumine and educate our own. We talk to each other about our emotions and, in the process, we teach each other something more about the subject. Given all this complexity in our communications, we still, as Aristotle indicated, know what an emotion is and even concur in the vast amount of our evaluations. Not many would deny that love is good, would they?

Some have tried to understand emotions by making a list of them and then seeking to understand each one separately. Seems like a good idea, except that none of us has yet fully understood love, for example, which is just one on the list. If God is love, no wonder. Each emotion cannot be understood by itself. Fear can only be understood against the background of courage, and anger against the background of acceptance, peace, considerateness, kindness, and a host of other emotions. Each emotion separates one feeling from another, and we need a bird's eye view of all the feelings to give meaning to an individual feeling.

Making a list is futile because we can't make a complete list. There are more emotions that have not been named than have been named. We will discover that emotions keep morphing into new combinations and subtle differences, and it would take more than a lifetime to keep up with the ones each of us alone experience.

So what is emotion? You may be satisfied with a dictionary definition like Webster's: "A physical or social agitation, disturbance, or tumultuous movement," or you may be better off saying, "Let's talk about what I feel, not how to define it in abstraction from my experiences." Why do we need to understand emotion? Here are some conclusions:

- Because it is so complex, and the more complex it is, the more we are challenged by our ignorance.
- Because it shapes all we are and do. With such authority and power, we can't ignore it.
- Because we need to manage it or it will manage us.
- Because without understanding our emotions, we can't get a grip on them to direct them or change them and, at times, we know we must. The more we understand them, the easier they are to grasp and be managed.

Will we ever understand emotion completely? No! However, that should not stop an ardent attempt to solve its mysteries and bring it to its knees, obedient to the purposes we have for our lives.

We should also note that all the questions our emotions raise are important to our understanding of who we are and the spiritual and ethical dimensions of our lives. We cannot simply explain emotions adequately in terms of what happens in our brains when an emotion develops. Emotions fashion our lives and therefore cannot be restricted to a neurological explanation. We understand them best in the context of our lives.

Emotion Serves Several Purposes

Here are some of the purposes emotion serves:

- It warns us about what is happening in our world, both good and bad. Emotions flag us that we are in danger or in love. Dr. Robert C. Solomon has written at length of emotions being intelligent engagements with the world. I would add, with the world inside us as well as outside ourselves. Therefore, if you train yourself and your child to react constructively to the world inside as well as the world outside, you and they are gaining an understanding of emotion that will lead to intelligent emotional choices.

- Each temperament is made up of different strengths which are driven by different emotions and, if we want the best results, we must use our emotions for the purpose of developing our strengths.

- Emotions reinforce our values. All of our values have emotional content or they wouldn't become our values. Importance, worth, usefulness, and accuracy are four of the standards that turn beliefs into values. The stronger the emotion, the stronger the value is to us.

- Motivating us and helping us motivate others is one of emotion's great services. Motivation is essential to both personal and social life. The most effective motivation is achieved when an intense emotion is cultivated to reinforce our strength and we feel doubly energized.

- It creates a sense of pleasure or pain — pleasure for the joy we need and the pain that educates and shapes us. Admittedly, both pleasure and pain can become excessive and damaging, but what would life look like without them?

- It fuels all of our actions or thoughts to gives them vitality and meaning.

Albert Camus, a French philosopher who wrote the famous novel, *L'Etranger* (which describes life as having no sense, useless, and meaningless — a very depressive, existentialist, nihilistic view), nonetheless surprisingly sees emotion as one of the redeeming factors of human life, making us truly and authentically human. However, he contradicts himself, because emotion has meaning, and life can never be meaningless with it. At least he makes the point that, even if we see no meaning in life, emotion can awaken it. Emotions may drive us to depression, but they can also lift us out.

We Feel or Experience Emotions

We know an emotion when we see or feel one. Or do we? Are we being fooled into feeling we know them with the little we do understand about our emotions, when by far the greatest part we don't know? Are they hiding their secrets from us? For many, the little they do know about their emotions is lulling them into a false sense of satisfaction with how they handle their emotions. Some are being driven to a false understanding. However, to those who don't struggle to understand more of their emotion's mysteries, their emotions become a closed book, rusted by familiarity and ignorance.

With each day, April was becoming more bitter. She was hurt by the harshness and, in her opinion, unfairness of her father's actions. He seemed remote from her, stiff and prickly, and he treated her mother to angry outbursts that shattered the delicate peace of the home. Being richly endowed with feelings, the pain and hurt of witnessing these outbursts and the ice of rejection that hung in the air forced her to make a choice.

Confronting her father had proved futile; consoling her mother's hurt only fueled the hurt inside of April. Withdrawing into her room or running through the neighborhood to escape the agony only seemed to focus her on the pain even more, and she noticed that she was tense even before she got out of bed in the morning.

April succumbed to what she saw as her only alternative. Perhaps she could become like a lobster with a hard, abrasive shell on the outside, protecting the soft delicious flesh on the inside from harm. As a human, she was soft on the outside, with a backbone hidden under her welcoming flesh — a flesh that was invitingly exposed to damage and hurt. This comparison became an analogy for the way she would protect her emotions, and it seemed rational.

She hardened her external responses and transformed herself into a thorny creature she hoped her father would see was the result of his actions and non-actions. You know, don't you: it had the opposite affect. More fighting broke out and the skirmishes were to her further loss. Emotions that are suppressed become stronger. Soon she became violent around the home and, yes, soon reports of her angry behavior at school found their way home. When her confused mother approached her about the reports, April flew into a rage. Her emotions were now demanding they find some solution.

It was a hard road back to being the tender, loving girl she too loved best. It was a road strewn with the rocks of angry emotions that demanded they be felt and negotiated before they would be calmed or successfully circumvented by focusing on who she was made to be. The road back led her also from ignorance of her emotions to a knowledge that gave her a new confidence to manage them intelligently in the future.

It's also our experience that we don't even notice all of our emotions, because some are so dominant that they overpower the feelings we have of the others. Also, we are so focused on the details of our lives that many emotions pass by without us giving them a thought. They capture us without our being aware of them or, if we notice, we react without concern. All of us are focused on life most of the time, not the feelings and responses we make to life's experiences, unless they bring sufficient pleasure or pain to get our attention.

Another reason why we don't notice our feelings is that we have become accustomed to them. Pleasure, unless it is dramatic, is just another internal surge of emotion that we expect. These reasons can create a familiarity with our emotions that causes us to be nonchalant about the static on our mind's communication lines so that we can't read our emotions correctly or, as we have noted, we don't recognize them at all.

However, we notice and can report most of our emotions. Even if we don't stop to think about them or identify them, we are aware of them as a backdrop to our consciousness. They are our lives and fill our senses; they are what we feel and experience; we just know they are us.

Some emotions we experience even become learned behavior and, as a result, form our character. Emotions seem to have a desire to stay and become us, particularly the ones whose design is to damage us. Even unwelcome emotions persist and tempt us to allow them to occupy our minds, to allow them to relax and make themselves comfortable while they absorb precious territory we need for more important use and while they attempt to become permanent residents. The proverb, "As a man thinketh, so is he," so impressed James Allen that he wrote the classic of the same name. Our mind is indeed the gymnasium where we are developed, or the lounge where we apathetically waste away our mental muscle.

Because emotions invade our conscious minds and shape our experiences, teaching emotional intelligence to ourselves or to our children will have a lot to do with making wise decisions and cultivating a mental discipline without which we will become mental putty. Some parents, for example, have not seen this connection, and their children grow up with undesirable beliefs and practices that spring from a lack of emotional backbone and disciplined self-management.

"I think I have ruined my children," said a 62-year-old mother. "I should have known these things. I feel so bad."

"No parent is perfect," I replied, "and it's not a matter of looking back, but looking forward. What we do today will cast its influence on tomorrow, so don't be depressed about what has happened. There is always today and a new day ahead."

Another thought hits us: why do we feel and experience emotions whether we want them or not? Can't we select what emotions we have? Later we will deal with this in more detail, but here's a quick summary:

- We can select emotions and cultivate them, if we want to. It's the skill of the actor to cry when the script calls for it.
- Most everyday emotions come unbidden, and we can't stop their initial surge. Our part is to decide on the best action, which may be opposite of our initial emotion: love instead of hate, for example.
- Emotions serve needed purposes, not the least of which is the mental and emotional exercise that builds the muscle of self-mastery.
- If we don't feel these unbidden emotions, we have no awareness of them and no ability to change them.

We should be thankful for our ability to feel our emotions. We are happy when we feel love, satisfaction, pleasure, and all the other beneficial emotions. If we could not feel our emotions life would have no pleasure.

Emotion Is a Force in Our Temperament.

Each strength in our temperament has emotions that drive it to fulfill its designed purpose, unless the emotion is contrary to the strength's true purpose (which results in the strength being distorted and perverted). Any strength without an emotion to drive it is impotent and limp. Courage, caution, independence, and imagination (to choose one strength from each temperament) are simply words or names — not even preferences — without an emotion of some sort giving them energy. A preference only develops if the strength is used, and it can only be used when emotion drives it.

Imagine courage without any emotional drive. I can't. Can you? Courage is the image of teeth gritted, muscles tensed, and a will as hard as steel, advancing into the jaws of danger undistracted. Emotion pervades every sensory cell in the SP strength of courage. So it should be with every strength.

The power of emotion makes our strengths all the more potent, and the more emotion we inject into the use of our strengths, the more powerful they become.

As a boy, Willy was passionate. He worried his parents, who thought that what they were seeing in their son was a loss of control when, in fact, it was a passion: the strength of an NF, filling their son's mind to the point where every fiber of his being was being called into use so that the passion would be all it could be. To Willy it was a meaningful rush of adrenaline that transformed him. He felt real and alive and wanted to sense repeatedly the thrill of his powerful emotions. He seemed to his dad to be trying to "burst his boiler," as his dad recalled.

Children will often try to experience the ultimate limit of their emotions. Adults who have learned to calm their emotions in the interests of controlling them (a false concept) avoid the upper limits of emotional expression by calling them dangerous. It's dangerous to climb a tree if you don't know how to hang on or you don't know how to come down again.

With the same sensation, adults often shy clear of emotional limits for a lack of confidently negotiating their emotion's possibilities. Social pressures are not the least of these influences on adults.

The strengths of each of the temperaments are waiting for us to mobilize them and confidently steer them into their stratospheres. The emotional content in your strengths will determine their limits and lessen their potential unless we become masters of the art of being intelligently emotional.

All our strengths can be powered by helpful or unhelpful emotions to achieve any purpose. We stand at the controls with our hands on the wheel of choice, masters of whatever destiny we choose. The emotions we welcome will strengthen or weaken our strengths, and this weakening is a result of poor emotional management that we don't think about. Choosing the right emotion is not easy and we will discuss ways of making correct emotional choices in a later chapter.

James dreaded his cautiousness which, as an SJ, was his strength, because time after time his hesitancy had lost him profitable opportunities in business and he felt he was a procrastinator because of it. He sensed that he was cursed by this strength. Not true. When the wrong emotion is steering the use of our strengths we often jump to this kind of negative judgment. The emotions of fear and dread that followed every failure for James had weakened his belief in the beneficial use of his caution to the point where it increased his timidity and lowered his self-confidence. Now he was avoiding its use.

The emotion of fear can dismantle any strength. "Let's deal with the fear and the misunderstanding that is causing the misuse of your strength," I suggested, and it worked. He became more confident and bold after a few prescribed exercises. Because he was an SJ, his boldness never matched the impulsive daring of the SP. However, he did not want to be daring, only courageous and patient enough to keep his belief in the value of being cautious, yet at the same time free to make sudden decisions when enough facts lined up and the risk factor was within his comfort level. A negative view (fear) of any of our strengths will hamper our success.

When an emotion that drives our strengths causes us to either misuse or overuse it (both damaging) we must abandon it for a positive emotion. I find most people wake up to the fact that they have changed and hurt their image only *after* the fact, instead of being aware of their emotions when they begin their damaging work. The biggest initial problem in most of us is emotional awareness. No other inner force so successfully takes us by surprise and dominates us like our emotions.

With children in particular, teaching them to abandon a damaging feeling is a matter of teaching them how to use the tools of intelligent emotions. Emotional skills are best learned in the positive use of our strengths. When learned in those formative years, adulthood blossoms early with potentiality.

Anita's temperament was SJ and she soon realized that her desire to please by being reliable and trustworthy was an excellent tool to manipulate her mom. She would offer to help and then demand a cookie or some other tasty treat. The emotion behind this behavior was, of course, the desire for personal satisfaction. The character she was building was not praiseworthy and would besiege her as an adult. A desire to help others must be built on the emotion to be of service, and this is what she needed to learn. She could learn this by learning to leave the reward to others and by not demanding a reward.

Our interest or fascination with something comes from the emotional drives that form our temperament. Golf fascinated me for years, but now the drive that it satisfied is satisfied in another way. It is the emotional drive in our temperament and its empowering desire that is the real motivating force, not the activity or interest.

The way to emotional intelligence is first by the pathway of self-understanding, understanding how we are designed to reach our potential via the right use of our emotions and discovering how we should use our strengths. Temperament is not some static quality that guides us. It is charged with emotions that either make it the most potent power for good or the worst destructive force for our personal demolition.

Emotions Can Last a Lifetime

Neuroscience has attracted a great deal of attention over the last two decades and when examining emotion, it focuses more on the short term emotional event in the brain, tracing the neural pathways, rather than the long-term or lifelong results. We should not see emotional events as only a fleeting episode. Emotions can last a long time and transform into moods and attitudes that may become part of a person's permanent lifestyle, creating, for example, a perfectionist or pessimist. Emotions may also last for only a few days or hours but affect all other emotions and events during those days and hours, creating changes that come and go and permanently transform our lives in moments. The complexity of emotional life is staggering when we conceive of it in its total effect on our lives in addition to our bodies. Neuroscience and its focus on the brain can be too simplistic and selective in its pronouncements concerning our emotions.

Emotions are not simply a brain event but a life event, recording how we see and react to all occasions, things, and life forms around us and in us. Emotions redirect our purposes in life, our relationships, beliefs, values, and to a large extent control our focus. What don't they control or affect? The study of emotion is not the territory of neuroscience alone but of all disciplines, not least, psychology, philosophy, and theology. It includes the personal understanding of life in all of its interactions with the world in which we live, and with how we are made and understand ourselves.

"But I just feel that way," Colin complained to me after he revealed that this had been going on for some time. "How can I change feeling this way when I have been taken advantage of?" He had been ill treated by a friend and it was not the first time he had felt the unfairness and the disloyalty of those he had trusted. The emotion of hurt had taken up permanent residence in his mind and he could not even comprehend feeling any other way. Moods, attitudes, and grudges are unwelcome tenants that try all the tricks to avoid eviction. When they stick around for some time, they feel so normal they fool us into thinking they are natural ways all humans feel. It had happened to Colin. "I am no fool," this NT reminded me, "and it makes no sense to trust people," he asserted with an emotional display that was quite unlike an NT.

He had to see that it was he who was causing the longevity of this unwelcome feeling, not the hurtful emotion that had set in and seemed natural, or those that had betrayed his trust. Another option (a possibility with promise) included exchanging his grudge for a healthy attitude that could dislodge the feeling of hurt and calm his bitter anxiety. When negative emotions hang around, we cannot remain the same; we must change them or suffer their consequences.

All emotions can live long lives. Love, grief, hate, and anger are well known examples. When destructive emotions do remain, we lose our freedom to be who we are and to live rewarding lives. When uplifting emotions like love remain for a long time, we become more loving and kind.

Biases and bigotry can also have lasting effect on the formation of our values. They can actually become our values. Once formed, the emotional content of these values are hard to eradicate. Seeing an undesirable emotion in our child as only a passing phase can be a mistake in judgment of larger proportions than we imagine. Helping the child change the emotion, not just the actions, is the only way to lasting change. And no one can do that for them; they must face the fight themselves. A caution for the parent: don't become an inveterate investigator of your child or the negativity that surrounds your parenting will become a problem of its own. More positive methods are needed.

Positive feelings can be permanent too, and their persistent replay molds our behavior and flavors our minds. Identify the emotions you want to characterize your life and use their cling and tenacity to build the future you want to live in.

Emotions Are Forces that Can Mutate and Change

An emotion can cross over and become its opposite in an instant. The speed at which love can swing all the way into a bitter hate, like into dislike, anger into respect, and grief into depression is a marvel to behold. It can happen before we are conscious of it. All we know is that we have become something else. This speed of change is rooted in a sudden change of belief and, because it is the way we are designed, if the belief is a powerful one, it can result in sudden conversions often seen in religious transformations. It is the content of the belief and its power, combined with the speed of our emotions that makes the change so dramatic. Other belief changes can result in a more gradual transformation, but no less powerful.

This changing from one emotion to its opposite will come into use when we consider "replacement," a method for the lasting defeat of unwanted emotions. If your child is exhibiting repeated behavior, it is because he is driven by a firm belief, and that belief is impregnated with a strong emotion of some sort. It may be good or it may be bad. Focus on changing the belief, and don't forget when replacing the new belief to accompany it with a very desirable emotion if you want real change.

Emotions can mutate into an almost endless variety of feelings that are similar and dissimilar to their parent feeling. These mutations can add variety and challenges to our emotional experiences, providing exercises for our growth and development, becoming our teachers and examiners, driving our development at times down narrow lanes with little flexibility as they keep testing us every day. Mutations are not changes from one species to another, from love into hate, but are changes within the emotion's current classification such as love changing into commitment or grief mutating into depression. They lighten or deepen, develop a new character, or gradually lose their distinctive emphasis.

This ability to mutate reminds me of the synergy drive in my car, which chooses any combination of gears for the changing road conditions, endlessly and smoothly. Emotions can change with equal frequency in response to current conditions but don't usually guarantee a smooth ride.

Nor is the ride unexciting. Emotions are always new. Yesterday's emotions spring up fresh today with ever-changing combinations, altering life's texture and flavor. If you want to see variety in full throttle mode, watch your emotions change in a fast changing environment. You probably won't be able to keep up with them.

Emotions also have the ability to change their "feel" as they change intensity. They can cause any emotion to alter its very nature simply by increasing or decreasing in power. Like becomes love, dislike slides into hate, and pleasure climbs into ecstatic joy as the emotion's energy waxes or wanes. But it is even more complex. On the continuum of like to love, the variety of "feels" seem infinite as the emotion gives birth to other emotions and our love becomes complex, like a well-made wine whose multiple layers of flavor blend seamlessly into a unique experience for the taste buds.

Puzzled, Karen came to me. "What is wrong with me?" she pleaded. "One moment I love this man and another I only like him, and then I hate him only to love him again? Her emotions were changing from one emotion to its opposite with intensity changes and mutations thrown in to further confuse her. But the intentions of her emotions were not to confuse; they were simply and accurately mapping the changes in the way she was responding to her world. To settle her mind, she would have to pay attention to the way her emotions were signaling her mental shifts and find the meaning behind these changes. Emotions report and make judgments at the same time. The meaning of our interactions with our world is found in their judgments of ourselves and our world.

Karen examined her emotions. When I love him, why is that? What has happened to my feelings? When love cools to like, what is happening? What am I feeling? Am I feeling a cooling of love or the disturbance of another attraction or distraction? The exercise helped her find the reasons for the shifts in emotion and her emotions educated her about whether she really loved this man or not. Emotions are excellent teachers.

The constant changes to their emotions can confuse children easily as well. Help them understand that they need to find a passion and then focus. Passions come and go, but not as fast as emotions; they tend to hold our life's ship on course for longer.

What is emotion? An amazing creation that seldom becomes static, as in a mood, and more often fills our life with spice and challenge. Emotions seldom turn life into a boring journey. Mutating emotions are fascinating studies in our reactions to our world.

Are Emotions Active or Passive?

Both! Sometimes emotions sweep over us and we feel happy or, on the contrary, blah, with seemingly no feeling of urgency to make us do anything about our present state. Sometimes they actively boil inside us, forcefully gaining our attention and urging action. Emotions happen *to* us, such as when we come face to face with danger or win the lottery, and we *create* them when we ruminate on the injustice of a situation. Emotions can also be *generated* by us, as when an actor enters the emotional state of a character in a play. So, there is no one answer or no singularity in an emotion's mode of operation.

Emotions create thoughts and sometimes thoughts create emotions. Anything can be the source of an emotion. When we daydream or imagine things, we can create any emotion we want. The INF, who recharges from the inside, often resorts to imagination to flood a drained spirit with hope and encourage happy feelings. For the NF, these emotions that power their imagination (a well-known strength of NFs) do their job very effectively. Again, we are facing the complexity of our emotional life.

It had been a long disappointing day and Jacqueline was feeling down, "really depressed," she would have said. The 50-minute trip home provided time for a dream while she drove down a quiet country road. She dreamed of being successful, of becoming the best salesperson in the town — no, in the state or, better still, the country. She imagined being flown to headquarters for her reward and proudly accepting the honor along with a spectacular banquet to cap off a night of significance, and all this replete with her emotions living out the dream. It was, to her, a totally unrealistic dream, but the emotions that were produced in her were not. They were what she needed — real and creating excitement along with a few tears — and she felt her depression moderate. Her newfound feeling of worth helped her walk into her home and report an unsuccessful day without being drenched in the despair of failure.

These were emotions that supported the use of her strong imagination and refreshed her, emotions she had generated for that very purpose. Generating pleasurable, active emotions can always be an NF's refreshment. But when we combine these self-generated emotions with our strengths, we actually *develop* our strengths. Our minds think we have used our strengths when we used our imaginations, and using our strengths develops them. It may be hard to swallow, but we can develop our strengths this way and fuel our motivation even while we lie in bed.

Another person's emotions can become ours, such as in empathy when it actively stirs the same feelings in us. Whether the emotions of the other person passively plant themselves in us or we create them ourselves is of academic interest.

Another example of someone else's emotions becoming ours is the meeting of minds in social exchange where the feelings of one person change the feelings of the other. Emotions limit themselves to no known boundaries and often, as in empathy or social bonding, surprise us.

Are Feelings Emotions?

Perhaps we can best answer that for our purposes by saying feelings are our conscious experience of emotions. We *feel* our emotions and that's the way we recognize them most of the time. When teaching ourselves or others intelligent emotions, first we must feel and recognize the emotion. This is easily achieved by asking, "What are you feeling?" "Describe your feelings to me, please."

Of course, this is a practical answer more than a theoretical one. There is little agreement about the difference between emotion and feelings in the various schools of thought. Feelings bring a degree of self-awareness with them, but sometimes feelings require the effort of a trained awareness to register their presence.

When asked "how do you feel?" many people answer, "I don't know." Confusion over naming or identifying the feeling is the issue rather than an absence of knowing that a feeling is present. Therefore, identification, not just acknowledging that a feeling is present, becomes the major issue.

We can be thankful that we have the conscious experience of our emotions even if we are frustrated at their appearance at times. I can't imagine what it would be like to have emotions and not have feelings, somewhat like driving down the road without a sense of movement.

Moods and Emotions

Again, we are on tenuous ground. For our purpose, a mood is a positive or negative feeling that we nurture and find difficulty releasing from our mind. Our thoughts determine the nature of our moods and, in turn, our moods influence our thoughts. This is why it is essential to keep a positive frame of mind and make life a positive reality. Of course, a mood can be a feeling of happiness — a good feeling, not just a negative one.

To a large degree, we are responsible for our moods, both positive and negative. We may blame circumstances or other people for feeling the way we do, but we are the ones giving the mood territory in our minds and that is where our responsibility comes into play. When a mood crosses the line into depression, we may find it very hard to eradicate. Any mood of long standing is going to put up quite a fight.

If we are aware of having a negative mood and want to get rid of it, we should ask ourselves "what are the negative thoughts I am nurturing?" Changing our thoughts is the path to changing our mood, as difficult as that may be. Some temperaments will find it easier than others. Most of us can identify our thoughts; what we don't realize is that when we identify our thoughts, we are also often making an identification of what is stimulating our emotions. Therefore, think of what you are feeling as well as what you are thinking and the task of identification will be easier.

All this underlines the fact that emotions permeate our actions and thoughts, both positive and negative, and if they are approved by us and nurtured, they create what we call a mood. Moods can last for minutes, days or years. They are clearly observed in children as they wrestle with their emotional pressures. Particularly in children, moods need to be addressed before they become entrenched habits.

Environment and Emotions

Does our environment, upbringing, and culture have a part to play in the formation of our emotional makeup? I often get asked this question. Answer — yes and no! They can have a part and when they do, what part is the question.

We have learned that our reactions or responses to our world are our emotion's judgments of that world. But these emotional judgments do not shape the basic framework of how we are emotionally designed. Our temperament will determine that. Our emotional judgments are the results of what we see of our environment and how our first impressions evaluate them.

The difference between the NT and the NF temperaments illustrates a difference in basic design. One minimizes emotion and the other maximizes its use and importance. The mold is cast by the temperament. The judgments our emotions make reflect both the drive of emotion in our temperament's preferences and our environmental conditioning. Unless pressured by other forces sufficiently to overcome our temperament's preferences, our preferences will win.

Culture (one of those environmental influences), for example, may make it acceptable or unacceptable to express an emotion under certain conditions. In that case, a modification of our temperament's preferences may take place. Even if culture or one's upbringing modifies our emotions, they don't eliminate them. The emotions may simply hide inside us, finding no outward expression. Though not expressed visibly or audibly, they are still there — hidden, not eliminated. For the NF temperament, outward expression of emotions may well be only the tip of the iceberg compared to what is hidden.

We can't blame circumstances or any other condition for an emotion because emotions are *our judgments* of whatever we encounter. It may be true that under certain circumstances most people are seen to have a particular emotion, but all that tells us about emotion is that people have similar reactions under the same circumstances, not that the circumstances are the cause of the emotion. We build values that factor into our emotion's judgments (the way they see our world), and we are offered the chance to accept or modify our emotions. Therefore, we are involved and responsible for their use.

"Should I leave my job?" Ricky asked, hoping for a confirmation of his feelings. "I go to work every day dreading it and feeling empty.   I hate my job.   The boss is a jerk! Everyday he irritates me and treats me as though I don't matter. I'm tired of it. I don't think I can continue to be angry like this anymore. My job is making me angry."

Ricky had several options. The one he did not have if he was to be intelligently emotional was to blame his anger on his job or his boss.   Anger was his response to all that was happening, an emotion he could confirm or condemn and he must own his responsibility for the option he chose.

That sounds inconsiderate and non-empathetic given Ricky's circumstances, but Ricky will never be able to master his emotions until he understands where personal responsibility lies and where he must position himself to do something about it.   Owning our emotion means positioning ourselves in the place of responsibility where we can affect a change and be the change agent if we so choose.   Disowning it is to take the stance of a victim, giving up the opportunity to be in control of the situation and resorting to blaming anyone and everyone.

When environment challenges us we can ask the question, "Do I want to control my life or shift control to my circumstances?"

Emotion and Ethics

Character is higher than intellect. A great soul will be strong to live as well as think.
~ Ralph Waldo Emerson

The understanding of emotion has always been an integral part of the study of responsible ethics. Ethics tries to define how we should live and what is the "best" life to live. Therefore, it must consider how emotions, via our actions and thoughts, will affect our inner peace and our relationships with others — both friends and enemies — and, of course, the thorny issue of what is the right or wrong emotion. Emotions are judgments of our engagements with the world around us and inside of us, and the right or wrong of these judgments is the concern of ethics too.

Today, right and wrong is often decided by popularity vote. Taking such a pole is defended by the argument that we are all free to determine our own standards of right and wrong and therefore, in a society, the majority vote is the only fair resolution of an ethical question. The emotions and arguments we choose to support our opinions indeed do decide the issue of right or wrong for us and are then used as the justification of our emotions. But right or wrong that is rooted in our own judgments means there are as many rights and wrongs as there are people, which destroys the concept of right and wrong altogether — a thought some welcome.

The other side would argue that our emotions or judgments are not always in our own best interests or that of society and, therefore, we should fix standards for right and wrong based on some more just measure. They would point out that in society, road rules are not decided by one's emotions or popular vote, but by safety standards which are a more objective measure of what is right or wrong. A popular vote would not stand up in a court of law when defending a violation of the code, they want to point out. The code is the standard for determining a violation. A jury must decide whether a code has been violated, not whether the code is right or not.

Others refer to God as the arbiter of what is right or wrong and hence the introduction of religion into ethics and emotion. When doing so they introduce absolute standards of right and wrong, like "Thou shalt not steal." These, then, guide both individual and societal standards. The measure of right or wrong is simply whether an act of stealing took place or not.

Religions have explained the good life and the noblest religious ideas have emphasized that the word *good* means what is right, or to use a theological word, "righteous". If you want to lead a *right* life, or you want your child to do so, then training yourself or your children to understand the right and appropriate use of emotion is fundamentally important to ethics. Emotion can lead to the good life or the bad life. One is intelligent and the other is not intelligent by ethical standards. Because we are assuming the need for intelligent actions that refrain from damaging ourselves and others, we are studying the need for intelligent emotions.

Ethics, for those who believe in God, is finding emotional empowerment from the "upward look," which is setting our minds on things above, meaning on God. Some see this commitment resulting in a "passionate inwardness," as Soren Kierkegaard would have us find truth and God. Whether in the subjectivity of our own hearts and minds or in the outward commitment of a life to love, service, truth, and God, or both, the so-called "good life" reverences and thanks God for the gift of emotion and builds an ethical life with the use of emotion's powers. Ethics and spirituality are quests in which emotions cannot help but take front and center seats.

For those who do not include the idea of God in their ethics, the good life is living the best life for their own pleasure or success (narcissistic) or living a simple life (another description of the good life) or yet again spending one's life in meditation, remote from the cares and demands of this life. Aristotle, the stoics, epicureans, and the existentialists offer their own definitions of ethics, to name just a few. For many, the good life is simply living to satisfy our own desires and interests or more nobly, to be of service to others. The good life, however it is defined, always involves the management of emotions in one way or another.

But emotions presuppose the need for responsible actions and choices, as we have already noted, and ethics speaks often of this responsibility too. All we do to teach ourselves self-mastery of our emotions is rooted in some form of responsibility concerned with the need to make wise choices. So the search for intelligent emotions cannot neglect ethics.

You might imagine that the question of what is an intelligent emotion is asked often in the coaching room. We can leave it to the client's own convictions (which must of course be respected) and we can, when asked, also give some guidance from the point of view of the effects of an emotion on us and others.

"Why was I castigated for expressing my emotions?" Rose asked. "I had a right to defend myself and how I feel, and all I did was raise my voice a little, and maybe I called him a few names I shouldn't have, but I have a right to what I think." Her defense went on for a few minutes and it was soon evident that the "defense" had caused a serious breach in a relationship she treasured.

What is unintelligent, at times, about defending our rights or expressing our anger? If we work from the premise that we are the only ones we can change and that we are responsible for what results from our actions, then there is an answer to this perplexing question.

It goes like this. An intelligent (though not necessarily a right or wrong) use of our emotions will achieve the result we want. Did Rose want to damage her relationship with Caleb? She said she did not. Did she feel that there might have been a better way to engage him over her feelings? She said, "Perhaps, but I acted in the moment and didn't give it any thought. I just followed the path of my hurt and anger." That can lead to the use of unintelligent emotions because it opposes the goal she wanted to achieve. We should also add: intelligent emotions will lead us to consider a path that is good for us and for others.

What could Rose have done? Well, the first path will take a little learning, but it is well worth the effort. She could have used the skills of intelligent emotions. Step one is, when emotionally challenged, always call a "time out" to allow yourself to think. Halt the rampage of your emotions. Walk out of the room if needed, or turn your back to think. Step two is to ask a simple question, "What is the best thing for me to do?" "Best" can include what achieves our goal and what is in line with our values or the right and wrong we believe in. We can challenge our emotions to be consistent with our standards.

When we pause and force ourselves to think, we cool (to a large extent) the emotion that is clambering for our action and we stop it from dominating our judgments. We also gain a measure of self-control.

This works once you have practiced it on all the little occasions when you are only slightly disturbed and have gained the feeling that you can do it. Sometimes you will fail, but not to fail is only for perfect people, and there are not many of them around. Emotion is not physical and, therefore, not easy to grasp. These two steps are a way to grasp it and stop its domination of us, giving us time to evaluate it.

And if Rose were to fail to seize the emotion and think? Ah! There is always a great alternative, a path still open to her, I suggested. It can be humbling, but who does not benefit from that from time to time? Rose could ask for forgiveness, which is an honorable path and seeks, after failure, to pursue the intelligent goal of restoring her place in the mind of Caleb as a person of integrity, even if not a perfect person.

Ethics is concerned with goals and the means to those goals. Intelligence is in finding the best way to achieve our goals and the tools to those goals that, if we include ethics, does not damage others or us — in fact, benefits both. It is hard for me to conceive of intelligence without ethics to guide it. Those goals and the means to the goals must find a path through the maze of our emotions or fail to achieve wisdom.

We cannot avoid the effect that emotion has on all ethical beliefs or philosophies. I bring my own presuppositions to the discussion and, because of my Christian persuasions, I see the use of intelligent emotions as vital in the cause of bringing love, peace, and joy to our own hearts, to all our relationships, and to our world. The question of what is right and what is wrong will always be an emotional as well as a rational and spiritual issue.

3 - The Emotional Mind

Love, music, passion, intrigue, heroism — these are the things that make life worthwhile.
~ Stendhal

Our understanding of how we function must constantly adjust to new data as science expands its knowledge of us and our self-understanding increases. Also, there is much that experience can teach us, information gathered from simply living our lives (like information we gather about a car when we drive it) and much knowledge which temperament, psychology and other academic disciplines have amassed, all adding to our insights.

What the mind is and where it is (if that really matters or can be known with any certainty) are subjects of much dispute. The theory that our minds (thoughts and feelings) are robotic and controlled by the physical operations of the brain does not do justice to the facts of how we live our lives, nor is it conclusive from brain research. But life is not concerned with such academic interests. We make our choices as though we are in control, and this chapter will explore the control the mind has over the emotions and vice versa. We are concerned with how we can live better lives.

Therefore, I will speak of the mind as if it can be influenced by processes in the brain but can also be the instigator of our thoughts and feelings, giving us this sense of control over what we think and feel. When we have control over what we think and feel, we can be responsible for our lives and become the master of our own destinies. We are at the wheel, not our brain.

At times we may feel out of control, directed by forces we can't manage, but we always know that somehow self-control is the norm we must return to. There is an inner urge to be the masters of our destiny.

Control is a drive seared into the core of the SJ temperament. Tony felt its power that day as he sat serious and defeated in my study. But something had gone wrong. His wife had left him, and although he fought to show it had not incapacitated him, inside he was crushed. Strangely, he thought to himself, it wasn't so much the loss of his wonderful wife that worried him most; it was his admission to himself that he had failed to control (there's that word again) an important area of his life. His self-esteem had taken a serious blow with his wife's departure. But as with events both negative and positive, a chain reaction in our emotions often takes place. He had also lost his sense of who he was and where he and his life were going. He had lost his direction and his destiny. Everything collapses when this happens.

However, Tony was still at the wheel. He could make decisions and gain his direction again, maybe even retrieve more than he had lost of his dream. His relationship mistakes were to be admitted, but his sense of self-mastery had not vanished because he still had the power to react in anyway he chose. All he needed was to recover his strengths and his understanding of how to use them effectively. This ability of the human mind to take control after loss and failure gives us our resilience and describes the non-robotic nature of human life.

Each will take away something different from this chapter because we read it through our own temperaments. Please note: If you are an NF or have an F in your profile, the knowledge this chapter contains will help you, in particular, to function with greater understanding, release, and confidence. For parents, you will find help in understanding not only how we all are made but how we are all made to function, and this will help you in the difficult task of raising that most complicated organism in the universe, your child.

The Ultrasonic Brain

We noted in chapter one that the emotions are the speedsters of the mind. Let's understand more of what that means. They act with such speed that they make the analytical brain's movements look like tired snails in comparison. Emotional reactions are measured in thousandths of a second and develop so fast that it can be impossible for us to be initially conscious of why we feel the way we do or detect the point at which the emotions begin. They flare, and only after they have surged do they report their actions in feelings that we can detect. We are grateful or disturbed in retrospect only. This fact can revolutionize the way we think of emotions. How can we be responsible for a surge we initially have no conscious control over?

Emotions often don't even stop to consider what should be done. There is no thorough examination of options or thoughtful weighing of consequences when the emotions react to an unexpected event. The focus is narrowed to one concern only and whatever is the greatest need is acted on immediately. We can be eternally thankful for this sense if a tiger appears yards away, headed in our direction with teeth bared, because we will be programmed for action by our emotions at a speed faster than thought and conscious refection and with all our faculties focused on only one concern — our safety.

When we "see" the tiger, a message, encoded in electrical currents, travels at ultrasonic speed to the back of our brain and is then routed to the cortex where the higher functions of thought and perception take place. In the cortex, the message is "decoded" and for the first time we know that it is a tiger we are seeing. Our emotions have already reacted and our system has already been programmed for action. Blood has been redirected to needed areas, such as our muscles, adrenaline has been ordered into the blood stream, and the heart has been instructed to beat faster. This and more occurs, all before we fully understand what is going on.

Implications

Let's consider the implications of this knowledge carefully. Are we responsible in this case for the initial emotion of fear that we are feeling? No, we can't be if we have been unaware of its initiation. We should think of it as an automatic response, a first impression of how our faculties perceived the event before action on our part could take place. We are thankful for such a quick response, of course, but cannot be praised or blamed for it.

Therefore, we should not blame ourselves or others for emotional responses that outpace our capacity to make decisions about them. We often hear people judge others for a sudden burst of anger or a fearful collapse as though they could have suppressed the emotion. Is that fair when the anger has yet to be evaluated and reacted to and the person has yet to make the choice of a right behavior? It may be alright to be angry or afraid, but we must evaluate our anger and then do the right thing, responding according to our best rational and emotional judgments.

How often has the emotionally sensitive person been harangued with accusations like, "Why can't you control yourself?" "What's wrong with you, can't you think before you react?" "Keep your cool, man!" "For goodness sake, can't you think?" The intensity with which a hurt is registered in all those who have deep feelings is hard enough to handle, but to understand that the emotions surged within them before they knew what was happening should give a new perspective and a sense of relief.

Many clients have expressed extreme disgust at the way they react emotionally because they haven't developed the control others expect them to have. They feel guilty, and it is difficult to explain to them that they are not guilty even after I point out that they did not have control over this first surge of emotion. The stigma of a non-understanding public can do great harm and distort life considerably. Let's walk through the right reaction we should have to a sudden automatic surge of emotion.

First, we should not feel guilty for an automatic reaction over which we have no control. Others should not hold us accountable for this first phase of emotional response, either.

Second, the emotionally sensitive and reactive person should enjoy the sense of relief it brings to know we are not to blame.

Third, the effort to control such alarms is futile if we have no control over them. We are trying to be something we are incapable of being. It is simply the way our emotions are wired. What we are capable of is evaluating our emotions and deciding whether to change them or confirm their automatic selection. We do this by thinking about them.

Fourth, we should, however, take seriously the fact that we must, and can, take a window of opportunity to do what is right in response to the situation after the message has been decoded by the cortex and we have processed the situation and understood how it is we should react. We may then have to reverse our reaction since careful thought may have told us our emotional reaction was ill-timed or wrong and it is in our interests, and that of others, to now act in a way we perceive is better for them and ourselves. Speedy emotions sometimes choose the right reaction, but sometimes our deliberate slower thinking processes must refine their decisions.

Patience with ourselves and others is what we can work on profitably. The instant reactions of our emotions serve a necessary purpose, but our ability to choose, think, and make rational judgments is where the responsibility kicks in.

The Window of Opportunity

A window of opportunity opens after our emotions have been activated and after the message has arrived in the cortex for evaluation. Only then can we begin to think about what is happening to us. When the window opens, the cooler breezes of rational thoughts blow in our minds, if we let them. To practice and learn the importance of immediately asking ourselves, "What is the best thing to do?" and thinking it through is what our ancestors meant when they encouraged us to count to ten before we reacted to a sudden event. They did not know how our emotions functioned, but they instinctively knew we had to think through the situation. They also knew that we could change our emotions after they had flared by reasoning with ourselves.

When we need to change our emotion for a better path of action, we can, without undue embarrassment, introduce the change with the phrase, "I'm sorry, I should be doing such and such," or "Let me change that...," or "On second thought..." Apologizing for a wrong reaction is no putdown, so we need not feel bad.

Changing the "automatic" emotional reaction when we first feel its surge is when we have the best chance to do so. "As quickly as possible" should be the goal of any attempt at emotional control. When we catch and change our emotions quickly, it builds our confidence in being able to master our emotions and it also engenders respect and trust from others. As we have discovered, the way we are built, we are not expected to always produce the right emotion immediately; we simply have to end up with the best reaction we can muster, one that does no damage to others or us.

We can't do better than our best, but with practice, our best will improve. If the emotion continues and we can't seem to arrest it to change our feelings when we know we need to change them, all is not lost. We must catch the next moment that can be seized to think and evaluate the emotion and then make whatever changes are needed.

Down with the ignorant thought that emotional reactions are somehow inferior to our reasoning powers or are a sign of weakness. Let's remember: emotions make life rich and meaningful and these uncontrollable first surges of emotion warn us of needed action and are part of our wise design.

Emotion is involved in our every thought and action, so building awareness of our emotions helps us to change them when change is needed. The trick is to be able to develop them, manage them, and use their power for our good and the good of others and stop them from escalating into a devastating storm. Grasping a window of opportunity is our chance to achieve this goal, and we will expand on it in detail later.

We Seldom Choose an Emotion

It seems natural to follow a discussion of the ultrasonic brain with the question "Do we choose emotions or do they choose us?" The answer is both. We have been discussing what happens when emotions choose us — the automatic first surge. Emotions are most often a reaction to our world and in all cases, when an emotion rises as a result of our engagement with the world, it is choosing us and surging in us without our having the opportunity to decide whether we want it or not.

However, we can choose an emotion. We can decide to do something nice for someone for no reason except a sudden decision to show love. In this case, the emotion is chosen by us — we initiate it. We do not believe we are being forced to show love. Our brain is not making us show this love; we decided to do it; it was our free choice. We do not live well with the thought that we are automatons that are controlled by our brains, at least we don't act as though we are. We believe we can control, change, alter, deny, and choose our emotions whenever we want. We have always lived with this consciousness. Anything else is unthinkable for truly free, self-conscious beings.

Consider the alternative. Either we are right in our understanding of how we live our lives or we are disturbingly deceived. To maintain that emotions always choose us and motivate us is to say that we are not creatures with a free will. It would be constantly de-motivating to believe we never freely choose to make a decision and that all of our actions are

61

programed by some force in us, emotional or otherwise. Just like we can't live without meaning, so we can't live without a sense of being creators of our own destiny.

Therefore, when we are confronted with danger and our emotions react first, we are offered an opportunity to make an evaluation of the situation and of our emotional response (the window of opportunity). When we choose an emotion rather than when it chooses us, we call on our rational faculties and make the decision before the emotion is initiated (the window of free choice).

We see it in our children. Sometimes our child chooses to tease a playmate and sometimes an emotion in response to what the playmate has done chooses them. Either way, they are called to make an evaluation of their emotion and decide what to do about it — a real struggle for the child. In either case we are responsible for making a decision about our actions. When we choose the emotion and act accordingly we make the decision first, and when the emotion chooses us, we must seize the window of opportunity that opens after we are aware of the emotion and its consequences. It is not easy training the most complex organism in the universe to think about their emotions because changing or even evaluating our emotions is not what we want to do most of the time.

The Ultra Powerful Mind

We all know that when we mentally give up, our strength leaves us. The brain is the physical organ that sends messages to the muscles to perform. If the weightlifter feels he can't do one more repetition but the coach yells in his ear, demanding he do one more, he seems to have the ability to do what he otherwise felt he did not have the strength to do. His mind forced another message to be sent and, with it, the belief that he must try — more than that, that he must do it. Only when we give up do we ultimately fail.

The book, *Into Thin Air*, by Krauchaur was an amazing read for me. It tells the story in detail of how on the day of the worst disaster on Mount Everest, the climbers struggled against a sudden squall in bitter cold and thin air to complete their climb of the mountain. Four teams of climbers were on the final face and trouble was inevitable, as too many climbers created delays at Hillary's Step, a place where only one climber can ascend or descend at a time. Those returning were held up when time was critical. It was on the way down from the summit that most of the fatalities occurred.

He tells how one of the leaders, an accomplished climber from Christchurch, New Zealand and who was leading clients to the top, had made a grave error of judgment (along with another leader of another party) by failing to keep their own safety rules. They had pursued their climb past the time they had determined it would be wise and the squall had overtaken them as they returned. Most made it down but some, like this leader, were overcome with exhaustion and cold. His last moments before he froze to death were a battle with his emotions. He was urged to remember his wife and child and keep moving for them. All possible emotional encouragements to keep going down were used, but without effect. He lost the most important power that we have, our emotional urges, and he simply laid down to die. His strength left with his last emotional urge.

So it is that our emotions are the most powerful element in our mental makeup. Without them we fail; with them we do the impossible. Our will has power, so do our beliefs; but without the force of emotion, none can stand and we fall powerless. Building strong emotions that will lead us to success is the single most important task for those who are called achievers or winners, or for those who live at the upper limit of their creative potential.

How the Emotional Mind Sees Reality

Is our mind confused about reality or does it leave us to judge what is real and what is only perceived as real? Answer: it leaves it to us. Reality is a relative concept because each person must determine what is reality for them and what is not. The reality for me is that I love broccoli, while for others, my reality is ridiculous. One person's reality can also be another's myth. Our emotions judge whether a remark was a deliberate insult or an attempt at humor as they try to perceive reality. Which is the reality? We decide.

Perception is the standard for our judgment of reality. For those who think in stark contrast, black and white, this fact is hard to process.

Of course, our reality may not be truth — it can be the biggest falsehood. Hence the need for our minds to be educated with more than our perception of reality. Truth is not something our minds are programed to see. We must learn what is right and wrong, truth or falsehood, and program it into our value system and our beliefs. Our minds perceive; truth is learned.

The formation of a perception is in itself a complex operation. Our experiences, the accumulation of past emotional judgments, and our hopes, formed by the expectations of the future, are some of the things that color and shape our perceptions. We are not always conscious of all the elements that mold our thinking, shape our emotions, and therefore form our perceptions. To this extent we are a product of our environment, and in this context our environment includes the forces of temperament with which we are hardwired. Our temperament is the basic influence on our decisions and perceptions. For example: The ultra sensitive NF may detect an insult while the practical SP may laugh at the perceived humor of the remark.

Our emotions, also part of our mental mechanism, are reading reality or perceived reality all the time. Did she feel I was rude or does she approve of my boldness? Is that the most beautiful sunset I ever saw or are the colors slightly less brilliant and attractive to me than the one I saw yesterday? Rob says this is the best chocolate cake ever, so why is it I am not impressed? How I perceive reality is the issue.

So, let's ask — are we responsible for the emotions that arise from our perceptions? Only if we choose to act on them and reaffirm their judgments. Whenever we make or affirm a choice we become responsible, not whenever we feel something or perceive something.

Our rational intelligence should be called into play to help us distinguish between insult or attempt at humor, for example. When we rely on emotions alone or on reason alone we can make serious mistakes in judgment. When we consult both, we are best fitted to make a sound judgment. We were given both and there is a definite design to how we are made. Teaching emotional intelligence is helping us and others to listen to both the wisdom of emotion and the wisdom of reason while our minds are being educated by the facts or the truth.

Emotion can also be initiated by intuition, which can be eerily accurate at times. Our emotions, when influenced by intuition, perceive reality and ask for our confirmation of their judgment in the same way as when they are initiated by our environment. The way we are designed to function is again calling for us to make right choices. It constantly pushes us by registering perceptions that we must evaluate. What our mind perceives may be right or wrong. Learn to evaluate it.

Does the Emotional Mind Overpower the Will?

We know from experience that our willpower is seriously challenged by our emotions. Love and fear will test our will every time. Our determination and tough-mindedness shake at their onslaught. Emotion can easily gain the allegiance of our will and use it in its service, making decisions all the more problematical. The strongest will has fallen to the call of love, and the most devoted has been known to sell his friend out for greed. Willpower is often the helpmate of emotion instead of its challenger.

Love, fear, and anger are some emotions that gain increasing power from a mind that obsesses with them. Each emotion demands the commitment of a 100 percent focus and feeds on the energy that focus provides. Previous decisions become obsolete and plans are scrapped when these, and other, powerful giants of the mind take over. We are under their control, momentarily at least.

Should we fear this takeover? We would be foolish not to. But of all the emotions that dominate us, love is perhaps the most demanding and requires our wills to sign an exclusive contract. Only if we do can love become all it can be.

Willpower, it turns out, is in turn fed and strengthened by emotions and has no power without an emotion gaining control of our minds. Therefore, of all the types, an F is able to be the most stubborn when their emotions take charge. It's the tenacity formed from the alliance of emotion and will that gives their emotions such power. The tough-mindedness of the rational thinker is based on their rational analysis plus their emotion to be right. But this is a world that is dominated not by rational thought, but by the strength of emotion, making the mind that is controlled by emotion the stronger mind.

"It seems as though the more I focus on being calm and the more I breathe and try to steady my nerves before I stand up to speak, the more nervous and panicky I become," complained this public speaker to be. "I sit there, heart pounding, hands sweaty, and I concentrate on every heartbeat and breathe, trying to calm myself. Why can't I just face my fear and overcome it? I have been told to face my fear and that's what I am doing. What is wrong?"

"Your fear has co-opted your will to do its wishes and, therefore, the focus of your will is creating negative energy that feeds your fear," I explained. Facing your fear only helps dispel the fear if you focus on believing you can overcome it, not on trying not to be afraid. The change in focus is a fine tuning but a necessary one. You don't want fear and the focus of your willpower in partnership if you want to be free from fear. You need faith and will working together, so place the focus on the right mental condition: faith, not fear. Your willpower serves whatever emotion is dominant in your mind. He thought, "So it's all about focusing on the emotion you want, not the one you don't want?" "Yes," I encouraged.

He had plenty of willpower as his persistence had evidenced. His fear had claimed his attention and, therefore, he was captive to his fear. Our emotional mind has a mind of its own. Focus it on the right emotion and it will cooperate with your willpower and serve your purposes well.

How we feel is often how we act. Emotion can, and often does, command the will. Therefore, be careful to analyze and evaluate all emotions, especially those that worry you or intrigue you. Focus on the ones that will build you according to the pattern of your temperament's strengths.

The Language of the Emotional Mind

Next we must learn that the emotional mind reads symbols, impressions, and overall patterns more than it reads reason and logic. This is why symbolic and metaphorical language, images, poetry, and any emotion-packed communication find a ready and instant response in our limbic system. This language carries rich and potent feelings that empower the imagination. Imagination, intuition, memory, empathy, and passion provide energy to the emotional mind.

A symbol can tell a story that words cannot, and the emotional mind readily translates imagery into feelings that can introduce expansive thoughts and excite our imagination. A smell can also awaken lost memories that are full of feeling without waiting for the slow process of thinking to reason its way to what that memory was. We feel the emotion of the event immediately. Also, just the sight of a sunset can stir our memories of experiences connected to other sunsets or to something the sunset suggests. Symbols unleash the potential of our imagination and the emotional mind runs with it.

67

A child will hear a sound at night and what the potential of the sound suggests is limitless. The mind runs wild with suggestions of this kind. Each suggestion is replete with emotions that can run the gamut from fear to fantasy. Whatever the emotion is, it will soon take the mind captive and it is the emotion that holds the mind prisoner, not the imagination. The child has to be freed from the emotion, not from a fertile imagination as some parents try to do.

We often feel something before we start thinking about it because we have an emotional mind that outpaces our thoughts. After the emotion has surfaced, we find our thoughts running rampant, but always in the direction of the emotion. Think of how this happens many times in one day. Love, trust, hope, fear, doubt, and anger are sparked by what we see, read, hear, and detect with our senses or create with our imagination, all before we think. Just the flash of fantasy or the whisper of a wish can birth a powerful feeling and our minds are off to the races. Life is filled with feelings, touching and influencing all our decisions. And imagination is not left out of being an instigator either. Imagination is an experience full of suggestiveness (not just an analytical thought, thanks to our emotions) and often leads the way to emotional experiences.

All Fs find rich meaning in their emotions, but the NF temperament, dominated by intuition and feeling, lives on the meaning the emotions give. In the NF temperament, metaphoric language, imagination, the love of symbol, passion, and sensitivity combine with intense emotion to make a temperament that reads the emotional patterns and images of life with heightened familiarity.

If you have a T in your profile and believe you are also good at "feeling" things, then double your degree of emotional sensitivity to understand the intense emotions of anyone who has an F in their profile. Symbolism is a language more suggestive to them. Life is richest for the Fs when they live the language of their emotional mind. This is not necessarily so for the Ts because they must feed on the facts.

Do you have a child who is an F? Then wonder at the unseen warmth of all things emotional to them and try to learn, at least in part, the language of their emotions by sharing emotive words with them. You can share in the wonder if you can't share in the expressions of their mental wanderings.

"I hate my emotions," Winston said. "People thought I was so celestially minded that I was of no earthly use, at least that's the way it seemed to me as a child. I'm a male and I'm not supposed to be this way. I've tried to think tough and speak prosaic-like, but it sucks the softness out of my heart and I feel parched, my emotions cracking in the heat of societal expectations. God made a mistake, didn't he? Trying to be what my friends expect me to be is horrible to me. There's a tug of war going on inside between what I should be and what I am, and I can't stand it at times. How do I make my emotions lie down?" I felt his pain.

It must be torture to have to live as though you are a mistake. Winston was a gifted student, majoring in Psychology in hopes of being able to heal himself. I could have saved him the cost of his studies, or so he put it, if only he had found out earlier that this was the way he was made and he was not perverted, just filled with an extraordinarily rich emotional mind that he could channel into many rewarding careers.

So, what have we learned? Here are a few points:

- Appreciate the richness of symbolism and metaphor and the journeyings of an emotionally-packed imagination.
- Seek to understand the mind that is set afire by such suggestiveness.
- Learn how metaphors suggest more than literal descriptions.
- Learn why feelings can so easily captivate our thoughts and are so hard to dislodge.
- Don't despise emotion even in the one who has such a hard time controlling it.

- For feelers, the meaning of life lies in their investigation of all things symbolic and metaphorical, in analogies and likenesses.
- Symbolism is more powerful if it suggests more emotion.

Associative Functioning

Emotions also function associatively in the mind. Whatever we are faced with in the present moment, our emotional system wants to know whether we have any similar memory, anything that might resemble the present situation, stored away in its repertoire. Emotions attract like emotions and associate them together in our minds.

There is no prolonged investigation of whether the association of any two experiences are really parallel. Careful investigation comes later when the message is examined by our rational investigative thoughts. Finding the connections between feelings and happenings is a fast way of seeing their patterns and making sense of them.

Associations are gathered in less than the blink of an eye, and our emotions respond immediately to comply with their job description — give an appropriate emotional response to all stimuli. The full text reads: notify us instantly of anything that may have an association with what we are feeling or could cause us concern or stimulates our sensitivities, and prepare the system for action whatever that may be.

Emotions such as fear and love are produced only after a fast scanning of any associative material. Whatever the associations with love or fear are in our memory banks, our emotional mind finds the appropriate response in the appropriate degree and generates it. This is one example of how our past influences our present regardless of our temperament. For the SJ, the past is scanned for facts and results and secondarily for emotive content, but for the Fs among the SPs, SJs, and NFs, the residual meanings from all their emotional experiences in the past are especially significant and the reaction to them is strong.

Often an emotion-packed memory is associated with several others and the response is then more potent. The response is also colored by all the relevant associative material, both negative and positive, that we have stored in our memories, and we can be surprised by how we feel and act at times when this kaleidoscope of emotional material suddenly creates new feelings.

First impressions can be right or wrong because our emotional mind reads all likely associations. But the important thing to our emotional mind is to err on the side of safety and protection in the case of danger and to our values and beliefs in all other cases. It is better to run from a tiger and find out later that it wasn't necessary than to become the tiger's meal. Quick association of all relevant material in assessing potential danger is the best policy. This response to danger is the same one I use when I see for the first time the person of my dreams across the room and somehow know this is the person I will marry.

Do you want never to forget those wonderful moments packed with intense feeling? Don't worry — they have been filed safely away and will return to thrill you again, maybe in another setting by association with a similar emotion. Powerful experiences never really die. We can rewrite their meaning in our minds but not really eradicate them. Things such as PTSD, abuse, and ecstasy are embedded in the emotional registry too.

Association is a key word in our emotional system. It is no oddity that creativeness is also energized by association. Not only is it a fast way to arrive at new insights, but it plays a large role in helping us heal from hurt once we have decided to give up our hurt, using all our past associations of healing experiences. The emotional mind is our great search engine of like feelings.

Inside Stimuli

We're emotionally set on edge when we are confronted with a life or death situation like a gun pressed to our head, but can our thoughts alone create the same emotional anxiety? Just think of the nightmare that woke you in a cold sweat, the scary feeling when you imagined falling from a ledge on the eightieth floor, the surge of anger when you thought of being unjustly treated, the memory of that car accident, or for some simply the thought of dying, and you can create the same emotions and sense of fear. It seems so real but the actual event is not happening to us. Our emotions are not reliant on outside stimuli. They pulse with the same power in the inner sanctum of our minds.

This stimulation of our emotions by our thoughts alone happens just like the real event, faster than our thought process, and can overcome us in a microsecond. Wherever the stimuli comes from, outside or inside, we are left first with only a small window of opportunity to grasp the chance to think through the situation and to make a responsible decision on what we should be feeling, thinking or doing. If we miss that small window, we must, as soon as we can, wrest our thoughts from the escalating emotion and examine it rather than submit to it. We then open up a new window of opportunity for our reason to take over.

We can observe something more when we awake from a nightmare. Notice it takes a few seconds to return to normal, doesn't it? The emotions remain real even after we are conscious of the fact that it was only a dream. Therefore, the stirring of our emotions is not dependent on an ongoing imagination. We have already realized that it is over. Emotions can operate independent of reality. They are seemingly a world to themselves, coming or going with or without will, existing with stimulation or without it. They can even creep up on us without conscious thought, as in a nightmare. Part of our confusion is the terms we use, which are not precise because it is so difficult to be precise about feelings.

Our emotions can also be set in motion by fantasizing. Unreal monsters frighten our children. Creatures that have no connection to what our children have ever seen or in any way have encountered appear. Science fiction films and horror movies that bear little resemblance to reality are stock-in-trade for scaring adult audiences. Emotions are not dependent on the world of reality or even anything we believe in to get at our emotionally vulnerable spots.

What are emotions, or how do our minds work if they are not dependent on reality? It's a question we humans still can't answer after millenniums of experience with ourselves and with life. That is, perhaps, not surprising since the mind we use to understand our mental processing is no greater than that mind itself, and therefore it cannot stand aside or above itself to gain a perspective.

To think of the emotional mind in physical or mechanical terms is to reduce us to being a machine of sorts and life to being a deception, neither of which we can live with. We think of ourselves as so much more and our self-image is not satisfied with being proud of a mind that engages in merely robotic meanderings.

If such limited perceptions of human life and genius are how we are to understand ourselves, we have also lost the magic and mystery of life and sold out all our creative wonders (such as intuition, imagination, emotions, and ingenuity) to mechanistic explanations. Do we not feel taller, bolder, stronger when we think of ourselves as more than mechanistic marvels, but rather as images that reach beyond the stars? Is not life represented to us more satisfyingly when we think of ourselves in terms of mystery? The emotional mind is beyond us, bigger than us, while it lives and moves in us and, as a result, we feel we are intricately a part of its magic.

An F child sitting in class or an F adult at a meeting can be distracted with no outside disturbance evident and suddenly break out in tears, or a sweat, or be otherwise far away at the whim of their emotional mind. Understand what could be happening to that child and what is happening to you when you lose your concentration and are transformed by these powerful emotions. The brain does not know the difference between what is vividly imagined in the mind and what is experienced in real life, and it can process both as though they are real. Have you asked yourself what we would be missing if emotions had to be connected to some reality that is currently happening before we could feel them?

So, the NF who is supersensitive and lives primarily in their inner world finds his thoughts and feelings can conquer him without time for him to stop the initial interruption, and he then punishes himself for being mentally incapable of the concentration others seem to have. Don't feel inferior if your emotions gain control of you. You only need to evaluate them and make decisions about them as soon as possible, and the more you believe in this possibility, the more you will be able to achieve this "after-the-fact" control. Your emotions bring both meaning and challenge to your life.

I wonder how many children have been reprimanded for such mental experiences that disturbed their attention in class, or scolded for waking from a wild and scary dream to upset a tired parent. The stronger the F, the greater the chances of such happenings. It's truly all in their minds.

We can learn much from our attempts in this section to understand the way we are impacted by our emotions such as:

- Emotions are not dependent on reality.
- Emotions can come seemingly without conscious provocation, as in a dream.
- If we don't catch the first opportunity to examine them, we can catch the next.
- The more we practice self-control, the stronger our mental muscle becomes.
- We would be impoverished by the disappearance of emotions that are stimulated by things inside of us and by nothing we can detect.
- We have not learned the whole story about our emotions yet.

Manipulating with Emotion or Manipulating Emotion

It seems to follow that if our thoughts alone can turn our emotions on, we should be able to do so whenever we want to. We can use this ability not only to bring a tear when acting in a play but to manipulate others when we want something from them. We use this technique many times every day for good and, sometimes, perhaps dubious purposes.

Children discover this ability early. First, they cry to get fed and it works repeatedly. It is simply a matter of learning that this display of emotion offers all kinds of possibilities and manipulation by the use of emotions becomes ingrained.

Then children catch on to the fact that they can make tears or anger happen at will, and they get attention or a cookie if they are good enough at the charade. What a discovery! The potential for this discovery is almost endless and as each year goes by, they hone their skills — who wouldn't with such an impressive upside? A downside is also learned, which helps to halt the use. When their manipulation is uncovered they find that people hate to have been manipulated. Harmony with others then vanishes. Consequences are unleashed and the practice becomes suspect at the very least.

They also find that others are manipulating them, and a simple discovery about their emotions and how to handle them becomes a complex problem affecting all their relationships. Intelligent use of emotions must come to the rescue or they are left with an inability to socially engage without causing hurt. We all started this journey as children and some have carried their knowledge of the power of emotions into a more sophisticated, and perhaps more damaging, use in adulthood. It is not easy to drop our manipulating endeavors but intelligent behavior insists we must.

Manipulating and Control

How do we call up an emotion at will — a tear perhaps? It's a form of emotional control. First, we must start thinking about a condition or memory that produces tears, an emotional event, a sad happening perhaps. Remember, thoughts can produce emotions. Then we must concentrate on the memory or imagined scenario that we have chosen. The more we focus on the emotion of sadness or loss, the easier it is to produce the tear. Only when we actually produce the emotion of sadness is the tear activated. We are exchanging one feeling for another, a process we must learn to use to be able to change one emotion for another. There was the feeling of the moment, whatever that was, and with the aid of only our thoughts we switched to another feeling. What powerful information!

There is no emotional intelligence without emotional control, and in this example of manipulating our emotions we have found how we control our emotions by thoughts or feelings alone, and we have also discovered how to replace one feeling with another. More later on this little gem.

Is manipulation found in one temperament more than others? Yes, simply because the more intense the feeling and the higher the sensitivity, the greater the temptation for using manipulation. The complex NF is the candidate again. They can be super-skilled at manipulating (but not always for selfish purposes) and yet still have a problem controlling their own powerful urges.

The NF will manipulate for love too. So strong is the need for harmony that when it seems to be fading, they will suggest their lover does not love them in the hope of eliciting a reminder that they are loved. Manipulation? You decide. Because this lust for emotional support is so enticing for the NF, it dies hard even in adulthood.

Changing Our Minds — a Form of Manipulation

Manipulating our emotions by changing our mind (an act common to many of us) is a built-in asset and we should use when needed it to wrench the control from an unwanted emotion. When we change our minds, we also receive for our further evaluation another emotion that matches the change of mind. This is the same as changing our thoughts, but we seem to be able to grasp it easier since we are constantly changing our minds due to distractions or the demands of our changing circumstances. If you are familiar with changing your mind, then use the same technique to exchange an emotion that bothers you for one that doesn't.

Changing our minds is how we can "manipulate" our emotions. How we allow ourselves to perceive the world creates a mental feeling and sets the mood of the moment. When I started writing early this morning, the sky was clear and the sun rose over the horizon, tinting the mountains with pink hues and establishing a warm welcoming feeling. My emotions perceived it as a warming of my spirit and I welcomed it. Two hours later, at the threat of an incoming snow storm, the sky turned cloudy, dark, and gray. My emotions changed with the scene. I first felt the drabness dampen my spirit, but then I deliberately manipulated my emotions by reminding myself how I love the eerie feeling of a gathering storm and the promise of snow flakes flying while the winds rake the countryside. So, I changed my mind and the thoughts of a stimulating storm pleased me and changed my mood.

Change your mind like this and your emotions change too. We are built this way so that with practice we can control our inner world. Don't lose this thought — we change our minds by changing our thoughts and then our feelings change. It will be the information you need to paint the colors of your inner world and shape your day.

77

Reason and Emotion Need Each Other

When emotions overwhelm us, we can't think straight. The mind feels fogged by the presence of feelings that push our thoughts around in our heads. NTs know this all too well and it is why they downplay emotions in favor of reason.

Is this wise and is it emotional intelligence or a form of emotional avoidance to downplay emotions in favor of reason? When we attempt to suppress our emotions, do we think more clearly? Different viewpoints on this issue are a major reason for conflict between the NF and the NT in particular, and to a lesser degree between the Fs and the Ts of all temperaments. Let's examine the issue of emotional "static" on the mind's rational communication lines and how reason and emotion are meant to compliment each other.

Emotion In Memory

Our memory is located in the emotional center of the brain, not in the area that controls reasoning. If there is too much emotional static on the communication lines, the analytical processes of the brain that want the memory to feed them the facts without distortion don't receive what they perceive to be clear messages. Are messages passed from the memory to the executive functions of the brain without some kind of emotional coloring? No. Our perception of the facts is always colored by some kind of emotion. Certainly, we know that our memories are stashed away complete with the emotions and all the sensory data that was relevant at the time.

Analysis and reason are perceived by the Ts to depend on an "accurate" (unemotional) interpretation of the facts. But since all facts have some emotional coloring, where do we draw the line between too much emotional interpretation and an acceptable emotional coloring of the facts? Both Ts and Fs have their own answers to this question. For the T, the communication must not be confused by any emotion and for the F, emotions are a necessary coloring of the facts in order to represent the facts accurately. Both perceive and interpret facts and emotions differently and one is not more correct than the other. However, it does make for disagreements.

Also consider that the facts stored in our memory can be saturated with strong emotions for one person while a memory of the same event for another may be of little emotional significance. Is it good for us to be designed this way? Yes!

If everyone saw the world and remembered it in the same emotional colors, it would be a dull world and provide little reason for discussion and interpretation. The infinite ways we look at the same event inspire creative thinking. So, in the world of memory we should view our different emotional content and colors as an ingenious design to propel the imagination and reason on the path to creativeness. We want the insights of an infinite variety of impressions, and emotion provides this.

Both Brains

Emotions can find their way quickly through a maze of seemingly conflicting facts and assess the big picture, whereas reason is slow to process the same data. But once directed by these emotional insights or judgments, our reason can wade through the details, aided by a sense of where they lead.

Dr. Antonio Damasio, a neurologist from the University of Iowa, has arrived at the conclusion from his studies that both brains, the emotional and the rational, are equally active in all our decisions. Without emotion and its interpretations about life, reason alone can be led up the path of what seems to make sense (the logical route) without all the relevant facts.

Remember, emotion needs reason as well to steady its surges and calm its off-course decisions. The first impressions of our emotional judgments can miss some details and reason. Even given that they are logically perfect, they can still err for want of all the facts or a misinterpretation of the facts. Both emotion and reason can be wrong, but emotion knows that its fast judgments must be subjected to a more careful analysis.

Emotional intelligence is better achieved when the Fs understand their need of reason's analysis, and the Ts understand their need of emotional insights. Just as two eyes add a dimension to sight that one eye cannot provide (depth perception), so both brains complete our perception of the facts and the meaning of life to us, positioning us in our relationships and guiding our lives.

We would all like to know just how our emotions and rational thoughts partner in the dance of decision-making and what their moves are. However, we still have a lot to learn about the interaction of the executive functions of the brain and the limbic system, especially the "hot" amygdala and its interface and contiguity with reason.

Emotions should not be experienced as fighting our rational thoughts or vice versa, but rather as being indispensable partners. So, let's add to our understanding of the relationship of emotion and reason this insight: mental health and agility of mind is found only in the subtle impact each has on the other.

The balance of reason and emotion in a family of Ts and Fs is not easily achieved. Respect for how we process decisions differently is what leads to family harmony and understanding. Many families whose members know only their own way of mental processing encounter continuous conflict. Ts hold tenaciously to the god of reason and Fs find their allegiance to the goddess of emotion hard to break. Neither should have to forsake their thoughts or feelings. Both should learn a healthy respect for the other's way of seeing things. The rational and emotional brains must align, motivated by understanding and respect.

Remember, all decisions are motivated by some emotion and all should equally be informed by reason. Bringing both emotion and reason to the table of decision is not necessarily going to solve the issue, however. The secret to satisfactory solutions is to find a mutual emotion that will guide both Ts and

Fs to a common goal. Emotions must be satisfied if agreement is to lead to mutually acceptable action.

Fearing Our Emotions?

Our tumultuous experiences with the volatility and power of emotion can teach any temperament to fear it. Anybody can be unnerved by an emotional surge.

A little child must also learn to manage these strange forces inside of him and not fall victim to them. When we fear our emotions we lessen the chance of positive outcomes. We have to struggle with our emotions and each person must find the way to calm them. No one can do it for us or learn it for us. So help your child through the struggle — don't try to take the struggle away from him. All of us must learn according to how we have been made.

- The NT fears the loss of concentration that a surge of emotions can cause, so they learn to fear the appearance of emotion at unwanted times.

- The SJ fears all the emotions that may cause them to lose control, causing them to experience the dreaded feelings of insecurity.

- The SP fears sadness and any emotion that robs them of the excitement of the moment. These emotions are the enemy of joy.

- The NF fears all negative emotions that cause them to explode or implode. Their anger, for example, can be stirred in a split second and at the wrong time, causing them a potential social catastrophe. But another fear looms big for the NF: the loss of self-esteem. How can they feel good about themselves when they can't seem to manage those crushing emotions?

Fear of our emotions only generates more fear and introduces other negative emotions to deal with. It becomes a self-fulfilling prophecy. As we have discussed, emotions mutate quickly and the struggle with our emotions escalates. We are not talking of the fear of fear, although that is also an issue in emotional control, but of the fear of emotion in general which appears in all temperaments.

Because all of us experience fear of our emotions in one way or another, NFs need not feel bad. Emotions in themselves are not a negative liability, rather they are an almost limitless possibility. Emotions are our friends and the door to things beyond mere logic and the concrete activity of our senses. They readily open the wonders and creativity of imagination to those who are sensitive to feelings. They are not to be feared, but rather wisely developed.

Since fearing emotions is a learned mental behavior, it can also be unlearned. Learning and unlearning is accomplished by mindfulness and conscious actions that if repeated enough, eventually can become almost automatic. Therefore, all is not lost if we are already fearing our emotions.

Emotions Believe They Are Right

The emotional mind believes it is right in its judgments. In fact, emotions don't hesitate to make their presence known and to act with a confidence that can take us by surprise. Tentative emotional judgments are virtually unheard of. We instantly feel our emotions are right in their judgments since the feeling dominates our thoughts and, whether the emotion is negative or positive, it is being presented so boldly to us.

This boldness is necessary. If confronted with danger, an emotional response that wavered and hesitatingly presented us with a suggestion rather than a command would not motivate us fast enough to escape or withdraw. Since emotions race the analytical mind out of the blocks, their boldness goes unchallenged until we can give thought to the matter.

Imagine the trouble children have when their emotions surge with such confidence and they consequently feel they are right. Are they not right? The child cannot conceive that he could be wrong. His emotions are bearing strong testimony. For the child, the harmonious functioning of both brains, emotional and rational, must be practiced. Children (also some adults) are still struggling on the learning curve. They must learn by experience that their emotions are often wrong and often right, and it is important for them to think about how they feel.

All emotions, even the emotion of falling in love, must be evaluated carefully and both the emotional and rational brains consulted or you may wake up too late, living with the consequences of a purely emotional decision. Teens have trouble with love, of course, and they should be learning when one of life's most powerful emotions assails them that they must consult both brains. What happens when the young adult has not yet learned to fully use the brains they have been given (both emotional and rational) and they make immature, uninformed choices? We often simply call it immaturity. Whatever we call it, it can be devastating.

It's not that we should consider our emotions to be wrong simply because their conviction that they are right could be a false alert. We would err much of the time if we did that. Speed, emotion's strong suit, is not necessarily a negative simply because it is accompanied by a conviction that its fast judgment is right, when on further analysis, it could be wrong.

The strong conviction that an emotional judgment is right is not to be lightly dismissed as immature either. Thoughtful evaluation of our emotion's convictions, coupled with being able to do the right thing after we analyze them, is the path to intelligence. The wrong path is disparaging all emotional messages because their judgments are fast and bold.

This biased attitude to emotions often tries to develop the ability to stop all feelings before they strike. Neither should rational judgments to be treated as though they are right simply because they have slowly processed the facts. Think again of how the speedy judgments of our emotions are often right, flagging us of our immediate needs. The only time to reasonably do anything about our emotions is after they strike, or in the case of conjuring up the emotions ourselves, before we give birth to them.

Intuitive judgments that can be valuable information and undetectable to our five senses make the point that reason cannot be considered as the final court of appeal. The world of intuition and feeling has its claim to wisdom too.

An emotion has a way of rationalizing its own judgments. It sometimes defends the rightness of its decisions by sheer force, overpowering our senses and leaving us baffled rather than allowing us the calm we need to reason our way to what is the best thing to do. Again, when facing danger or hurt, the wisdom of this sense of urgency and conviction should be obvious.

We can also notice another feature in emotion's claims to be right. If the emotion is negative, like the fear of being hurt, then negative rationalization of the fear usually dominates; if a positive like love is present, then positive rationalization usually dominates. The nature of the emotion, positive or negative, determines how it presents its justifications to us for us to accept them. Simply asking the whether this feeling is negative or positive can, in most circumstances, give us a clue as to whether we should believe it or not.

These facts are teaching us that emotional intelligence is learning how to free ourselves from the grasp of our feelings long enough to objectively evaluate them together with the situation that gave rise to them. Emotionally gullible people who believe their emotions without examination are emotionally unintelligent.

Can I Think Clearly with Emotion?

For some, to think clearly when they are emotionally stirred is a major concern, so we need to try to understand the issue better. They (the NT in particular) have become convinced that emotions cloud their thinking, and they can. The solid evidence that emotions can impair our thinking is in our experiences. Therefore, with this irrefutable evidence, these people reject all emotion as damaging to crystal clear thinking. However, we must not identify what *can* happen with what *always* happens.

Although emotions can cloud our thinking, they can also clarify our thinking. Take anxiety, for example, which can carry our mind into a very dense fog. Anxiety is a heightened fear, an animated form of alertness. We need a certain amount of pure mental alertness to be able to think clearly, coherently, and lucidly.

The alertness we experience when thinking clearly is a form of attentiveness that needs an element of emotion to drive it. The emotion is found in the reason we are paying attention. The right amount of alertness, not too little and not too much, will enable us to evaluate our emotions about the facts we are considering and make a sound judgment. So, emotion can both energize and clarify our thinking. However, we know only too well how too much emotional alertness creates a hyper sensitivity and clouds our minds. If we add fear, it demands our full attention and full blown anxiety results.

Fear can also play two roles: it can paralyze our minds or empower our minds to think with precision. How often have we felt a surge of fear accompanied by an accurate assessment of what we needed to do immediately? Both an emotion and, as a result of the emotion, a clarity of thinking has occurred spontaneously. A powerful, captivating emotion has thought emotionally and with clarity.

Hopelessness, on the other hand, performs one role, demotivating us so that we can't seem to bring ourselves to face the task of thinking at all. Emotions clearly have their role in creating both fog and clarity in thinking, so if we want to be intelligently emotional we cannot accept the maxim that emotions only cloud our thinking and only reason clarifies it. As I have been arguing, both emotion and reason together are the mental tools to create clarity and power in our thinking.

What about positive versus negative emotions?   Love is a positive emotion, but we all know that love can be both blind and very insightful.   Positive emotions can jam the mental communications or illuminate them.   Fear is generally regarded as a negative emotion, but as a motivator it can contain great wisdom.   There is no rule that says positive emotions always contribute to clear thinking — they don't. Neither do negative emotions always contribute to fogged thinking.   Positive emotions usually help and negative ones usually hurt, but that's as far as we can go.   Again, clear thinking is a matter of using both emotion and reason and evaluating their contributions to the argument.

The real truth is we don't think without emotion.   The very desire to think through a problem is a motivating emotion. We think with a purpose and the purpose contains an emotion of some sort. We include reason in our thinking for the obvious benefits reason can offer.

The Mind's Power Source

Emotions are also the powerhouse of the mind.   That's why they drive us and our actions so easily. They get the first shot at all incoming messages and we have to battle a rising tide of emotional pressure as they try to have an impact on us with their message that they believe is right. In the NF, this rising tide amounts to an inner tsunami at times.   Why is it that emotions are so forceful?

Our emotional reactions to what is happening in our world must counter force with force.   To escape imminent danger (the situational force) we must react with a force that is sufficient to impel us out of danger's reach (the force of a powerful emotion, fear). Emotion holds the key to the control center of all of our amazing chemicals that power our bodies, such as adrenaline or dopamine. Emotion can also energize our thoughts with what feels like the speed and brilliance of a lightning bolt.

The more emotional energy we have, the greater our influence over our world. It can be a quiet determination or a loud outburst. Being the most complex of all organisms, doesn't it make sense that we should be given the greatest power to shape our world? And we have — emotions.

Our interactions with people (consider world events that hinge on opposing ideologies and morally opposite goals) are all energized by emotion. Think of the lover who, when it seems foolish to pursue his dreams anymore, wins his loved one's heart in the end by the sheer determination and skill of his emotions.

Emotions not only power our brain, our relationships, and our lives but have power over our environment as well. The explorer battles on against impossible odds, in pain but driven by hope. In the end, in spite of circumstances that have destroyed those with lesser emotional persistence, the force of his determined emotions takes him where no one has been before. His environment has succumbed to the relentless drive of his emotions. It makes sense that we should have a power that matches the dignity and potential of our natures. Observation of our capacity for greatness suggests we are made in a higher image. For good or ill, our world and our achievements are inevitably shaped by our emotions.

Fighting these escalating tides of emotion within us can help us learn emotional toughness. In the gym, the less weight we lift, the less muscle we develop. So it is in our inner lives: the less we struggle, the less we develop emotional power. The design that says we must struggle against our emotions as well as ride triumphantly with them to become stronger calls us to our greatest and keeps our potential ever in front of us, urging us on to more.

This argument suggests that for those who have struggled less with emotion's powers or have already captured them (usually those with a T in their profile), there is sense in not criticizing those who seem to bend under the weight of their emotions while deep in the heat of the struggle, or those who are still fighting for control, or those who will never give up the struggle to attain yet more power from their emotions. The struggle is where the building of great resources and superior strength is taking place.

Also, when thinking of the power of emotions we must understand that the struggle against them also teaches us self-control and personal discipline. Know where the power comes from and the benefits of personal control.

Part 2

4-Emotions That Drive the Eight Energy Centers

Human subtlety ... will never devise an invention more beautiful, more simple or more direct than does nature.
~ Leonardo da Vinci, *The Notebooks (1508-1518)*

To ignore, repress, or dismiss our feelings is to fail to listen to the stirrings of the Spirit within our emotional life.
~ Brennan Manning, *Abba's Child*

The word *temperament* suggests emotion to most people and some would even insist that temperament is emotion. When we talk of a person having a strong temperament, we mean someone who is forceful, determined, emotional, or maybe even angry. All of these are emotions we are identifying as a person's temperament. We certainly identify a person's dominant emotions as their temperament's strengths. We can see the emotion more readily than their inner urges or strengths, but we are not altogether right because the emotion with which we power our strengths is not the same as our strengths.

The meaning of the Latin word, *temperamentum*, suggests temperament is a "correct mixture," adding a new thought to our definition of temperament. The Latin definition is correct. Each of us is given a correct mixture of strengths.

Temperament is our strengths, not the emotions that energize them. To energize is the role of emotion in temperament. It is, therefore, important to know what strengths we have and to use the correct emotion to drive each strength intelligently. We can disturb the correct mixture by using negative or inappropriately matched emotions. Or, we can employ the wrong amount of emotion. Both result in us living in self-made weaknesses.

Here's another mixture we find in temperament. When Briggs (the mother) and Myers (the daughter) created the first temperament questionnaire, the Myers-Briggs Type Indicator (MBTI), they sought to find out what mixture of extroversion and introversion we have as well as the mixture for each of the other three areas of personality they were examining: sensing and intuition, thinking and feeling, and the two lifestyles (J and P). The result is seen in the pairs of numbers we have for each of the four categories.

For the extrovert/introvert category, we may have almost even numbers and for sensing and intuition, the numbers may widely diverge. These numbers indicate the mixture of each variant we have in our temperament. All of this is valuable information about who we are. We are not fully extroverted or fully introverted; we are different mixtures.

So, are close numbers or divergent numbers the correct mixture? What causes the mixture to be close or divergent is not our preferences but the emotions that drive them under each circumstance. In some people the driving force behind their preferences is strong, and in others it is weaker. It can also be a damaging emotion or a helpful one that is driving the strength of, say, supervision.

Whatever the mixture or numbers, it is a "correct mixture" because the mixture forms the temperament of the person and stamps them with their own wonderful uniqueness. However, we can modify these numbers if we choose for various reasons, such as to relate to someone more effectively. This is why we see people change somewhat as they age or when they are under new circumstances. We can never change our letter from E to I or S to N, for example, because our temperament remains hard-wired, but we can act toward an extrovert as an extrovert even if we are introverted. This accommodation is something we can become more adept at doing through practice. It is a temporary adjustment that enables us to be all things to all people.

We will begin by examining some emotions that drive the strengths represented by each letter. The letters will be E or I, S or N, T or F, and J or P. You will need your four-letter profile from completing the Temperament Key that appears in the first Appendix to benefit most from this chapter. Focusing on your letters and understanding the contrasting letter in each category will give you the best introduction to understanding the mixture that is you.

Viewing some emotions that drive each of the eight energy centers (letters) and then (in the next chapter) viewing the emotions that form the core of each temperament will add yet more information and understanding to the complex world of your innerkinetics. It's your inner world and the interaction of your emotions that shape your innerkinetics positively or negatively.

Each of the letters report, as I have indicated, on energy centers in our lives: think of each of your letters that way. Our inner life (or life itself for that matter) is more than energy, but it must have energy to motivate and move it forward. Emotion is a form of energy and drives each of the eight preferences to lead us in the direction our lives are intended to go.

Many people who come to me are worried about the feelings that seem to control them. For example, Jacob's problem was a persistent puzzle to him. "Why can't I make decisions?" he asked. "People tell me I am a procrastinator because I have to think about the decision and let it settle overnight before I can bring myself to decide. I keep thinking the right decision is obvious, but I hesitate and think of how it affects others and how I feel about it and, honestly, it's a real struggle to decide. Am I a procrastinator or what is this? Am I somehow twisted or something?"

Emotion drives us, and it was driving Jacob. He was tormented by its interference in his life. His experience is normal for all Fs. That piece of information was a relief to

Jacob. When he understood emotion's role in what appeared to be procrastination, he realized his emotions were also aids in making better decisions and that information then showed him how he might be more intelligently emotional.

E or I

The first center, the one that determines our extrovert/introvert energy source and method of its replenishment, is recorded in our profile by the letters E or I.   Extroverts are chiefly energized by people and things outside of themselves, whereas introverts mainly energize from within.   These preferences are strongly driven by emotions.

The Emotional World of the E

For the extrovert, emotional connections with another person supply the extrovert with a rising level of energy, lifting their spirit. Emotions like to sympathize with others, and they build their inner level of alertness and energy when they do. Here are some of the emotions that stimulate the extrovert:

- Love, especially when it is intense
- The simple excitement of connecting, which can border on an addiction for some extroverts
- The relief of having someone to talk to (this need for the extrovert occurs whenever their inner batteries begin to lose their charge)
- The calming feeling of flow that talking produces
- The mental stimulation from sharing ideas or information about their world with others
- The warmth and excitement of physical encounters
- The lift that a smile brings

- The stimulation from the urge to investigate — the curiosity addiction
- The promise of intimate interaction

The introvert will feel all these emotions too, but will find them draining in too large a dose. Talking, connecting, even too much intimacy can rob the introvert of energy — not so the extrovert.

For the extrovert, the stimulation of sensing and engaging with things, not just people — especially exciting things — can charge their batteries fast as well. A trip to the amusement park or a ball game will certainly do it. All the emotions that result from social encounters and physical stimulation team up and can overcharge their batteries so that they become hyper-sensitized.

An extroverted child can often be observed in this over-replenished state. If it happens just before bedtime, the parents can have a trial on their hands trying to keep the child in bed. For the extrovert, a full charge is normal and an overcharge can easily be attained. Please note that the emotion of excitement plays a large part in replenishing this lost energy.

"When I'm drained, I feel the urge to reconnect with my friends, to meet new ones, and just to feel the thrill of people and that electrifying charge of excitement again," reports one extroverted person. Again? Yes, again and again for the extrovert — the need will never end.

"I feel my emotions being lifted and refueled for more adventure as long as an engaging encounter is in the offing," said another extrovert. Expectation recharges.

Estelle looked forward to it too, "I don't mind feeling drained, because it's like having a spat with your partner and then comes the thrill of making up." Once charged, extroverts burn up their energy without fear of being unable to recharge. The opportunities for meeting people and experiencing things is always somewhere near. Have you ever observed a little child falling down repeatedly and laughing as they get back up? They are getting a charge, a lift to their spirits. Recharging is fun for the extrovert.

For the extrovert, the emotions that arise from long exposure to excitement and lively interactions, from the feeling of being popular, and from the tug of social opportunities recharge them best.

Note: It is not just the excitement but the other emotions that are generated in and by the excitement that are the fuel in the extrovert's tank.

The Emotional World of the I

That man's silence is wonderful to listen to.
~Thomas Hardy

The introvert is both powered and drained by emotions, only it seems drained more often and with greater speed. First, their battery is very seldom fully charged. When feeling full to the introvert, it is actually only about two-thirds full. When empty, it is dead empty. The reason is that they are more easily and constantly drained and it is hard to attain a full charge in the normal routines of life.

They can seem to be less excitable, more morose or serious and somewhat removed at times, all of these emotional conditions caused by the draining of their energy. "Why are they not excitable like us, enjoying the ride of life?" ponders the extrovert. They are enjoying the ride, but not in the same way. For an introvert to experience outright ecstasy is unusual and if they do, it passes quickly as they fall back to reality with a thud. This downside of the emotional spectrum can more often be experienced by the introvert than the upside, but the feelings of recharge are just as satisfying as the extrovert's sensitizations.

"I love being alone where I can dream or read — it's so refreshing. Extroverts, to me, seem not be in touch with themselves or something," Lester told me with a warm reserved smile. He was not unhappy. He had found how to have pleasure in a more solitary fashion.

Since introverts recharge best in solitude, the introvert is affected by different emotions that have mostly the opposite effect than the extrovert experiences in the recharging process. Recharging is mainly a peaceful venture for the introvert, or at least they hope so.

In the privacy of their own space, they feel the calming effect of disengagement, the peace of solitude in some sequestered nook, the stirring of inner life in their mind as they draw on the stimulation of ideas and concepts. They sense the deep abstract movements of the spirit, the refreshing loss of distractions, and the stimulation of a mental vacation. They enjoy the reduction of meaningless chatter and savor the reduction with great pleasure. A connection with themselves and their inner world, the tranquility from the lowering of stress, and the return of optimism to a hurting spirit sapped of its vitality by the constant external grating of a hectic world, bring peace.

The "peace" can be exciting as well, however. They may read or watch a program and, for some (the NF), they are always comparing themselves to everything they see and hear. Going for a walk or run, savoring the wonder and beauty of nature, connecting to its pulse, and dreaming of the future possibilities are treasured exercises for the drained and drooping introverted spirit. Emotions flood their minds in all these simple practices even if they don't stir the body. A quiet body and an overactive, stimulated mind can bring emotions of great delight.

This quiet side of life and the tranquility of "my own space" quells the disturbances that have chafed the linings of the introvert's soul. Harmony with themselves and their world is what they want. They feel the beginnings of exhilaration as the spirit of quiet confidence edges up slowly, increasing feelings of self-worth and bringing feelings of hope that glimmer optimistically in their minds. Recharging is fundamentally the restoration of a battered person whose bruises are not likely to be seen by prying eyes. Privacy, quiet, reflection, and learning fill the reservoirs of hope and create warm emotions.

Sigurd F. Olson, whose books on the wildness of the Boundary Waters are so refreshing, demonstrates the enjoyments of the introvert. He would spend weeks plying the lakes and trudging the trails, and in the evenings, he would thrill to the sound of the loon, the noises of the woods, and the lack of all other distracting interferences. It is when we reach down into the unfrequented depths of a quiet spirit that the creative surges of an undisturbed imagination rise to refresh us, and he of all men knew this pleasure of the introvert.

The introvert does not have the edge on intuition, but it seems they come into contact with it the most. "People who are intuitive have the edge over those who are not," Olsen writes and credits the solitude experienced in a quiet mind and a quiet place to his familiarity with it. There are many joys beyond the prattle of voices and the clamor of attention-getters. Introverts know these emotions well.

"The love of learning, the sequestered nook and all the sweet serenity of books," wrote Longfellow who drew on introversion's pleasures in his poems. And, ah, those books. A book requires imagination, turning type into pictures in the mind, and draws its pleasures from emotions that it can stir in a mind as no other source can. For some introverts, a book has to be a paper book: the smell of ink on paper, the physical turning of pages, and even the favored bookmark give great pleasure. The electronic reader can be a cold reading device for them.

Introverts must find their own happiness. "What angel in my own remote childhood taught me when alone to be happy?" wrote the British poet, Walter de la Mare. He continues, "What gratitude could repay such a boon?" These writers were happy, very happy and proud to be introverts.

All the emotions of extroverts and introverts enrich our lives, and both serve up their pleasures in different ways in different regions of life, the outward and the inward. If we disturb the recharging process or demand they recharge another way, we interfere with their emotions. Unsatisfied emotions introduce pain.

The Effect of E or I on Emotional Health

It is a testimony to the power and purpose of our positive emotions that they can energize us so easily. Pause and think of the opposite, the negative emotions that result from an undercharged or a flat battery. Negative emotions drain whatever energy we have left. If we are suddenly faced with bad news or the loss of a friend or a sickening report, our inner batteries can drain and and we feel the depression of sadness in minutes or even seconds. We even feel it in the pit of our stomach and can become ill if the news is too deflating. The effect of negative emotions on our health is not to be underestimated.

Energizing often takes place in seconds, as does de-energizing. Like breathing in and out, the constant oscillation from having an energized spirit to underpowered and back to powered again seems to happen endlessly on some days. We charge and then drain, oscillating with apparent ease. We notice it in children. A child can be up one moment and down the next. A sudden disappointment can drain them so fast they are left gasping — especially the introverted child.

Have you noticed that an offer of ice cream can miraculously recharge your child in an instant, but if the cause of their being drained is still around they can be de-energized, sad, and morose again before the ice cream is eaten. Only the deep emotions of the human spirit charge or deflate with such speed and persistency. Ups and downs are normal for us all, but we must watch out for the downs that flatten our batteries or those of our children and risk our health.

Constant depression that would deflate us everyday is avoided because of this forced need to recharge. When we feel ourselves becoming depressed, we find a way to restore the energy we are losing and we recharge again. But if one deflating experience after another assails us without an opportunity to recharge our failing batteries, we are almost certain to be drained of all life-giving feelings and then we are left gasping for refreshment or, in more serious cases, the desire to live. The loss of self-worth can also rush in like a tide and obliterate our happiness before we know it. Would you believe that even the thought of stress, let alone the reality, can bring on an emptying of our inner power? Thanks to the urge to recharge, whether we are extroverts or introverts we recharge many times a day and are saved from the devastating effects of a flat battery.

Maintaining a charge is what we must accomplish to create stability in our lives — the calming feeling of being on an even keel. The seas of life will challenge us, at times overwhelm us, or grant us the peace of placid waters one moment and toss us wildly about the next. We must find time to restore our emptied resources and manage both the vagaries and ecstasies of life or run the danger of shipwreck on lifeless shores. It is our responsibility to heed the urge to refresh our dwindling resources or to make sure we see the need and do something about it.

Why do we need this recharge? Ask an extrovert who has been locked up in solitary confinement and you will get a dramatic answer. Mental health is threatened when we cannot recharge. It feels like we are dying inside. The extrovert who is denied contact with others or the introvert who is denied their recharge in solitude will fight for what their spirits need, even resort to violence. For both the extrovert and the introvert, replenishment of needed inner energy must be achieved and feels good as the life of the spirit returns.

These two categories, extrovert and introvert, have seldom been questioned since they are so easily observed. Carl Jung thought them to be where we focus our energies. More correctly, they are where we go to replenish our energies.

A family of four extroverts kept trying to lift the spirit of the youngest child, an introvert. They would burst into her room when she was alone and drench her spirit with lighthearted chatter. The parents would keep insisting that she should show excitement at being with her siblings, and she would only burst into tears when accused of being antisocial. If they thought their accusations would persuade her to change they were very wrong. "What is wrong with our youngest child?" they asked themselves without finding an effective solution.

She became more reclusive even though she was seeing a psychiatrist regularly, and she showed all the signs of depression. When she pleaded for them to build her a room in the detached garage, they consented only because they did not know what else to do to help her and in the hope that it may lift her spirits.

Her mother soon discovered she was cutting herself and when both parents finally sought help, they discovered how they were denying her the space and pleasure of recharging her depleted spirit. Unknowingly, they were only making matters worse by their criticisms of her introversion. Only when they began respecting who she was and started on the road of understanding someone so different from themselves did things change. She bounced back, and only an introvert can imagine the relief she felt when she could recharge in her own way and not be the subject of criticism.

Extroverts and introverts need the refreshment of their very different emotions. Understand the different plights of each and encourage them to take time to meet their truly human need — a mental health requirement. The need to feel alive in our spirits is as important to health as the need for our bodies to feel their strength.

S and N

Sensing and intuiting (S or N) are two different ways for gathering information from the world around us and both have emotions that drive them. These two ways of being informed about our world form the great divide in the four temperaments, two temperaments being Ss and two being Ns.

Outward and Inward Emphases

Again we find an outward/inward contrast of preferences and emotions like we find in the extrovert/introvert category.

The S finds gathering information outside of themselves more to their liking, using their five physical senses. The facts of life around them that they detect with their physical senses mostly satisfy their informational gathering needs. For them it is comfortable to live in this external world, manipulating, controlling, and experiencing its many enjoyable stimulations. Their emotions, which are inward, are stirred by their engagement with the world outside of themselves.

"As long as I have someone to talk to and information on those dear to me, I feel satisfied," one SJ typically reported. The news of friends and family can be all-important to an S, and they wonder why others can live happily without constant contact. The others, the Ns, live inside themselves and emerge, so to speak, with less urgency to check the "mail."

The Ss are very observant because they are focused on the realities that are seen, heard, touched, tasted and smelled. Practice makes perfect and the Ss get lots of practice from dawn to day's end by observing their world and filing the information they gather. Seldom do they pass by an object without noticing it. The pride that arises from accurately remembered details is an emotion not as familiar to the Ns (one they wish they had).

On the contrary, the N prefers to focus on how they feel inwardly about things and events, and since the focus is inward and they are often lost in thought, they can easily pass by an object and not notice it (such as an exit sign on the highway) or even bump into it (such as a chair that has been moved). Intuition, this inward sensing (the eyes of the soul, some call it), is used reliably to guide their passage through life but not to avoid those physical objects. Emotions that satisfy and challenge them arise from the use of their intuition, imagination, and empathy. Ns trust these gut feelings and insights. When they are lost in thought, they are lost in their minds and any thought that comes to mind is focused on and examined for its potential emotional and rational rewards. Therefore, insights and intuitive information are seldom missed.

The Ss focus their information-gathering energy on the outside world, while the N prefers to check in with the effect the world is having on their inner life and then spend time enjoying it. Emotions accompany both outwardly-focused and inwardly-focused preferences.

For Tom, it was in the physical engagement with his world that his emotions were most pleasantly aroused. He was an S and the emotional charge of all things external, such as the thrill of the slope as he pointed his skies downhill over the moguls and twisted and turned his way in a sensory paradise, made him feel most alive.

Not so for Mandy. She would accompany him to the ski ground with different expectations. After a run or two, she would retire to a quiet corner of the lodge where there was a view of the mountain and, with a good book and a hot cup of coffee, she would find the real pleasure of her day. The emotions of pleasure deep inside rewarded her intuitive spirit in spades.

Emotions of the S and N

Since emotions that are aroused by connections with the world outside of themselves seem to dominate in the S, we can find plenty of examples. Love, an obvious one, is given generously by the S to other people in deeds or loving actions and not so commonly expressed in language. The loving deed is seen as adequate if the S is not notified to the contrary. Of course, the S loves to receive love in any form it is given.

However, love in the NF is talked about more because it is the constant rumination of their minds in all their close relationships. "Am I still loved?" they ask themselves. "Is there still harmony in the relationship?" And when it comes to receiving love in the form of loving deeds, they think to themselves, "Can I depend on the loving action of another to reflect their true feelings? I would like to *hear* they love me too, just in case I am misunderstanding their deeds." The N's attention is on the feeling of harmony and any loss of it is immediately registered as disturbing. Therefore, emotions generated in the virtual world seem to dominate for the NF in particular.

The other N, the NT, is not focused on emotions per se and, therefore, is not affected by their presence or absence as much as the NF. They can tend to be less disturbed by the absence of loving expressions as long as they know everything is alright. They also tend to express their love less.

The Emotions of the S

Sensing persons who are mainly focused on the world outside of themselves are driven by the emotions they feel as they react with the world and often in the very moment they are experiencing them. Love, fear, hate, and jealousy, these and countless other emotions are concretely experienced and expressed, often in a very useful, practical way.

The Ss defend the practical use of their emotions, pointing out that if our love, for example, is not practical it does not satisfy or even pass the test of real love, meaning a love that can be sensed and experienced must also be in some way practical. "Please show me your love by helping me," they silently ask. They also imply, "Who would not like a lover to remember your birthday or your anniversary?" Love is seen most assuredly in the husband who labors above the call of duty to provide and

Emotions that Drive the Eight Energy Centers

the wife who works outside the home and also does her part of the home's duties without complaint. These expressions of love are most often the true expression of love to the S. Not that Ns don't appreciate such devotion when the S gives it, but on its own, deeds are not enough for the NF.

Since emotions are our way of dealing with the world and responding to its events and to our interpretations of them the Ss believes their emotions. Their emotions are a part of the real world they live in and they construct their views of what is happening, has happened, or will happen around their emotions. An S can be very quick to react to events and to people, taking the experience and the emotions created by their engagement at face value.

What is seen, heard and, consequently, felt is believed because it is seen, heard, and felt. Why not, since it meets the demands of our physical senses? If someone makes a statement, rather than looking for hidden explanations and motives, they believe the person said what they meant, and surely they must also be held responsible for what they have said. It's as simple as that. The emotional interpretations of the S are, then, part of their dominant orientation to the outside world.

Therefore, in the case of the S, their emotions are also rather easily observed and understood, since they respond in a concrete form to what most people (Ss are more than three quarters of the population) are also responding to. The response is most often accepting at face value what their encounters suggest. When we say Ss are easier to understand, this is one factor that explains that observation.

Of course, "easily read" does not mean they react according to a few obvious emotions. There are numerous reactions possible to, let's say, a car cutting them off on the freeway. It could be rage, upset, mild concern, an urge to call the police, a feeling of dislike, hate, or simply despising the offending driver.

On the other hand, if they approve of the act, there is an almost endless set of emotions that start with being attracted to the offending driver's nerve, the thrill of speed or the call of danger. No list would be complete because of the complexity and subtlety of our ever-changing emotions. So the emotional world of the S is not simplistic even if their reactions and interpretations of what is going on may be straight forward.

When one emotion is observed, other emotions can also be drawn into play, creating a flood of emotional responses. The world of emotion in the S is many-faceted and never fully understood by another person. Give up? Don't. Ns experience the same things in life, even if their inner drives are different, and therefore they can read people with a high degree of accuracy. With practice they will become adept at knowing how the S feels.

The Emotions of the N

From the world of the S's practical emotions we move to the world of the N's dominant intuitive and secretive emotions. Theirs is the inside world, as we have said, with inside information being dominantly attended to, further complicating their rich emotional life. Emotions are still a response to the world, but in the case of the N, it is the world inside their own minds, embellished at times by imagination that is shaping their lives.

It's a real world, even if it is only a virtual world. And to the mind of the Ns, it is as real as the world outside of the mind that we are all too prone to label as the only "real world." Remember, it's well known that the N can run into an object like a chair and, being lost in their virtual world, exclaim that they never saw it.

So intense is their focus on the inner world that the sign on the freeway goes by unnoticed, the reason for going to the store is lost, or the name of the book is forgotten as they strain to experience and process their mental meanderings and all the emotions they produce — a colossal task. Just because they live in their thoughts and feelings does not mean they experience less or feel no emotions from their thoughts and feelings — just the opposite.

Rob can't remember how many times he has had to endure a stern reminder of things he has not observed or remembered with the same clarity as his "S" wife's well-practiced observational skills. He knows it reinforces his feelings of being very different. In the face of her charges he feels he is being reminded of his inferiority. Note the word *feels*. It's the emotional response he has to what she says, not the lack of remembering, that stirs him. He tells me that when his wife forgets something and he reminds her, she brushes it off with an excuse and seems to be unaffected by the momentary loss of her native skill. Her emotional response is minimal.

The emotions produced in him and her for the same failure feel like opposites and they are at least very different. It's not just that Ns are more affected by their not registering what their physical eyes see; it is how they are affected by not noting what they see that creates the different emotional response.

The N is troubled by the loss of respect in the eyes of the S and the lowering of their self-esteem, which is always a main touchstone of happiness for them. An over-indulged sensitivity also brings on the feeling of being judged. This "thin skin" can be hard to thicken; some achieve it and some don't. The solution is not always the obvious attempt to be less sensitive; rather it is to strengthen their self-image. A low self-image is always the breeding ground of blossoming, negative emotions.

The N's sensitive emotions are actually enjoyable to them. At times the S can't fathom why. They don't see these secretive, internal emotions. They have little knowledge that the feeling of low self-worth can, with the same gift of sensitivity, be changed in an instant into feelings of pleasure. The N's imagination can change anything at any time.

Their inner world can change as fast as the outer world, but the change can't be observed by others. Living in their minds also means they can create any kind of world they like, regardless of the conditions of the world outside. They can feel and sense the pleasures of anything that is imagined vividly enough. So vivid is their imagination that it is hard for them to detect at times whether the experience was limited to their mind or actually experienced in real life. The emotions are the same.

They can also imagine the darkest world of self-blame, a world where they and life itself is worth nothing, where utter despair is no phantom passing in the night but a nightmarish monster.

Imagination does not discriminate. Bright or dark thoughts are equally vivid and remembered with equal power. If only the S would understand this and not berate the NF, in particular, for their long struggles at rising from their feelings of worthlessness, helplessness, and hopelessness. Rise they will, if not clinically depressed, and even then they will also rise if hope glimmers again. The NF is particularly vulnerable to the dark emotions that plague our souls.

The emotions of the N are, of course, hard to detect unless they choose for them to be displayed, and that is not very often. Sometimes the N can successfully hide emotions from all those around and later, when they do emerge due to some unbearable internal pressure, people will express surprise at why these emotions surfaced at a time unrelated to any event that might have prompted them.

"Why don't they live like us?" the S puzzles. "Be an open book; let it out." The N either does not want to (hidden is safe) or can't face the potential hurt. Their emotions can tangle them in a web of embarrassment, real or not, and they fear their exposure with a passion. Just being misunderstood is a form of hurt for the truly sensitive among them. They have adopted private lives since they knew from the beginning that they are vulnerable to hurt.

The Ns can even fear their own emotions because they are so powerful. If they allow them to be expressed, they know they can escalate and create all kinds of havoc. Such emotional eruptions can dominate their minds in an instant. Later they will probably regret such ill-chosen displays. Depression can also be just this, being taken emotionally captive.

It's hard to draw a precise line between the emotions of the S and the N, since both have an inner world and live also in an outer world. It is also difficult to understand all Ns in all cases because the NT and the NF, as we will see later, have very different responses to the invasion of emotion. The difference between the S and the N, to generalize, is largely a matter of degree and a matter of how they experience their emotions. However we see it, it makes a huge difference in how they live their lives.

Simply think "outer," the physical side of life and the contentment with stimulation from the outside for the S. Think "inner," mental musings, looking behind the facts to the meanings for the N and you will understand their emotions most of the time. The S and the N produce divergent life experiences.

T or F

Thinkers and feelers (T or F) is a way of differentiating between two ways of judging the information we gather from the world around us and within us. Thinkers favor the use of analysis, reason, and logic in their decisions. Feelers, while using logic, must also consult their feelings. What must be noted is that both think and feel.

The choice of the words, thinker and feeler, is unfortunate since they give the impression that thinkers don't feel and feelers don't think. Both can be logical and reasonable, but the feelers sense the need to consult their feelings before a final decision is reached and also to consider the feelings of others in the process, which the thinkers may or may not do. Certainly the thinkers do so to a lesser degree.

For Pam, it was a simple choice. She was a T. The car for the best bargain and with the most favorable gas mileage and warranty was the obvious choice. "The facts make it clear that we should buy that blue one over there," she dogmatically stated. "I don't like blue, but it's the best deal for our money," she continued. More tentative was her husband's response, being a strong F: "I like the red one," he softly said. "We have to look at it every day and the red is more appealing to me," and then he added in self defense, "It is nearly as good a bargain and, besides, our happiness is worth something, don't you think?" Without pausing and realizing the weak spots that a T would instantly notice in his argument, he pleaded again, "And don't you want to take our feelings into account?"

He'd been here many times before when making decisions, but his feelings always led him into the same trap again. He knew how she was so practical, sensible in her judgments and, to him, lacking in feelings at times. Unfortunately his emotional appeal and her logic were not going to meet happily.

After a verbal fight and having to leave the dealership without a conclusion, the decision still hung in the air like a poisonous gas, choking their relationship. All was not solved until they came to an understanding of each other and how to respect their opposite ways of evaluating and deciding. Then they would have to find a compromise acceptable to both.

In this section we are considering the emotional energy generated by decision-making, and what strong energy it can be. Emotions obviously play a large role in this important energy center of our lives. When Ts and Fs are in conflict, emotions often reach the overheated stage, and not just for the Fs. It is ironic that the temperament (NT) that does not prefer to consult emotion uses emotion in battling for the win in an argument, and the one that emphasizes emotional facts (NF) uses reason to defend their emotions.

The Emotions of the T

"Do they have any?" wonder the Fs. Yes, everyone has emotions and uses them. Ts place the emphasis on analysis and rationality, not on emotion. Once they feel comfortable with their assumptions about the facts, they then proceed to truth via the precise path of logic. In their view, the path requires little emotion.

However, it is not devoid of emotion because emotion is driving them to walk the path to discovery and truth. Without it they would have no motivation. No discovery is ever made that does not utilize emotion, except one made by pure chance. It may be the prosaic emotion of having to be right, or a normal feeling of curiosity, or maybe a questioning skepticism that drives the T to a decision, but they are assuredly driven by emotion.

Some Ts will keep insisting that they are not emotionally motivated. These people are simply self-deceived. As we have found, emotion is an unavoidable motivator of the human system, whether observed or not. Other Ts besides the NTs regard emotion as unintelligent and they, too, are in error.

I remind you again of these facts about emotion to help you gain a perspective on the important place this element wields in our profile. Ever since Aristotle, we have been led to believe that we are rational creatures. Of course this is true, but it is only half or less than half of the story. We are emotional creatures first and foremost.

Emotions with their judgments can be a direct path to truth since emotions are facts of life and can make wise decisions. Once made, they have an impact on all we do and think and they often form our beliefs about what is true and false. We reject them as always unintelligent to the detriment of our lives. Don't exclude their wisdom; rather let them take their rightful seat alongside of our reason.

For all Ts, their struggle is to understand the equality of both reason and emotion. The emotions that drive the worship of reason are the emotions that honor accuracy and preciseness. Emotion, however, reports whatever it senses and often does not pause for a lengthy evaluation before notifying us of its findings. Hence, the Ts can think it an inaccurate tool and the more so, the more it stirs their feelings of inaccuracy.

Add to this that the Ts don't favor fuzzy edges to anything in life and have a difficulty coming to a decision about anything that is not clear cut, black or white. Pride in intellectual preciseness can make some feel intellectually superior, which is an emotion that can blind them to the importance of emotion's role in decision-making.

We must not see these emotions as entirely negative, however. Skepticism, if it has positive goals, can drive us forcefully to creating a world of better ways and more useful inventions. Nor should we strive for a balance between the use of emotion and reason since balance is not usually motivating and often a compromise. It is always a matter of walking the path of reason while evaluating the urges of emotion.

The Emotions of the F

"Do they ever think?" ponder the Ts. Yes, they do, but not without feeling. Feelings are front and center to the Fs, demanding attention, coloring decisions with their judgments, showing concern for both the past and the future and insisting that they be a part of all the F does.

Strong emotion for the F can create a kind of brain-lock so they can't even function well, but this is the extreme. In the little child who is trying to manage compulsive feelings, their emotions can create traumatic tantrums and memorable meltdowns that last for long periods, and even result in the child turning purple and gasping for breath. In the adult it can incapacitate and de-motivate them entirely or produce anger reminiscent of childish displays. When the emotions take over, the F can lose all clarity, freeze in fear, and focus painfully on their feelings.

Such extremes should not elicit judgments of being weak. The bearer of strong emotions fights a battle with them that others know nothing of. We all tend to criticize those who are influenced powerfully by emotion because the Ts seem to handle these same pressures and struggles with ease. Admire the fight of the Fs to master their emotions; don't criticize the warriors. Those who are emotionally challenged should receive our comfort, encouragement, and our patience. However, SJs and all Ts often judge severely those who don't control their emotions like they do. It's truly a case of "Judge not, lest you be judged," since the T, like all of us, is in no position to claim perfection in the handling of their own emotions. The F is not to be victimized.

However, feelings do pose a big challenge that must be managed and not allowed to manage us. For many, it is a lifelong battle for mastery. Emotions are far more difficult to change than rational thoughts or even ingrained beliefs. They have a logic of their own and, having judged the situation, our emotions cling to what they believe is right. Powerful feelings surge and take control to motivate the person, but when they are the wrong emotional judgments, they must be challenged. Even when they are not wrong, they must be managed within acceptable boundaries.

There is no point in trying to name the kaleidoscope of emotions that Fs feel; they are legion. Justice and fairness, empathy and concern, for example, can show themselves anywhere on a continuum from rage to gentle pleas, creating numberless expressions of each emotion. What we can productively point out is that, for the F, their emotions mostly center around feelings that protect themselves or others from hurt.

We have already defended the need for emotions to be considered in all our decisions, and the Fs play both offense and defense with them to make themselves heard. An emotional person is often not taken seriously and, for the Fs, that is a very unjust act that they resent and that can produce another burst of annoyance. Their emotional outbursts are not to be defended, nor should they be condemned.

Encouragement and patience, to remind you, produce better results.

Another contrast between the Ts and the Fs should be placed in sharp focus. Decisiveness is not owned by the Ts. Both Ts and Fs can be decisive or indecisive. Typically the Ts can be indecisive for lack of emotional motivation, and the Fs can be indecisive precisely because of emotional motivation.

"Why can't you make up your mind," yelled the inveterate T to his partner who was full of feelings. "OK," she responded, "What's your decision, then?" There was a pause.

"Well it all depends," he began, and I could sense he was trapped by not having enough facts to make an accurate decision that his own demanding rational standards required. "I don't know, I'll need more facts," was his much subdued reply.

"And, I'll need more time," she retorted with growing confidence. "You find the facts and I'll find the time!"

This graphically illustrates that we all make our decisions by our own standards, whether they be rational or emotional requirements, and both should be honored and given space to operate comfortably.

J or P

The final two choices are lifestyle preferences (J or P). The choice of words is again unfortunate since the J stands for judging while the P stands for perceiving. In reality, the J does as much perceiving as the P and the P does as much judging as the J, making the distinction meaningless. I know that the words have a technical meaning, but because the words are so obviously misleading to all except those with privileged knowledge (and even then their applicability is somewhat questionable) we will simply call them J and P and fill the letters with the definitions of the two lifestyles.

As energy centers, these two preferences are first about coming to closure (J) or keeping options open (P). The result of these two choices is for the Js a more hurried and deliberate lifestyle that likes order and process, while for the P's, life is more laid back, impulsive, and less orderly. One will organize life more and the other lean toward going with the whim of the moment. There appears to be more need for energy in the lifestyle of the J and they are often cited for the early heart attack.

Emotions drive each preference, J and P, and they also flare quite volcanically when the lifestyles clash. Control of emotions rather than development of their strengths is most appropriate here. In relationships, the Js must move toward greater acceptance and appreciation of the P, and vice versa.

Emotional Dominance in the J

Dominant in the J is the feeling of urgency. Let's get it done now. There is a fear of not getting things done and having the unfinished tasks back up and produce anxiety. This urgency is fed by the need to achieve, a sense of pride in work accomplished, the treasured sense of relief when progress is made, and the strong desire to be on time and not be further stressed by being late.

These drives can easily be overdone, creating tension, high blood pressure and other issues, all raising the level of emotional strain. Emotions are easily seen in this lifestyle. Too much emotional pressure can drive the J prematurely to anger. It is often the anger of a threatened lifestyle.

The emotions of the J lifestyle seem to surge in the direction of achievement and getting all the tasks of life done. Peace is found in the completion of all needed details, but this also means peace is only realized in a structured life where it takes its place alongside of all the other urgent demands.

Emotional Dominance in the P

The Ps are ruled by stress-reducing emotions for the most part. What can't be done today will wait for the morrow. However, when the impulse hits them, the adrenaline must flow as the compulsion of the moment is attended to.

Fear of making a wrong move is more dominant in the P lifestyle. So, when they make a decision, they can be plagued with the uncertainty that they may have made the wrong decision. The craving to go with the flow and enter a peaceful, happy mode of existence is disturbed.

Their relaxed mode tends to stimulate a host of pleasant feelings like calm optimism, the urge of pleasure, the desire to play and enjoy. The P in the different temperaments — SP, NT, and NF — will stir quite divergent interpretations of these emotions, and in the NT, perhaps only ripple the surface of emotional calm.

Again, we cannot list the emotions of the P since, for them, any emotion can be called to the frontline of experience at any time, all decided by the conditions of the moment. What we do know of the P lifestyle is that their emotions all tend to flow in the direction of finding pleasure and calm and appear most often in the impulse of the moment.

Conclusions

We have examined the way the individual letters, representing the energy centers of life, display the emotional forces behind them. The variety of emotions that a different profile can induce and their divergent meanings to each type make for a rich human experience while creating challenge. Hopefully, we understand that such a challenge offers the chance for growth.

Understanding each other in terms of how we are emotionally driven is the way to lay a solid foundation for the enjoyment of a relationship, and relationships are the result of emotional bonds. Perhaps, we have also given more meaning to how emotions, more than reason, fashion who we are and give us appeal to others or initiate judgments not in our favor.

We must now understand the combination of two letters that describe the four temperaments and drive to the core of who the types are.

Intelligently Emotional

5 - How the Four Temperaments See Emotion and Use It

Do not let another day go by where your dedication to other people's opinions is greater than your dedication to your own emotions!
~ Steve Maraboli

Answer me, you who believe that animals are only machines. Has nature arranged for this animal to have all the machinery of feelings only in order for it not to have any at all?
~ Voltaire (Francois-Marie Arouet)

For almost two and a half millenniums, the four temperaments have been our most useful, accurate, and user-friendly means of understanding each other. Those four temperaments can be identified by the letters, SP, SJ, NT, and NF in the letters of the Myers-Briggs Type Indicator and all the temperament key's that use them. Almost 2,500 years is a compelling story, as David Keirsey put it.

Temperament is our innerkinetics, as I like to call it, and has revealed to us the core of our immaterial make-up, our inner strengths. Inside that core are the driving forces of emotion that shape the use of our strengths. This mix of temperament and its drives, powered by emotions that fashion our drives, makes for an almost infinite possibility of variances in human personality. The remarkable thing is that, given this infinite uniqueness of each human psyche, we are still recognizable in four distinct groupings. Each grouping (temperament) reveals a set of strengths that show distinct patterns of preferences that result in typical but not identical behavior for that temperament. Similar emotions appear in each temperament, driving its strengths and further fashioning its behavior.

Some people hate to be categorized or asked to identify their temperament. "Don't put me in a box," they scream. We all understand the appeal of being different, but are we being told by these people that we have no similarities that group us? Physically we do and psychologically we act in ways that bare great similarities to how others act. If this were not so, psychology would not be able to study human behavior; our differences would mean each would have to be studied with no reference to how another might act under the same circumstances with the same environmental conditions. What a weird concept to suggest we are in no way similar to others. I am looking out my window and I notice that the grasses on the hillock all have leaves, but not all leaves are the same, and although the specimens of one species are not identical, they certainly show identifiable similarities.

Love is recognizable as love even though its forms are infinite, and this is true of all our emotions. Therefore, with good reason we will talk of the groupings of strengths and emotions we call temperament (four boxes) and study their patterns in humans (one big box into which the four boxes fit).

Each of the four temperaments is represented by two letters that condition and affect each other. To read the emotions of the temperaments (as we have just done in the previous chapter) as simply a sum of each letter loses a great deal of information. Here we will look more closely at what the combination of the two letters and the temperament they reveal tell us about emotion. The four temperaments will be your best method to quickly understand yourself, your child, or your significant other.

Key Elements of Emotional Intelligence in the Temperaments

To remind you, the four temperaments referred to in this book by the letters, SP, SJ, NT, and NF, respectively correspond to Galen's *Sanguine, Melancholic, Phlegmatic*, and *Choleric* and to Keirsey's *Artisans, Guardians, Rationals*, and *Idealists*.

Each of the Ss, SP and SJ, are at opposite ends of the fear spectrum. This does not mean negative fears control the SP and SJ, although they can, and when they do, both temperaments fall apart. Fear is not necessarily a negative emotion. It can be a positive lifesaver for example when, because of an intuition, we feared to put our savings in the stock market just before it crashed. Fear of loss, such as when we fear we will miss the plane if we don't hurry, is not a negative emotion but a positive empowering feeling that gets us there on time. We can't live successfully without fear. On this positive side, fear motivates us, saves us, warns us, and makes us more intelligent.

Invaluable to us in all our efforts at success is this fear spectrum I am about to introduce, which can help us identify where our emotions are on a continuum. Both ends of the spectrum, one representing almost the absence of fear the other the presence of a real fear, are named for the positive emotions, optimism and caution — one dominant in the SP and the other in the SJ. Optimism is just as much a contributor to success as is caution or vice versa.

Therefore, do we need to attain a balance between optimism and caution for the greatest chance of success? No! The result would be a median where traffic flows neither one way nor the other. A lack of optimism or caution when we need one or the other spells motivational disaster. Success is not the achievement of averages. The circumstances for significant achievement usually require extreme optimism or extreme caution.

121

The SP displays the intelligence of optimism and the SJ that of caution. Each must be who they are and know when to hold back or press forward with their strengths.

The Fear Spectrum

SP<--->SJ

Optimism<-- >Caution

Emotions Charged With Optimism	Emotions Charged with Caution
Courage Impulsiveness Freedom to Express Spontaneous Change Effectiveness Lightheartedness	Concern Order and Preparedness Consistency Worry, Anxiety Logistical Efficiency Seriousness

In the SP, optimism is the core of their emotions and in the SJ, caution is the guiding heart of their emotions.

- Neither is negative or emotionally unintelligent.
- As with all the emotions of the SP and SJ, a balance is not the way to impress.
- Each circumstance and challenge will call for more of one than the other and the SP and SJ must learn when to hold back or push forward with optimism and caution.

The Sensitivity Spectrum

The NT and NF are dominated by opposite emotions on the sensitivity spectrum. The NT displays the intelligence of calmness and the NF, that of passion. Each must be who they are and know when to hold back or press forward with these emotions.

The need for calmness or passion is often not clear at first glance. When faced with a tiger, is calmness or the adrenaline of passion needed most? It depends. An extreme of calmness can lead one to freeze up, and an extreme of passion, to panic.

Sometimes success can be achieved with either, sometimes with only one. What is characteristic of each is the level of intensity both feel inside. To be calm requires effort, as does passion. The NT is visibly less reactive to challenges and the NF is more reactive.

NT<-->NF

Low reaction — Calm<---------- >High reaction — Passion

Emotions Controlled With Calm	Emotions Controlled with Passion
Reasoning Questioning Determination Independence Efficiency	Sensitivity Idealism Imagination Personal Significance Empathy

In the NT, calmness is the core of their emotions and in the NF, passion is the nature of all their emotions.

• Neither is negative or emotionally unintelligent.

- As with all the emotions of the NT and NF, a balance is not the way to impress.

- Each circumstance and challenge will call for more of one than the other, and the NT and NF must learn when to hold back or push forward with calmness or passion.

A dominance of optimism, caution, calmness, or passion in a person's behavior can help identify their temperament. Watch for the dominant emotional condition under normal circumstances and you will have found a short-cut to a tentative identification of the temperaments.

Either end of the spectrum can be emotionally intelligent. Being optimistic is no more or less intelligent than being cautious. Being calm is no more or less intelligent than being passionate. We are all made to display intelligence through our dominant emotions.

Understanding the key elements of emotion in each temperament is our next task.

Emotion in the SP Temperament

Few things are more powerful than a positive push. A smile. A word of optimism and hope. A "you can do it when things are tough."
~ Richard M. DeVos

Philosophically speaking, SPs act like Epicurians, or what is now more often called Hedonists in the field of ethics. Don't let philosophy scare you. We all live by some form or mixture of philosophic maxims. Philosophy is merely the understanding of our world, ourselves, our origins, and how we should live.

Epicurus would have us live for pleasure but not a life of pleasure that is out of control. He advocated pleasure in moderation. Hedonism, on the other hand, lays more emphasis on pleasure and less on the control of our lives. Some SPs are true hedonists, running wild with their emotions, and some condition their use and enjoyment of pleasure to fit the circumstance as Epicurus would advise. Not all SPs are extremists.

Epicurus, who was a copious writer, completing about 300 books (or so we are led to believe), lived from c.341-270 B.C. in Greece. At about 30 years of age he opened a school where he taught philosophy. He believed temperance combined with a simple life should lead to the greatest pleasure, so we would classify him by this definition of his teachings as a mild SP. His beliefs were founded on pleasure being the greatest good. An SP's love of fun, excitement, and their desire to drain the last drop of pleasure from each moment places there philosophy of life in the same broad category.

Whatever you do to escape pain and anxiety and find a simple pleasure, Epicurus would advocate. However, don't abandon yourself to pleasure because that could lead to even greater pain and fear. These are two of the most relevant thoughts, for our purpose, that governed his teaching and his life. SPs are best when they discover the control of their urges as Epicurus advocated.

Optimism Championed

Painting a picture of emotions in the SP temperament will give us a better grasp of how emotions shape them, and optimism is the dominant heartbeat. The upbeat, pleasant countenance of the SP gives them an obvious optimistic image that should be encouraged. It sets a positive mental stage for any encounter with an SP. When feelings of courage fill them and an adventuresome spirit propels them, they can be moved to fearlessly attack the impossible.

"Never done it before," is not a negative feeling to the SP; rather it prepares them for action. Physical stimulation then fuels their senses, filling them with the will to explore and achieve. Variety is also essential to keep their optimism fresh and alive.

"Let's go" "No time like the present," "Don't worry; it will all be okay," "If we wait we may never get another opportunity," and "Come on, what's wrong with you?" are phrases an SP regularly speaks with conviction.

This optimism is a belief. They really mean to egg us on and help us experience the offerings of an optimistic outlook.

All this optimism leads to excitement. Excitement challenges optimism for being the core of the SP's emotional makeup, but it is optimism that feeds the SP's excitement. If you believe in a generous world, optimism is an outcome of that belief and the belief itself feeds optimistic behavior. Excitement follows. If you are drenched in worry and pessimism, excitement is not even on the menu. All the emotions that mold the SP temperament's urges are moistened with optimism.

When optimistic, we are given more courage to attempt the impossible and surge bravely ahead in the face of difficulty. The optimistic bungee jumper leaps off the platform, showing courage, expecting a thrill, and wishing to add to its intensity by escalating their positive beliefs. You will not likely find them fearfully falling off the platform, scared out of their wits. Optimism restrains fear and liberates the courage of the human spirit. "Join us!" cries the SP.

Risk is not the same for the optimistic spirit as it is for the pessimist. The attitude toward risk determines the emotional nature of the challenge. Life is fashioned by your place on the optimism-caution spectrum. We all fashion our days by our emotions, so don't look disapprovingly on the SP's risk-taking attitude. They have discovered a path that, for them, leads to happy choices. Boundaries are to be tested — another risk-taking attitude. Optimism explores and tests the known and the unknown, the unknown more than the known. "How dull life is when we limit ourselves and our adventures," says the SP. Hence, risk draws them and they only need to add the temperance of Epicurus to keep them from a damaging, foolish action.

"Another day, another risk," shouts the SP. "Another day, and I'm already feeling a little anxious," says the SJ. "Another day for mental explorations and independence," states the NT. "Another day, another passion," cries the hopeful NF. When finding direction for your own life (or that of your child), make certain you add an element of optimism to the quest — your own brand, of course. Try to risk a little even when you are nervous; life will eventually force you to.

But optimism is not without decisions and the SP mind is tactical, skillfully finding the best move out of the current choices that face them. Optimism without tactical brilliance loses one of its best aids. To see the next tactical move with electrifying speed and feel the confidence it brings is the natural ability of the SP.

SPs are driven with a creative talent. At their core they are artisans and often artists, with an optimistic mind that guides them without fear in this world of creativity. What lies beyond the possible calls passionately to the SP. Their artistic creations are often breathtaking and to some considered outlandish as they challenge all boundaries. The emotions of an optimistic mind is behind it all.

The possibilities presented by tools extend their bold spirit to the mastery of things and abilities. They refuse to believe that there is not more to be experienced. A standing record is not the last word. When Roger Banister broke the four-minute mile, the SP was less surprised than the SJ. "Is the three-minute mile simply another achievement not too far in our future," reasons the SP. Nothing is impossible! Do you feel the wisdom of their mental optimism? "No," says the SJ, "all things are not possible. Be real!"

Your reality is not mine, the SP says in response to the SJ's caution. Besides, if we settled for such a philosophy of life we would still be in the dark ages. The war of optimism versus realism wages on.

To live optimistically, the mind and the body must be free, and the SP worships at the shrine of freedom. The land of the free and the call of the brave indeed chimes in every beat of their hearts. Bondage and boundaries, they believe, are for prisons. "Don't fence me in," they cry. Spontaneity and the freedom to follow one's impulses is the drumbeat of the SP. Optimism cannot follow the rules since the rules are limitations and need to be constantly tested and revised. SPs do not see themselves as a herd of cows, content to feed in a defined pasture. They are the nomads among the temperaments, wandering off into the world and beyond, if possible. This interpretation of freedom scares the SJ. It also gave rise to Epicurus's call for moderation in pleasure and optimism. Optimism is an emotion with boundless energy and even optimism is to be managed.

Fun and carefree abandon are the rewards of a truly optimistic attitude. As Epicurus put it, pleasure is the goal, and the SP agrees. But carefree abandon advocates no caution. Therefore, a more intelligent optimistic belief is that we are here on this planet to enjoy life and all the planet offers while protecting optimism from itself when it overreaches. It is our world, a gift from a generous God, and why show disregard for such a gift? It is true that there is more to life than pleasure, but at times the SP cannot see beyond the obvious call of their optimistic emotions.

Pain is to be avoided unless it is endured on the path to greater glory, such as the athlete pursues. A morbid endurance of pain is not for the SP. Morbidity is not optimism — it is surrender to pessimism.

So the optimism that infuses all the emotions of the SP leads also to an individualist spirit and a craving to find their self-image expressed uniquely, but never without an audience to appreciate their skills. This picture of the SP's emotional sprightliness should entice a respect and a longing for more of the ecstasy that optimism offers as well as a warning of the dangers of its overuse.

Positive/Negative Emotions in the SP

It seems as though all the emotions of the SP are positive and it's true that all their strengths are positive, but not all the emotions that drive their strengths are always positive. Of all the temperaments, positivism is best displayed in the SP because the SP exemplifies the positive life. Thank them for their fresh, optimistic spirit and encourage them to generously share it with us. Optimism can be negative, though, if it is overused or misused as we have just noted, and then it calls into use the negative emotions that damage others and us.

The threat to their ultimate happiness is this overuse or misuse of optimistic emotions. Any emotion can be misused in any temperament, but in this case, the overuse is what most needs tempering with caution. If you are reading this in the hopes of helping your SP child to develop emotional intelligence, focus on their overuse; it is also a misuse. And don't forget to approve their love of optimism or you will run headlong into resistance. Optimism feels good to all of us unless we are wallowing in self-pity and self-blame. To your SP, it feels right and they won't understand your opposition. Teach them that optimism feels best when spiced with a little caution. Constant guidance feels like restriction to the SP, but a wise mixture of approval and instruction will go over and reward the giver as well as the child.

It seems as though optimism entices us to overuse it because of its appeal. As we have seen, it colors all the SP's emotions, so the danger of overuse lurks in the use of any of their optimistically driven emotions or strengths. Overuse is determined when an emotion or a strength damages someone else or us. Therefore, the measure of health is always the damage it is, or is not, doing. We can escape the possibility of damage if we love others and ourselves truly and purely.

129

Pleasure is a self-centered emotion and so are excitement, impulse, and self-expression — all SP strengths. The SPs must be encouraged to examine the way their actions are affecting others. With care, optimism can then keep itself pure and other-centered.

I have quoted the Greek philosophers often, so a reference to the all-wise words of Jesus is in place. He said, "This is my commandment, that you love others as I have loved you" (John 15:12, RSV), a love that was immortalized in dying for others. Truly, selfless love is the goal of the emotionally intelligent SP.

How SPs Can Best View Their Optimism

Optimism is to be enjoyed because optimism is:

- Being hopeful about the future. For the SP this is mainly the immediate future. We can't live mentally healthy without hope of some sort. The unknown future is tamed with hope.

- Being confident. Confidence breeds faith and ushers in the possibility of success. Confidence builds strong faith, and faith in a world we can't control is what we must live by or we worry ourselves into failure.

- Seeing ourselves or others as successful. Success is the hoped-for fruit of optimism.

- Being expectant. Expectations are the ripening of hope. Optimism is the excitement that enjoys the present and does not fear the future.

- Based on grounds for its existence. Optimism that has no reason for its existence is no more than a wish.

- Seeing the silver lining when others can't. The German philosopher, Gottfried Wilhelm Leibniz, optimistically held that this world was the best of all possible worlds. How did he know? He chose to believe this, and all optimists choose to believe in the best rather than the worst. He died without real recognition, still writing and with nearly all his works unpublished. Now that's an optimist to the end.

- The belief that good will ultimately prevail over evil in this universe and the belief that we must always choose the best.
- The Latin from which our English word "optimism" comes simply means "the best thing."

All temperaments should temper their strengths with some form of optimism.

Emotion in the SJ Temperament

I have learned to use the word "impossible" with the greatest caution.
~ Wernher Von Braun

Caution, not exuberance, should be our fiscal motto.
~ John Chafee

Distrust and caution are the parents of security.
~ Benjamin Franklin

SJs are Stoics of a sort, philosophically speaking. The Stoic philosophers taught that we should not let emotion run our lives. We should keep emotions restrained in the sense that we should be able to free ourselves from their pull and also learn to accept whatever happens with a kind of somber fate. They firmly believe that being in some form of control is the way to deal with our troublesome feelings.

Perhaps the most influential Western philosophy before the rise of Christianity, Stoicism swept over Greece and Rome and dominated thought until Christianity, which was sympathetic with some of its beliefs, replaced it with a more optimistic world view. Zeno, said to be the founder of Stoicism, lectured from a painted porch, or so the story goes, and the "stoa" (porch) gave its name to the new philosophical school. He was a student of Plato before he started his own school.

Stoicism is more cynical about the world and serious in nature than Epicurianism (the general mental stance of SPs). The SJs reflect this seriousness. Stoics believed that everything is determined by the gods or fate and we can't change it, so learn to accept it or control it as best you can. We only damage ourselves and destroy our happiness when we try to change things. Freedom is in not struggling. Those who struggle are imprisoned by their struggles and are not free. If you want to be free, try to be indifferent to everything and then nothing will disturb your inner peace. In contrast, this is not a mental attitude that an SP enjoys, though. A similar disregard for pain and disturbing thoughts is also found in Buddhism.

Another strong parallel between Stoicism and the SJ way of life is their sense of responsibility. We are responsible for all we do; society is not, nor are our parents or our environment. Therefore, mold and control your world as best you can while taking full responsibility for all that happens.

Caution, the Emotional Core

Finding the emotion that drives the SJ temperament was not difficult. SJ strengths such as concern, being prepared, a responsible way of life, doing what is right, social respectability, the love of routines, rules, and logistical behavior seem to spring from the attempt at emotional control that is evident in the feeling of caution. When this emotion is overused, fear, worry and anxiety are the negative byproducts. All three are closely related and all stem from fear of one sort or another. Caution is the attempt to avoid the damage of negative fears and the unpredictable extremes of optimism.

The emotions of the SJ promote a serious view of life. At first glance they are more serious than the sprightly, freewheeling SPs. But seriousness is not a bad thing, nor is caution. It is much needed and the SJ constantly feels the SP has not even been introduced to it or even cares for it. The SP's attitude to life can make the SJ nervous.

Caution leads to being solid, respectable citizens, observant of the laws of society, and concerned not to upset the equilibrium of order. Everything that society needs is carefully weighed and controlled so that, supposedly, no waste or misuse results. Waste, too, is a result of inadequate caution. The world is not as the SP supposes, a world of plenty, says the SJ. Rather it is a limited world whose resources can be drained, and then what? To the SJ no one else seems to care and the observation increases the drive for cautious actions. We must show the restraint that responsible caution would suggest, hoarding essentials for a rainy day, protecting all things from harm, opening our doors to those less fortunate, warding off the evils of chaos, promoting all things good, and continuing the traditions that have brought us safely to our present paradise of order. This is the agenda of all worthy and honorable citizens.

The SJs take upon themselves the responsibility of creating a cautious society for everyone else. Haven't you noticed that an SJ parent is the epitome of cautious care? Caution is constantly promoted to their children as the essence of duty and responsible ethical behavior, but this approach can have a negative ring to it. They protect passionately against the possibility of trouble. Protecting the good by keeping out the bad makes such good sense to the SJ because the emotion of caution is dominant. This also means keep busy, because the idle mind is the devil's workshop.

"I have work to do."
"Can't you see I'm busy."
"Don't interrupt me."
"When we have done our work, not now."
"Of course I care; I'm overwhelmed now can't you see?"

These and all of their cousin phrases pour from the mouths of these serious, cautious caregivers of society.

Living in the real world is a byproduct of a cautious attitude. Why would anyone think that people should live any differently, so SJs can't understand the unreal world of imagination or the fanciful world of dreamers. Fantasy has no connection to caution, for them. It builds a house of straw — useless in the real world. Caution, however, keeps its feet on the ground. Keep life grounded in reality, their pundits say.

Dreamers are wasters of one of life's greatest gifts — time — and time is very important to the SJ. "Always keep your eye on the clock," they advise. Time wasted is time never to be retrieved. Who can live successfully in the real world without all senses alert to the unexpected and the dangerous; it seems impossible to them. The real world passes by all who don't live circumspectly. (You may have noticed that faith, hope, and optimism are not in the forefront of the SJ's mind. SJs need to be reminded to inject their realism with optimism, because optimism is the framework of faith and hope. They must often move more to the center of the fear spectrum for healthy living.) Being cautious, but less so, will do it.

Caution prefers the status quo which the tried-and-tested are dependent on. That way you avoid mistakes and many dangers. Conservatism is honored because it is more cautious than liberalism. Liberalism gives to people the encouragement to probe new ideas, and all new ideas are suspect until they have passed the test of time and been proven to be consistently reliable. Liberalism is simply not cautious enough for the SJ. "Why commit to the untried and uncertain?" says the SJ. "Why not?" says the SP whose liberal bent irritates the SJ no end. Change, which is always a nervous time for the SJ, must be measured and accepted only with cautious steps, making sure of each move. How do you proceed with caution when facing something new? Very slowly and cautiously, of course. The emotion of caution calls for "steady as we go."

Emotionally cautious, the SJ feels the call to be society's architect and guardian. We are guardians of all the precious things of life, they remind us, and a guardian sets impenetrable walls of care around the treasures for which he is responsible. Often in their passion to protect others, they do not notify others of changes they make, and their intentions then result in conflict and hurt.

The feeling of having to have control of things and people keeps excitement and risk-taking to a minimum. It results in trying to offset the ever present possibilities of trouble (an SJ's agenda) as opposed to facing the challenge and winging it (the SP's mode of operation). Both have their place, but one is driven by caution and the other actively seeks the risk of adventure, so SJs and SPs move in opposite directions, each motivated by admirable emotions.

We all know prevention is better than cure and this cautious attitude encourages a preventive approach. In the SJ, it has attained the status of the default emotion, activating without thought or consideration at times. "Be careful now," are words you will hear a myriad of times from an SJ mother as she seeks to prevent any and all trouble from happening to her children.

Caution gives birth to protecting, inspecting, preserving, supervising, providing, managing, controlling, and the host of other administrative functions we have been referring to. Administration is itself a cautious activity and SJs, as the emotion that controls their core might suggest, are born managers of life's affairs.

Caution is a negative emotion with a positive goal. The SJ believes that we must first deal with the negative happenings and possibilities and then, if there is time, turn our attention to the positive. Guard against failure first and then we can be free to think of success. The positive attitude for the SJ is that they have not lost sight of it — it is just relegated to second place. The SP, in contrast, wants first to deal with the positive happenings and then, only as needed, handle the negative arrivals. The emotions are polar opposites and drive two very different behaviors that leave the fingerprint of opposite lifestyles.

A fear of out-of-control happenings and of depressing results drives the SJ to drink, as the saying goes. But don't forget that this fear is also driven by a passionate care and love for family, friends, and country. So, the SJ is not just scared of bad happenings but concerned for a good and controllable life. To dub the SJ as entirely negative is the gravest of misunderstandings. Caution can give birth to a tenacious love with the best of intentions in all things.

It's ironic that in the steady trustworthy SJ love should partner with fear in making things safe and secure for the world. If you have trouble understanding this remember, fear is not all negative and love is not always positive. In the SJ, the two can meet on the common ground of cautious concern for others.

In SJs, reliability and responsibility are positive attributes motivated by the fear of failing themselves and others. The whole idea of living cautiously is to avoid failure. When they fail, they whip themselves and the feeling is a loss of personal integrity. SJs possess a temperament that provides a clear sense of who they are and how they are supposed to live; therefore any deviation from this path is detected readily and it pains them. When this happens they instinctively act more cautiously.

As a result, caution builds rules and regulations that act like fences to keep the SJ (and hopefully all others, too) from straying into danger. Fences are devices born of this emotion and of cautious planning. However, we see in the SJs and their strengths a need for cautious living which permeates all of their thinking and planning. Only when foreign pressures prevail will they abandon caution for the moment. This emotion and its incessant demands is why the desire for consistency and sameness characterizes them.

If we are motivated by a need for safety and security, then a work ethic that says we will do whatever it takes to be safe and secure develops. The SJ soon becomes a workaholic, propelled by the fear of things getting out of control and entering the horrible world of chaos. Even a desk that is chaotic can rob some of them of sleep. The random, impulsive world of the SP causes nervousness, and they worry over a lack of order and of not being able to see results, which shakes them to the core. The emotion of caution drives their great ability to logistically plan and operate.

All the feelings of caution and concern for order arise also from the SJ's disdain for chaos. The historical need for this emotion has always been with us and is in the development of language, which goes back to early Greek Mythology where the Greek writers thought of Chaos (Khaos) as the first created being from which the first deities, Gaia (Earth), Tartaros (the Underworld), and Eros (Love, the life-bringer) emerged. That chaos could be conceived of as a living being is frightening, and if chaos was the first being that was created, life is doomed to failure unless we approach it with great care and caution. Truly an SJ fearful philosophy.

The Greeks' feelings led them to describe chaos as the empty space between heaven and earth that was neither one thing nor the other. For anything to be neither one thing nor another is for it to lack direction, purpose, and a cautious controlling hand. This disorderly state shakes the SJ's foundations and a nervous fear results that asks how this could have happened if caution had been observed.

The Greeks also thought of chaos as a gloomy mist surrounding the earth and yet again as the goddess of fate, images that confirm to the SJ that chaos is the most horrible state in which to live. Extreme caution is needed to avoid the evil disorder of fate and create the comfort of order.

Chaos is the opposite of the Hebrew/Christian God and, therefore, it is no surprise that SJs fill churches where chaos is not to be feared from their God. The ancient Greeks, who were intelligent humans, struggling to explain their feelings and organize their thoughts about this world just like we seek to do, saw chaos as almost inevitable because of its frequent appearance in human affairs. The SJ trembles at that thought, but the Greeks also saw chaos as having no saving virtue, and with that the SJ passionately agrees.

The mental processing of the SJ also bears a relationship to their desire to be cautious and avoid the devastation of insecurity. To do this they think logistically, as I have mentioned. One thought follows the other in logical progression until their goal has been achieved. It is a practical logic, the first step by practical necessity needing to precede the second step and so forth. If the mind is logistical and sequential in the way it operates, the emotion that loves order and security and calls for caution is the driving force of all this systemization. The SJ must run on the rails of clear operating procedures or risk leaving the tracks and wrecking their lives. The signs we see in parks that warn us not to leave the trails can stir the SP to do just that, and the SJ to talk disparagingly of the people who won't keep to the trails.

Order and careful calculations give the SJ the appearance of being a solid unmovable rock. Underneath this well-deserved image is the tremor of fear. To be afraid is to court worry, anxiety, and pessimism, all waiting in the wings to shatter their image of solidarity.

A shattered SJ falls into worry and negative fears all too easily. The overuse of caution creates this negative fear and what produced a steady image also crumbles under the mental seismology of anxiety and pessimism. Caution lost is the breaching of the dam. The SJ must protect their emotions from such loss and fight negativity if they are to shine in all their strength and glory.

Positive/Negative Emotions

When a sailor sails close to the wind, the slightest change in wind direction can empty the sail of wind or whip the boom to the opposite side of the craft, potentially causing panic. It's all a matter of sensing the slightest shift in the wind and responding quickly. The possibility is true of the SJ who applies too much caution. They can stall, or fall off wind quickly only to struggle with the negative result of their actions.

Caution is laudable, but too much causes the human ship to flounder. More optimism is the remedy. The SJ views optimism with a mild suspicion (some with scorn) as though it is the greater problem. It's not. Too much caution is the culprit in that mindset. A deliberate attempt to change this mental bias will make the SJ the master of his world, accepted by all as prudent and full of faith. The change must include a tactic for more optimism and hope and the willingness to face change and win the challenges rather than try to avoid them altogether.

The SJ's Love of Caution and Control

Caution is an emotional tool used mostly to control the emotions and is not to be thought of as the goal for the construction of a successful life. It is only a mental tool that the SJ develops as a helpful strength. Tooling a book, for example, is the mental task of designing it and forming its structure, and caution can be one of the tools, if wisely used, in creatively designing our lives. It is seldom used by the SP and often overused by the SJ, as we have noted.

"Tool" is Old English for "tol" which comes from the German meaning "to prepare." Caution prepares us for the unknown and the potentially or actually frightening experience. To be prepared (the SJ's motto) breathes the atmosphere of caution. But note the warning: over-preparedness is the SJ's downfall, halting progress and making the means the end.

The SJ must note that tools, whether physical or mental, are purposely functional by nature, not the end product, nor is caution meant to be developed into an inflexible lifestyle. The ability to walk through life cautiously with confidence, feet solidly planted on the ground while making good speed toward a better life, is the SJ's needed contribution to a successful society. Caution, when not overdone, steadies their aim and calms those around them.

Need to Be More Playful About Their Emotions

A remedy for the love of too much cautiousness is more playfulness. Playfulness loosens up our mental tension. With the SJ child, more play can be the path to more happiness as long as the SJ does not become obsessed with controlling the play and turning it into an exercise in supervision or an over-enthusiastic inspection of other people's actions. Letting mistakes happen is part of learning, and over-seriousness can hinder their learning. The SJ child will pick up the mood of the parent and if too serious, will suffer from the overuse of caution.

Just as the SP can take a play out of the SJ's book, the SJ can seek to incorporate more lightheartedness into their life in order to avoid the dangers of fear. Enjoy! Make time for play and when playing, learn to do so with passion. Enjoy, play, enjoy, it is a great recipe for the SJ.

How SJs Use Their Emotions

Emotion for the SJ is a practical tool. They use it in an endeavor to control their world. An attempt to control our world, we all agree, is needed. People and things, if left to themselves, can explode or implode. The SJ parent knows this and can be absorbed with correcting all the things that go wrong so that the child will, they believe, become a useful member of society. However, they forget that being useful is not necessarily the standard for fitting into society and obeying its mandates; nor does usefulness naturally arise from an over-cautious controlling of events and people's lives. Creativity, the opposite of control, is by nature a kind of "out of control" activity. It is finding beauty not yet expressed and ways to do things that are unusual and pleasing.

Successful SJ artists have broken into the world of art and blended caution with optimistic creations that, with restraint, stir the emotions. Encourage the SJ to experience all that is new and to crave a little for what is different. They will be released from their seriousness and structured life to find some freedom of spirit. We will never make them into some other temperament; they will always return to their solid core of SJ dependability and reliability, caution, and care.

The imaginative and the fanciful is also a world to be explored, if only cautiously, by the SJ. Its rewards will help curb the overuse of concern and practicality.

How SJs Can Best View Their Emotions

Caution is to be enjoyed because caution is:

- A safety measure against loss of control.
- Not the opposite of optimism, which is pessimism.
- A control on wild, irresponsible freedom.
- An expression of how we care about ourselves and others.
- A safe way of facing change.
- A controlled way of introducing the new.
- A way to steady our nerves.

Emotion in the NT Temperament

In quietness and in confidence shall be your strength.
~ Isaiah 30:15

To him who looks upon the world rationally, the world in its turn presents a rational aspect.
~ Georg Wilhelm Friedrich Hegel

All people see the world through their own temperament. Writers, speakers, influencers of people, all color what they do and say with these inner drives. So, when a philosopher or teacher explains life and the world, we are seeing it through his temperament. This, they can't escape doing.

Plato was an NT and when it comes to ethics, he truly painted the subject with what appears to be his own temperament. His ethical stance started and ended with rational arguments. Plato taught that if we know what the good life is, we will act accordingly (not necessarily true). Living the good life, as he put it (the life that brings ultimate human satisfaction), is an intellectual adventure similar to learning mathematical truths. Would to God it was. All ethical situations would be easy to decide. However, NTs find a real comfort in reducing ethics to reason. But many people with reason seriously doubt that living the best life is simply a matter of rational behavior. How do you weigh in?

One comment would be: we can't totally reduce ethics to reason because we are emotional creatures and act out of emotion as much, if not more, than out of reason. Emotional reasons also have their place alongside of rational motivations. Therefore, the NT's struggle to achieve emotional intelligence is mainly about giving emotion its rightful place in their minds and then in their behavior.

143

NTs are also in the tradition of the Stoics when they seek to free themselves from passion and all emotion. This is, as we have noted before, an impossible stance. Emotion tints all we do and think. Not all NTs see their lives this way, but the inner drives to make sense and be logical and to honor all things cerebral causes most of them to see ethics in a strictly rational way.

Calm Is the Desired Emotion

Emotion tends to amplify our responses, and less emotion — the feeling of calm — quietens their disturbing chatter, or at least this is the NT's perception. A calm interior will likely produce a calm exterior. The less internally reactive we are to events and the people around us, the more we can calmly evaluate the best response to their challenges. All this makes sense to the NT and seems to be reasonable to most of us.

The emotion of calm is, of course, to be highly praised. Concentration is not shattered by calm; focus can be intensified; periods of prolonged thought that are needed to forge strategies are more easily produced. The inner peace calm produces keeps other disturbing emotions at a minimum. This is very satisfying to the NT.

However, calming ourselves on the inside requires great discipline. "Yes, I know," the NT replies. That mental control is what they do best. Even if their emotions are raging, they typically call on the calm of mental discipline to hold off falling into emotional panic. Have you ever noticed an NT child watch the emotional turmoil of his parents? There's a remoteness about his gaze. He seems to wonder if maybe the stork dropped him off in the wrong home or even on the wrong planet. How did he end up with a race of people that seem to honor emotion and bow to its every whim? Intelligence has surely nothing to do with emotion, he thinks.

NTs don't mean to be cold when they appear calm, but calm can feel cold to the warmer temperaments — very cold. They feel warmth does not exist if it is not being expressed. The NTs are simply using their cool emotional core as a defense mechanism against becoming the same as others — emotionally captured — a thought that is troubling indeed to the NTs. They know that if they let their emotions express themselves fully, they would then find it hard to control them. In childhood, they felt the tug of wild emotions, and because they are designed to be cool, calm, and collected, when they reacted to the emotional disturbance, they felt compelled to learn the lesson of calm early. Emotions can quickly run away with anyone who does not resort to serious control measures. An NT who displays wild emotions has become afraid of them and hasn't learned the lessons of calming his spirit.

Emotions are also best controlled the instant they appear. They can escalate at warp speed, and if given a moment's consideration, we can well fall victim to their sudden judgments. The best protection, the NT believes, is to view them as aliens in an otherwise intelligent race. Keep them quiet! Slam the door of acceptance in their face and make sure you suspect them of evil, always. Perhaps this is overstated, but to the observer of the NT's passionate exclusion of emotion it seems to be near the truth.

Staying calm calls for mastery of the rise and fall of emotions and it all starts with the beliefs we have cited. "Emotion is the culprit if this is not accomplished," says the typical NT. Therefore, emotions are best kept locked away and accessed only when absolutely necessary. They know emotions must have some purpose, such as when they fall in love, but the daily usefulness of emotions evades the NT when they see their devastating results in people that can't control them. Maybe they serve a purpose — something like that of a human appendix, they think. Humor aside, NTs know of emotion's purpose but choose to treat their feelings with suspicion and rejection. After use, they desire to lock them away again.

Reason is king and the king's rule must not be threatened. Logic is all-important and leads the way to objective truth, or so the belief goes. This tribute to analytical reasoning makes them tend to honor reason and dishonor emotion.

The result of this outward display of the mastery of emotion can give them the edge in a discussion or debate. It makes them seem superior to others in intelligence and mental ability. The pure, uninterrupted operation of their brains is the goal of their mental lives. All people with an F in their profile envy this ability in the NT. When emotionally unintelligent, the NT despises his own show of emotion. However, emotional intelligence, as we have already seen, is not a denial of emotion.

Calm is a complex emotion. Sometimes it is cold, sometimes warm. It can be developed by disengaging from people or from circumstances that create disturbing inner pressures, so the NT withdraws on occasion to maintain equilibrium.

Skepticism, even of a positive nature, can contribute to a calm exterior. This could be one reason why skepticism is part of the package of strengths the NT displays. The skeptic refuses to respond with a sudden emotional display, always withholding judgment until all the available evidence is in. Even then the skeptic can remain noncommittal since more evidence may still emerge. A premature decision, to the NT, is a shameful thing.

Questioning also helps the NT to remain calm. The more questions one asks, the more one holds off making a decision or forming an emotional judgment. It keeps the mind busy exploring alternatives and moves from one focus to another, lessening the chance of rumination on some troubling issue, which inevitably stirs the emotions. Why, what, what for, with what purpose, how, when, where — an endless flow of inquiries keeps the NT mind moving forward.

As children, NTs often appear to be the champions of the little word "why." It is all for the purpose of understanding their world. Once understood, the world is less challenging and that brings calm. Attaining a steady mental flow, as in a deep, slow-running stream, makes it easier for thoughts to pass through the mind and be thoroughly examined en route.

Curiosity and an investigative spirit can assist the show of calm that the NT is known for. All Ts can make a show of renouncing emotion and stifling their feelings, but the combination of strengths in the NT makes them the master's of this art. For curiosity not to disturb the calm, the element of surprise must be removed or managed and this is another achievement of the calm spirit of the NT.

To remain calm we must look ahead and strategize. Ezekiel's eagle is the far-seeing one, as Stephen Montgomery (Keirsey's editor) has it. (Ezekiel saw humanity in four faces: the lion, ox, eagle, and man. The eagle is the parallel to Hippocrates' Phlegmatic or our NT.) Seeing the distant probabilities gives the NT the opportunity to scheme, calculate and strategize what might or could happen and prepare a plan of approach. Step-by-step, the future is penetrated and visualized with a controlled intuition that helps keep them ahead of the game of life, strategizing the next moves.

Theorizing is part of developing a strategy too, and the NT is at home in developing abstract theories in the calm of the mind. A theory is aimed at exploring the unknown and, if we believe in an explanation of the facts we have observed, we take away the sense of surprise and fear that an unexplained event can induce. Mental calm results.

When we value a calm, controlled approach to life, we soon build an image which we now have to maintain. The NT takes pride in maintaining this image. We all try to develop and maintain an image of some sort. They are proud of their coolness under pressure and, therefore, they guard it by pursuing calm whenever pressure arises. How else should we live, they ponder.

In this quest for a calm image, even the demands of time are rejected if they disturb. The NT's relationship to time is a fascinating study. Time marches on and waits for no one. It brings new things to our consciousness as it flows by incessantly. Distractions that constantly challenge the calm emotion in the mind of the NT can be too much to handle, so they wall themselves off from time's demands and focus on a project, trying not to notice the attractions and sights that flash by in their peripheral vision as each present moment passes. The determination of the NT is well known and they can concentrate fiercely. Focused, always focused, they can narrow their vision and shut out the disturbances and then prove to be hard to awaken from their mental seclusion.

One more aid to calm is the NT's understanding of facts. Facts are thought of as distinct from emotions. Facts, to the NT, are just that: facts, bare facts, skinned of all their emotional flesh. Some facts come with emotional content and they must trim the emotions away first to get at the facts. One may question the facts, but they are all given the same unemotional status until proven, and then they become the bare exhibits in the museum of the NT mind. All conclusions are based on these bare facts. To the NT, only bare facts are the building blocks of theory and the foundation of all the NT's strategies. Just give me the facts, they urge.

Emotions, on the other hand, constantly change and must be continually reevaluated and questioned as they morph into other emotions and intensify in a split second. To the NT, they are slippery facts of life, if facts at all, and ever-changing facts at best. Calm cannot handle such constantly changing elements without its peace being threatened.

Calm depends on establishing a mental condition where little changes; a constancy that is itself calming. So the NT must limit themselves to facts and their plain interpretation of them if they are to retain the emotion of calmness. The NT will plead, of course, "Please don't call calm an emotion; we prefer to think of it as an absence of emotion!"

As we study emotions in the NT temperament, we can see that nearly all of their strengths are infused with, and fashioned by, calmness, and if the calm is absent, the NT ceases to be who they were made to be. A serious loss of self-image can result.

Positive/Negative Emotions

When not wanting to be disturbed by distracting feelings, it seems unnecessary to distinguish between positive and negative emotions. Both can disturb. We must remember, the emotions of an NT have a positive goal just like those of the SJ. To one it is the maintenance of calm, to the other it is the control of caution.

Negative emotions that take away the NT's calm and make them explode in bursts of anger like other temperaments seem only to be experienced when they are challenged beyond their ability to control. Positive distractions are likely to result in the NT reacting negatively to being disturbed. Disturbance of any kind is a negative occurrence.

Losing control, as we have said, is for the NT a shameful experience. It stresses their high self-image and the feeling of low esteem can be truly frightening to them. If an NT child or adult repeatedly gets angry and reveals their anger in outbursts, something has deeply troubled him. When they burst into uncontrollable anger they experience almost as powerful a surge of emotion as the NF. For the NF, such displays arise from powerful feelings that live near the surface. For the NT, the surfacing of powerful emotions is a flag that something has gone seriously wrong because it is so unusual.

Emotional upheaval in the NT can also result from a loss of pride or personal identity. Once they fail to believe in their mental excellence or superiority, they can fall apart. A change in how they feel and think about themselves directly challenges their peace of mind. What they think about themselves is the prime cause of their calm or lack of it, more so than what others think about them.

What To Do About Their Love of Calmness

Encourage it. Calmness is a positive emotion. Because it lives at the low-reaction end of the sensitivity spectrum, it is strongly motivating to the NT. An extreme on the spectrum is very motivating to any temperament, so the calmer the NT is, the more they feel its useful power.

Calmness mystifies, making people wonder what is going on inside the person who is calm. It frightens some people, particularly if they are sensitive to what others think of them. This gives the calm person the edge in a discussion or argument.

For one person to remain calm in the midst of turmoil makes them the "go to" person. NTs are often appealed to, to calm emotional turmoil. Their calm can also have a healing effect.

Excitement can mist the mind and agitation can cloud it even more. Therefore, for the NT, remaining calm can be what they love most about their temperament. It motivates them strongly, for motivation in any temperament always develops and encourages the use of their strengths.

However, calm is not a state that increases communication or helps when others want more information from the NT. So the NT's love of it should be tempered with an understanding of its negative properties and how it can lessen communication.

To be more open to recognizing and accepting the emotions of others can lead the NT to a more rewarding social life. In accepting emotions and including them comfortably into their daily lives, the NT should, perhaps, begin by appreciating the emotions they see in others and by discovering how these emotions bring different and rewarding meanings to life. Accepting them in others is a start to accepting their worth in themselves.

A calm exterior can also be interpreted as cold and that perception will not serve the NT well in creating relationships. It can be felt as a disapproval of others whose emotions run at a higher temperature. All temperaments bring worthy contributions to human experiences and they all crave being approved and accepted. The NT's calm may not do that and, therefore, they can be at a distinct disadvantage in winning approval from others.

Release of Emotion

The NTs must convince themselves that release of emotion is not the same as loss of emotional control. The emotions of an NT can enrich their interactions and their theorizing. While still remaining in firm control of their emotions, they can open the lock-box and let them be seen at least.

Being perceived as emotionless gives the impression at times that they do not care. Emotions that do not see the light of day do not embellish and enhance life either. Remember, emotions bring meaning to life and its interactions.

Sometimes, when suppressed, emotions can eat away at our integrity. Unexpressed approval or disapproval can make us feel the beginnings of cowardice and fear. There are times when emotions must be expressed for us to feel good about ourselves.

How NTs Can Best View Their Emotions

Calmness is to be enjoyed because calmness is:

- The edge in debate and discussion that often disrupts the opponent's thoughts and plans.
- A control factor in the tumultuous world of emotions. This benefit gives the NT the image they prefer.
- The producer of clarity in the mind.
- A way to keep distractions at bay.
- A mystifying quality that keeps the rest of the world guessing at one's stance, purpose, goal, and effectiveness.
- A help when sorting out facts that have powerful emotional content.

Intelligently Emotional

- A direct cause of inner peace.
- Sometimes, an indication of intelligence.

Emotion in the NF Temperament

Passion is energy. Feel the power that comes from focussing on what excites you.
~ Oprah Winfrey

Passion is the genius of genius.
~ Tony Robbins

Nothing great in the world has ever been accomplished without passion.
~ Georg Wilhelm Friedrich Hegel

Years may wrinkle the skin, but to give up enthusiasm wrinkles the soul.
~ Samuel Ullman

When it comes to emotion, NFs are both expressive secretive. Emotions constantly make their presence felt, and although they do not have to be outwardly expressed all the time, they record their influences and judgments with certainty on the mind of the NF. Feelings warm or chill their mental landscape constantly.

To continue the theme of how each temperament has been observed in philosophy, NFs are Aristotelians, in part. The "good life" lies in achieving happiness, says Aristotle, and we ought to behave in such a way that we enjoy a life of happiness. *Eudaimonia*, his word for happiness, originally meant the presence of good spirits and later, in Greek thought, it came to mean happiness attained by gaining virtue, or at least a life of value that rewards us and others. So, the good life to Aristotle was truly the virtuous or good life. It was for Socrates also, since he taught that the good person was one whose life was aimed at the good and at the rewards or punishments that would await him in the next life.

For NFs, virtue, ethical behavior, and goodness are an important part of their passions. Ethical and spiritual concerns feature in the temperament. They can become very passionate about all things good. Inner feelings of happiness and fulfillment are related to this pursuit of what is right and good.

This involves feeling happy and contented, and for the NFs with their powerful emotions, sometimes being happy demands a lot. Aristotle's famous statement, "No man can be happy on the rack," suggests that suffering is not the source of happiness, nor is a life without hope. For the NF, life without hope is the ultimate misery.

Aristotle, like Eusebius, also holds that pleasure, although it ought to be pursued, must be pursued with moderation. Giving attention to our emotions can be overdone. Many an NF has been wrecked on the rocks of his own emotions. Aristotle is very much like an NF, focusing on meaningful happiness, happiness that produces the good. Fun, excitement, and pleasure that has no depth or significance is futile, a mere waste of time. To the NF, emotions are rich with meaning and ethical goodness.

Having no shortage of emotions and mining deeply their riches, NFs are known for their passionate expressiveness. Emotions were once called passions in philosophic literature. The similarity of meaning in the two words, emotion and passion, should be obvious, or so thinks the NF.

Emotion/Passion

Passion plays a very large part in life. We could say it lies behind all the temperaments' emotions, motivating them. Thought or feeling without some degree of passion soon dies. For the NF, passion is so dominant in their inner composition that they have earned the right to own it.

The NF's core emotion is passion. Because emotion stirs them so deeply and pervades all they do, being passionate feels right and without it nothing is represented adequately.

Passion, Central to All NF Emotions

I have stated in my book, *INNERKINETICS*, that to me one of the major poles around which the NF's strengths form is sensitivity. It is a basic factor of their makeup. Therefore, it is expected that behind this hyper-sensitive temperament resides the emotion of passion. Sensitivity is responsiveness and passion is a high-powered emotion that sweeps all before it and responds to all that is sensitized in the NF's virtual world and real world. Emotions then follow the trail of the NF's passionate sensitivity.

Their passion will at times be displayed for all to see and is largely responsible for making them the influencers of people that they are. Emotion influences, and when it pulses with the agreement of reason, it is unassailable.

NFs seem to possess the ability at times to camouflage their emotions or be secretive about them. In fact, they want to assess their emotions inwardly at times and feel the power and result of them before they make them public. They must test their effect on their world. Are their emotions going to please or create disharmony and pain? Once released, the passion that resides in all emotions stirs the blood and pumps adrenaline into the blood stream with what seems equal velocity to the way fear alerts us. Passion can be both constructive and damaging, but whatever it is, it is soul-shaking.

Passion is enjoyable and warm, never cold and uninviting unless it is inspired by hate and fear, in which case it can be frigid. When filled with passion we ride high on emotion's mountain tops and the exhilaration rewards us regardless of the reason we are passionate. It fulfills and intoxicates the NF. Becoming addicted to the adrenaline rush of emotion can be a real problem as well as a blessing for them. The NF seems never so healthy, alive, and well as when they are pulsating with positive passions.

For both the adult and child, avoiding the love of power found in the emotional rush is an important lesson the NF must learn. Because the emotional operations of the brain are more motivational and dominant, they can quickly override common sense and responsible behavior. Emotions can be used to overpower others for less than noble reasons.

Jackson was in his teens and had never been taught to restrain his emotions. Whenever he was hurt or unfairly treated, he flared with the force of a human volcano bent on getting his way. He watched as others quickly retreated for their own safety, leaving him an empty battle field. An insatiable thirst for the power he felt drove him to explode at even the slightest sign of wrong. He was addicted to the power of his emotions.

His addiction required that he change the metal programming of his mind. The acquired taste for power is a stubborn feeling and difficult to dislodge, so it took hard discipline over time to build a greater thirst for love and kindness. He had to undergo a change in his identity as well as an understanding of the downside of his love of power. This downside of powerful emotions is the temptation to use them to control, manipulate, and scare others, often in the interest of personal ambitions. When emotions are positive their power can influence a world for good, when negative, well... Hitler is an example of the use of emotion's powers for personal gain. Mother Teresa and her selfless sacrifice and passionate love is the opposite example, the one all NFs are built for.

Transferring passion to others is the goal of much of the NF's behavior. Passion that lifts the downtrodden or heals the depressed, and encourages the spirit that has lost hope or whose expectations have faded, making their lives miserable, is the NF's world. It fills the barren heart with optimism, beats with excitement for some worthy abstract goal, showers the unloved with love, and opens up the mind to grand future vistas.

This is the NF's reward in life. Passion aimed at lifting and helping others gives NFs a charm and warmth that is unmistakable. But above all, it makes them the indispensable encouragers of all human goodness and love. Always, passion in the cause of the good of others impresses NFs with their potential and with a vision of why they were created with such emotional fervor. To use these emotions with all their power in the cause of the good for others is the NF's destiny in this world.

Furthermore, passion fuels their friendliness and desire to please everyone. The belief that NFs can't please everyone takes some determination and effort to beat out of their passionate minds. And when the conviction that they can please everyone is vanquished by reason (since they truly cannot please everyone) it returns to claim its residence in their hearts again and again despite the lesson they learned. If it is not possible to please everyone in a single speech (NFs can be persuasive speakers), they passionately believe that one-on-one they can influence and please anyone. "All things to all people" is their golden rule.

Again, a warming emotion inside of them of being meaningful in the lives of others is born from the effort to please. It is typical of emotion that one emotion morphs into another or one gives birth to another until a whole family of emotions are stirring the heart. NFs, rich with feeling, sometimes aim at having a full house of emotions that all support each other in the cause of affecting others.

However, as we have noted, their passion is not always seen because of fear. They hide it, sometimes embarrassed that it may be seen as inappropriate, weird, ignorant or shallow. They keep it inside, careful as to where to let it be seen and timing its release with care. Embarrassed passion results in deep hurt, and they must avoid this at all cost since hurt is debilitating to them. Watch an NF carefully and you may see evidence of a calm that signals the hiding of pleasure or of pain that warns of an intense joy or a brooding anger. Emotions that are pent up inside are time-bombs ticking away that may be set off at any time. They can be ignited at any moment by some stray spark.

If the build-up of emotion on the inside is pleasurable, it waits its release in a flood of expressiveness, thoughts of satisfaction and thankfulness pouring out, laced with verbal superlatives. The release is a satisfying moment of ecstasy that warms inexpressively the pleasures of the heart.

Often they hide their emotions because their passions are so personally motivated that they know they will be lectured, ridiculed, or misunderstood if they make them known. They bar the gates to their private castle and withdraw the bridge, tightly protected from the scorn they fear will come from even their closest companions.

Locked up inside, however, the passion does not fade. It boils and creates increasing longing and emotional heat. At this point in its inner development the NF must evaluate it. "Should I hate this buildup of emotion and try to stamp out its fire," asks the NF, "or should I open the gates and flood the world with its qualities?" If they do not choose a path, the tension will find its own moment of freedom and burst out, perhaps inappropriately.

They often punish themselves for having such strong passions, because they can be very troubling. A passion that is destined not to be released creates pressure as it churns inside, and the agony of an unreleased emotion is finally the reason for the passion's death. Every NF will witness to the many unborn passions they have let die for want of safe and profitable birth. How do they kill them? First, by blaming themselves for their cultivation. They blame mercilessly and finally in the lows of self-depredation; they bury them and then slowly rise to face the next challenge. Or they turn to some distraction or to an opposite emotion and cultivate it with an equal passion, leaving the first emotion without breath, strangled in its own passion. All this may seem unbelievable to the other temperaments. They must learn the complexities and vagaries of an NF's inner cogitations if they want to be held close in the NF's heart.

Why do NFs have all these passions? It seems that everything they put into their minds turns into an irresistible passion. Yes, that isn't far from the truth, and a love/hate relationship can soon develop. They love passion for its warmth, its creative powers, and the meaning it brings to their lives. Life is passion and passion is life. How can they do without it? They don't want to. And they often have cause to ask, why does the world pour ice-water on the emotions that they, the NF, find so warm?

Yet lurking in its pleasures are its pains. They hate the hurt of negative passions. They are always hurt by negativism in any of its forms. Unless the NF becomes bitter and estranged from his true self, all that is damaging to others and to himself ultimately stirs his hatred.

Because of the NF's desire to avoid hurt, a subtle plan can be hatched to calmly, without notice, change what people are doing to them and bring healing instead, if possible. This attempt to protect themselves by influencing others to change is again an indication of the way the NFs are aware of the power of their emotions. Surreptitiously, they dress up their attempts so as not to cause detection or rejection and then they release them. Field testing the responses of others to their emotions is another appropriate way to evaluate their plans. In this way they attempt to be as "cunning as serpents and as harmless as doves." Sometimes they succeed, sometimes they don't.

They are aware of the damage crushed passions have on their self-esteem too. Awareness does not always result in action, however. Always comparing themselves to others, they judge harshly all "unworthy" passions and doubt themselves to the point that many a worthy passion is not risked a public appearance. As foolish as this procedure may be, the avoidance of the hurt of dashed expectations overrules. They soon identify the people who are the most likely to form the bucket brigade that douses their imaginations. They then speak less of these unaccepted passions, except when the passion boils over and cannot be contained.

The desire to be a person of integrity molds much of their secretive behavior. However, since their desire to please and their longing to be full of integrity often conflict, they must choose between pleasing and being inwardly consistent. Whichever is the strongest passion in them will win, although if they choose to please over being people of integrity, guilt follows and they can punish themselves without mercy.

Emotions of any sort are hard to reject. The NFs emulate their cousins, the NTs, at times and can train themselves to mask their passions even to the point of producing a calm, cool exterior that is indistinguishable from the NT's calmness on casual observation. Long experience with the demands and pains of emotion can make them great managers of passion at times, but never always. The NF's passion is too strong to always be kept under control.

Being introspective complicates passion even more. They ask, "Is it justifiable for me to feel this way? How do others deal with this? Am I better or worse than others?" Introspection is driven by the emotion to please and be significant, never insignificant. It is the desire to excel that intensifies much of their introspective activity.

Furthermore, their intuition acts as intelligence for the release or withholding of their passions. But these very insights into another person's needs can spark other virile passions when they are supposed to be gathering information on whether to release or withhold their passion. They can intuit that another person is possessed of a need that derails their original plan, and their passion can be lost in this new discovery. It's all very complicated for the NF. Life is a constantly changing scene of emotionally packed surprises.

Living inside their minds means the NFs constantly search all of their emotions and thoughts for any sign of disturbance or pleasure. Add to this the sensitivity and productivity of their imaginations and anything can go right or wrong in seconds. The NF's mind is a factory, producing endless thoughts and feelings that they want and don't want simultaneously. The result is a constant struggle to make right choices or when they tire, to go with the flow of their feelings wherever they may lead.

Being natural perfectionists, their passions must be right. But, emotions are not always right. Much personal criticism occurs as a result. "Why do I feel this way; what is wrong with me?" they ask themselves in severe disapproval. They have to learn to tell themselves that perfect is an unattainable standard and has to be conditioned by reality, and that emotions are often snap decisions, first impressions that cannot be expected to be right all the time. Emotions do not claim to be right all the time, only helpful and a starting place for further evaluation. Teach yourself and your NF child these facts, slowly and compassionately.

Visions are created out of passion and passion, in turn, drives them. A passionless vision is a contradiction in terms to the NF. How can it be worth anything if an emotion is not driving it? Anything passionless is not worthy of the NF's time or their effort. Besides, there is so much to be passionate about that life is filled with passion's demands. A possibility is a passion too, if it appeals. The future is scanned constantly for pregnant possibilities and the right or wrong one can redirect an NF's life in seconds.

Always in search of personal growth, NFs are natural self-actualizers. If the idea promises growth and self-development, it can be powered by passion. The passion to be better fills their mind, and if no other concept is identified, this one will do. They are never good enough unless they are momentarily savoring a victory or what is to them some meaningful accomplishment.

Perhaps by now you have understood that the passion of the NF arises out of the very depths of their souls. Wanting to be soulful and bond over deep experiences, they search all their lives for this inner satisfaction and meaning that other temperaments don't dream of doing.

If we accept that passion fires all of the NF's emotions, we can understand their emotional sensitivity more and their intense inner focus.

Positive/Negative Emotions

For the NF there are a million positive and negative emotions, most unidentified but not unfelt, and many that emerge from just one original emotion that can be either positive or negative. And seemingly, many can be experienced at nearly the same time with crippling speed. Again, complex is the word for the NF's emotional experiences. All people have complex emotions but none like those that produce the inner storms that can ravage the peace of the NF. It is the negative versions of their emotions that disrupt them so easily and cause them so much concern. They live for the positive ones.

Anything can become a negative. Love, with all of its positive contributions to life, can be negative if focused on a negative object or indulged in with an inappropriate intensity. The NF will tend to love someone who hurts them and cling to that love with a passionate desire to purify it, where another might abandon the object of their hurt quickly. This pattern can accompany any emotion for the NF.

Belief in others is almost a given for the gullible NF. Not so a belief in themselves. Self-doubt is a result of their low self-image, caused by an over-passionate and over-expectant perfectionism. A strength can easily turn into a liability.

It's not just perfectionism that causes their constant self-doubt, but also what Keirsey sees them as — idealists. Idealism is the creation of a goal or an image that the NF admires and aspires to with passion while it lies just beyond their accomplishment or is not even possible in an imperfect world. Always beyond their accomplishment, it challenges them to even greater effort or visionary belief. If it lies within what they can see they are able to achieve, it is not the ideal by definition. So, the ideal and perfection are almost synonymous to them. How can you succeed with such unattainable goals? Talk about shooting themselves in the foot before they begin the race!

Negative emotions are characterized by the absence of noble features. One would think that the NF would, therefore, abandon them with haste. Not so! Because to abandon the negative emotion of self-blame, for example, which seems to have no real redeeming feature from one point of view, can be to run headlong into destruction of the NF's idealism. It is their idealism that is one of the strengths that drives them to better things and self-blame aids in motivating them to better things. They must accept blame for their failures because that is their responsible way to regroup and try again, their feelings tell them. Is this reasonable or even emotionally wise?

I have often had people say, "I don't understand this in them," and no, you perhaps don't. It's not a means of self-destruction as is supposed by those who don't experience the same feelings. Rather, not to blame themselves means to them that they must lower their standards (an illogical conclusion) by failing to hold themselves to their high expectations. They hang on the horns of a dilemma: destroy their perfectionist and idealist tendencies, which are fused to their imaginative pursuits, or be illogical. Follow their emotions or their logic, which? To all but the NF, this sounds like foolishness and an unnecessary battle.

Realism, with which others of a more earthy bent (SPs and SJs for sure) would wish the NF was more richly endowed, is not the opposite of fantasy or imagination, but of idealism. The SP and SJ, because they are champions of a concrete, down-to-earth realism, don't understand the NF. At the same time, the NF, being the champion of an idealism (the first cousin of perfectionism, and second cousins of fantasy and imagination) which is fueled by passion for all that is mystical and spiritual, feel the SP and SJ just don't seem to understand life. Think that one through if you can. You won't, without understanding the emotions of some NFs. It's not unraveled by reason but belongs to the changeable path of emotion.

Making sense is not the NF's only standard of emotional conduct.

For the most part, NFs do not hold others to these idealistic standards, but if constantly hurt by others, they will transfer their perfectionist expectations to those that hurt them and heap blame on them, only to later apologize with a deep sense of guilt. If deeply disturbed, they simply withdraw from those who hurt them while at the same time finding that withdrawal very difficult to accomplish.

So, the NF can be as much the exemplification of negative emotions as of positive ones and finds emotional intelligence in the positive expressions of emotional self-management. This is achieved best for the NF via the road of struggle to emotional maturity.

Trust of Passion's Powers

When hurt, the NFs will defend themselves with as much passion as they display in the use at other times of any emotion, sometimes more. If you don't want to displease others and you try your best to accommodate their inconsiderateness, but you are constantly getting hurt by them, a burst of defensive anger is likely, and to the NF at first it seems appropriate. Yes, and anger is a means of self-defense that the NF trusts. Their explosions can be dramatic enough to force a stop to the hurt others are imposing on them, whether that hurt is intentional or not.

The problem for others in understanding this passionate display of displeasure is that the NF usually bottles up several episodes of hurt before they explode to release all their pent up pressures. The final (latest) hurt, though at times minor (the straw that breaks the camels back), gives rise to anger that may be totally out of proportion to that incident. For the NF, however, it is often — not always — a cathartic cleansing of hurt and the release of tension that is alone a kind of healing. Crying is also cathartic. Others who don't understand don't see it that way, and again the NF remains to them a mystery.

So, passion is treasured for its defensive powers as well as its motivational and creative energies.

Control of Emotions

All this emotional sensitivity is, on the one hand, a great benefit. The purpose is to give the NF temperament a giftedness that has no emotional and imaginative equal. Creative solutions to human issues often require such passion and sensitiveness. Because there is both a positive and negative benefit to their sensitivity to emotions, control is essential.

The way to control their passion needs more explanation. Control, however, is not achieved by expecting the NF to "suck it up." That's an SJ's modus operandi and an ignorant approach to the NF's control of passion.

The NF will benefit most from the chapter titled *The Three Paths to Intelligent Emotional Behavior,* plus living progressively more and more in their strengths and using the tools of choice for emotional intelligence. Assets need management and emotions are rich assets.

How NFs Can Best View Their Emotions

Passion is to be enjoyed because passion is:

- Enjoying pleasures and opportunities to their extreme
- Strongly feeling the pleasant inner warmth that the mind and heart can create
- Feeling truly alive
- The adrenaline of the soul
- Motivation at its best

- The door to creativity
- The secret to discipline
- The meaning in enjoyment
- The ultimate power of the human spirit
- The drive to discovery
- The light that leads though the darkness of doubt
- The sustainer of hope
- And much, much more

Part 3

Intelligently Emotional

6 - Three Steps to Intelligent Emotional Behavior

Our civilization is still in a middle stage, scarcely beast in that it is no longer guided by instinct, scarcely human in that it is not yet wholly guided by reason.
~ Theodore Dreiser, *Sister Carrie.*

Conquer your passions and you conquer the world.
~ *Hindu Proverb*

The first quotation above introduces us to the first step we must take toward emotional intelligence — reason. It also points to the common fallacy of our Western society that reason (without emotion) is all that is needed for humans to be at their best.

Isn't reason enough? If reason prevailed in all of us, wouldn't it succeed in making a just and caring society and intelligently emotional beings?

In this chapter we will learn how to operate and weave together the three basic methods for emotional control: reason, action, and replacing one emotion with another (we will call this step simply "replacement"). These three steps comprise one of the most intelligent designs found in our human system. Our reason, actions, and efforts to replace an undesirable emotion with a more desirable one also provide us with multiple methods to manage our emotions. In managing and developing our emotions we will be challenged with making the right decisions at the right time.

Intelligently Emotional

They were on the ski slopes. Jan was pumped with adrenaline and couldn't wait to get off the gondola at the top of the mountain and feel the excitement of a long downhill run through the crowded lodgepole pines, which reminded her of a crowd of admiring spectators. Her friend, Janus, was not so impelled. He delayed her after they got off the lift and wanted to spend time at the top of the world while her impatience was growing. At first she hinted to get going, as she put it, and then as her unexplained anger rose she became quite upset. A heated exchange followed. Pointing her skis down the black run, she plunged toward the valley far below, leaving him standing there with an emotional fire of hurt burning in his chest. It might have been the start to a bad day.

Fortunately, this time, he was intelligently emotional. He knew the damage emotional hurt does to self-control and, remaining where he was, he took a deep breath and grasped at his mind for the space to reason. He thought, I am not going to lose control. I will show her how mentally strong and stable I am. He thought again. To try to catch her and start cooling her emotions, if he could, did not seem to be right for some reason. The timing was wrong. That was it: he would let her descend and let the excitement of the run cool her mind. He then realized that he needed to be charged with an emotion other than anger when he met her at the lodge. The best way to do that was to think of her attractiveness and what he so much admired and loved in her.

All this passed through his mind in a jumbled but sufficiently structured way as he stood there forming his plan. Down the hill he sped, thrilling at the speed and challenge. Moments later he slid to a stop alongside her as she waited in line. With a broad smile he showed the excitement that he knew she must be feeling and promptly said, "When we get off at the top this time, it's off to the races, agreed?" With noticeable puzzlement she agreed, and so the day became one to remember for both of them. He had saved the day with the use of all three methods.

To be challenged like this is to be forced into constantly being the designers of our own selves and destinies, unable to blame others or circumstances for whatever we become. As a result, we grow and become better and more intelligent managers of our lives.

We will get to know each of these methods and some of the ways we use them in combination to become intelligently emotional. We must use them intentionally and creatively because they are not automatic functions. Repetition breeds familiarity, which makes it easier as time goes by.

Reason, action, or replacement can each instigate a change in how we feel, but reason is, for most, the logical starting place. However, only when all three steps are mastered and intentionally used can we really claim to be intelligently emotional.

Each temperament will learn the mastery of their own emotions in different ways because each must follow their own blueprint for the motivation they will need to change their emotions.

A Brief History

Attempts to answer the question of how we can control our emotions and learn emotional intelligence have been made throughout recorded history. It's not a new quest. Individuals, religions, and ethical systems have all given their answers.

Surveying the history in the briefest of ways, we can get some perspective on how we as humans seem to believe we function and how we have answered this question. Not all the steps or methods (reason, action, and replacement) are emphasized by all ethical systems, but there is some real agreement. You can make your own evaluations of each as this is not an attempt to reason the right or wrong of each system.

(If you are not interested in this historical survey skip to the section headed "Reason.")

Our Western World and the Superiority of Reason

Since Aristotle claimed we are rational creatures, the Western world has not questioned this assumption and has accepted it as a basic fact. Reason has proved "adequate" in the world of scientific discoveries, commerce, and life in general to demonstrate its superiority to most Western people.

The following points for the superiority of reason in controlling our emotions are often cited but are not necessarily adequate in representing reality:

- Reason calms our emotions.
- Reason is cool; emotion is hot. Cool heads are better than hot heads.
- Reason is a slow and deliberate process, uncovering more relevant data.
- Reason slows us down, which is beneficial to achieving emotional control.
- Reason, not emotion, can be trusted because it provides a logical analysis of what is the best action.
- Taking time out to reason is like taking time out in sports to arrive at the next best move.
- Reason is the more advanced function of the brain.
- Great minds are great thinkers.

The case seems closed to most Western thinkers, and there is little sense in questioning reason as the way to the best life even though most of the above points can be challenged. But is the case closed? Are these assumptions, that reason is the best way to control our emotions, all there is to say? To Western thinkers who are steeped in the disciplines of logic, reasoning our way to emotional control makes best sense and works, at least to an extent, for most people.

But remember, there are other ways that can also be effective, and using all three methods may prove to be the superior route to the intelligent use of our emotions, or so I will propose.

"How then should we live?" is the pragmatic philosophical question asked by all great thinkers, and it tests the validity, or usefulness, of any philosophy. If we can't live by our beliefs, or if they are not helpful to our functioning at our best, they have failed us. Our beliefs always affect the way we live and the way we live in turn affects our beliefs. We all somehow intuitively sense that if we can't live successfully with our beliefs, they must be discarded.

We also know that if we can't manage ourselves and our emotions well regardless of our beliefs, we have failed to live intelligently. The greatest of thinkers and ethical systems have been concerned with both how to live and how to manage our impulsive emotions.

The Western world has triumphed in scientific advances, but in comparison to other cultures a case can be made that in the face of this progress, its people have not advanced beyond other cultures in achieving superior behavior. Unintelligent behavior that damages others is as rampant in the West as it is in the East, and some might argue more so.

The family unit where most of the emotional and social lessons are modeled and learned is falling apart in the West, leaving young people with sad models of fractured relationships and emotional failure to guide them.

Reason alone has proved inadequate to solve our emotional problems. This we must concede. Learning how our actions can contribute to success and how the intelligent control and use of our greatest intellectual power (our emotions) works is an urgent need for both the East and the West. Here are just a few historical notations.

Eastern Intellectual Thought and the Superiority of Right Actions

Let's take a quick journey into some of the world's cultures and observe what they emphasize.

In Eastern intellectual thought (often of a religious nature), the quest for emotional control is no less important. Managing emotions is a universal concern. Therefore, in the East, all philosophies and religions are in one sense or another trying to find the elusive secret of how to manage and control the emotions and the powers within us. It's the "how to" that appears to be the ultimate goal of all Eastern teaching just as it is in the West. We could note that all ethical systems succeed or fail at the point of application.

Three examples from Eastern intellectual thought will show us how the East has emphasized action as a means to control emotions.

Buddhism
First, Buddhism, which advocates a letting go of all desire and offers an eightfold path to enable us to do so, emphasizes our actions as the path to success. Desire is an expression of emotion and in Buddhist thought is the cause of all suffering. Eliminating desire is difficult, but we are told actions can aid us. The "how to" for Buddhism is found in an eightfold path of mental and physical actions (mental actions are not the same as reason):

1. Correct views

2. Correct intention

3. Right speech

4. Correct action

5. Acceptable livelihood

6. Right effort

7. Mindfulness

8. Mental development by means of right concentration

These actions and mental conditions are designed to produce an intentional karma (karma is the ethical results of a person's good or bad actions), not an unintentional or accidental one. According to Buddhism, cruel or unacceptable actions create bad karma and good deeds create a positive karma. Clearly Buddhism is presenting us with a "how to" based largely on physical and mental actions.

Bhagavad Gita
Second, an example from the *Bhagavad Gita*. Here we are told that avoiding bad karma can be achieved by several different yoga paths (yoga calls for physical actions that help condition both mind and body). Karma yoga (one of several yoga practices) teaches that if we can focus on doing our duty (actions) without any regard for the results of our actions, we can better divorce ourselves from desire, which is said to be the source of all evil including our emotional evils.

An example would be if we are wrapped up in the present moment doing what is right and are not concerned with the outcome of our actions, we can perform better, producing better karma. An athlete might agree, as may someone harassed by a crippling fear. Focus on the actions of the moment and let the chips fall.

Therefore, the "how to" that is most emphasized in the *Bhagavad Gita* is focused on the actions of the yoga practices and on rituals.

Confucianism
Third, is an example from Confucius. Confucianism teaches that our lives are to be lived with reciprocity as our number one goal. Confucius phrased reciprocity negatively: "Don't do to others what you would not want them to do to you."

Approximately 500 years later, Jesus (Christianity is variously thought of as an Eastern and Western religion) phrased it positively, "Do to others what you would have them do to you."

Both are statements advocating reciprocity and emphasizing the importance of right actions in obtaining intelligent emotional behavior.

Obviously the positive version of reciprocity is more demanding than the negative version. Not to do to others what we would not like done to us does not call for the performance of positive actions of love, while doing to others as we would have them do to us invites us to see the need for loving actions as well as the avoidance of harmful, negative actions. The teachings of "how to live" successfully in the Analects of Confucius clearly stress right behavior. Once again actions are emphasized.

Self Control in East and West

Some sort of self-control or self-discipline (right actions) underpins the Eastern methods, whether in Buddhism, Jainism, Confucianism, Daoism, Islam, or other ethical and religious systems. Yoga, in its various forms, as well as meditation or any other form of controlled ritual is regarded in these beliefs as necessary to gain control over the emotional urges. Desire is seen as the reason we need self-control.

In various forms self-control, meditation, and mastery of one's life are also found in all Western philosophies and religions from the Greek philosophers to the Christian Scriptures where self-control is said to be the fruit of God's Spirit. Everyone seems to agree that to control emotions and live acceptably, we have to be active participants, using self-control, which means actions of some sort. Actions such as perseverance, meditation, prayer, coping tools, and visualization (intense imagination) are all aids in developing enough willpower to enable us to win the battles with our emotions.

The West (Judaism/Philosophy/Christianity)

The West has emphasized reason, right action, and occasionally replacement as important steps in gaining emotional control. The ethical systems of the philosophers from Plato onward and the Jewish and Christian Scriptures differ in where the source of our strength comes from that enables us to be emotionally intelligent. All call for actions and beliefs even though the ethical requirements vary widely and significantly. It has, as I have already emphasized, been assumed by many philosophers that reason alone will prevail in all educated humans even though history and current world happenings don't bare this out. That assumption obviously lacks something.

The replacement of one emotion with another is a strong emphasis in Christian and Jewish teachings and in some ethical systems, even if in practice Westerners have not followed their own teachings very well. The reason for failure is perhaps the invasive belief in Western life that everyone can pursue their own standards of behavior based on their own perceptions and desires of what is right. This is blended together with a strong belief that no one is to be judged as having inadequate or wrong beliefs. The judicial system in the West, however, runs counter to these popular beliefs. It makes judgments based on how people obey the set laws of society and endeavors to hold them responsible. So, there is a tension in western philosophy.

In summary, what we see is agreement that actions are important in reaching control of ourselves and, hence, also of our emotions. Reason is emphasized more in the West, and replacing one emotion with another is not nearly as widely stressed.

First Method — Reason

… reason, more than anything else, is man.
~ Aristotle

What is a man,
If his chief good and market of his time
Be but to sleep and feed? a beast, no more.
Sure, he that made us with such large discourse,
Looking before and after, gave us not
That capability and god-like reason
To fust in us unus'd.
~ Shakespeare

Change your thoughts and you change your world.
~ Norman Vincent Peale

Returning to reason, let's see how it helps us use our emotions intelligently and let's learn how to use it. It is not the same as thinking because some thinking can be unreasonable. Like all of our abilities, reason can be used in rational or irrational ways.

We have thought about how the brain develops and processes an incoming message from any of our physical senses: namely, how it travels in "code" to the thinking area of the brain where we decode it, understand it, and think about it, and how we first respond to it by our emotional centers. We are built so that we respond emotionally to most messages before we think about the message. Our emotions therefore, provide us with a suggested path of action that we are to think about and confirm or reject.

Reason is indeed an important step. Here's why: When we understand why we are feeling the way we are, we can reason the right or wrong, the appropriateness or inappropriateness of our feelings. We don't think first and then feel. We feel and then decide whether to change our feelings.

Reason can, and often does, correctly choose the intelligent course for our subsequent actions. It is also the path most written about when discussing emotional intelligence and the one most followed in the Western world. "Be reasonable" is the advice given to the emotionally distraught, which means: think before you leap! Get your thinking right and all will be well, is the idea. Good advice if you can make it work when your emotions are rampant.

I want to highlight reason's importance first because of its unique "window of opportunity," our first chance to evaluate and direct our emotions. This window of opportunity is the key to using intelligent emotions via the path of reason. We should all try to grab it and let our reasoning powers help us determine what is the best emotional response.

Reason's Window of Opportunity

After our emotions have reacted to whatever the event was that sparked them, we are provided with a window of opportunity to evaluate and respond to our emotions. If we don't grasp this opportunity, we lose the first and best chance at checking the escalation of our emotions and managing them.

Speed is everything in grasping the window of opportunity. As soon as we feel an emotional response (surge) we should ask ourselves three questions:

- Is this the best response to make or is there a better one?
- Am I responding at an appropriate emotional level, or am I over-responding or under-responding based on the circumstances?
- Is this the right time to let my emotions be seen in this way?

We are inquiring about the "best response" the "appropriate response," and the "timing" of our response.

Developing this as a habit before things soar out of control is an essential tool in achieving emotional wisdom.

Asking, "Is this the best thing to do?" is using the gift of our rationality to solve the possible escalation of our emotions. Let's see it in a life situation. We will focus only on one moment in this exchange where asking what is the best thing to do illustrates the use of reason.

An exchange takes place between Pattie and Lance. Lance detects Pattie is upset, or at least irritated with him for something, perhaps for asking what she meant by her cryptic remark. He doesn't know the real reason but feels the cutting edge of her remark.

"Why are you so irritated with me?" asks Lance.
"I'm not irritated."
"Yes you are, I can hear it in your voice — you are irritated. Why do I upset you like that? Tell me."

At this point, Pattie's emotions are rising too and she can grasp the window of opportunity and think. She has a choice. She can think to herself: the best thing for me to do is to make sure this does not develop into a fight and, besides, I want this relationship and I will only be disturbed if it escalates into an all-out brawl. She can also choose another path, namely, to actively defend the fact that she did not feel irritated and it's Lance that needs to apologize for even thinking she might be upset. His remark insinuated that she was mad at him.

If the relationship is what Pattie values most, the reasonable response would be to calm the exchange now and not escalate it with her defense of her position and perhaps even add her own insinuations. The latter would be unreasonable because it would not achieve her goals. She could choose to say:

"I'm sorry if I came across sounding irritated. I didn't mean to because I am not irritated at you. Please don't worry, I am sorry if you thought I was."

This has the best chance of cooling a potential escalation of both of their emotions and wisely achieves her goals. It does not amount to a confession of guilt because she says "I'm sorry IF I came across that way." It declares her real intent and that is to avoid any misunderstanding or the escalation of their emotions. It is intelligently reasonable. To have persisted in claiming she was not irritated and then pursue defending herself would almost certainly return offense for offense. Who knows where the exchange might go from there.

Lance then has the opportunity to respond with assurances of his acceptance of her apology. Pattie will have made the most reasonable response in line with her goals for the relationship and be proud of the intelligent emotions that her reason helped her select.

After the emotions have cooled, Pattie might attempt an explanation of why he might have misunderstood her. Reason will have triumphed.

We need this window of opportunity to be able to examine our emotions and their response to how we engage with the world. Thankfully, our emotions do not escalate while we focus on thinking about "What is the best thing to do?" or any of the three questions. We grasp this window of opportunity while we intentionally think about our best response.

Our emotions allow us this window of time to consider if we should make any adjustments. This time-out to think is when we must use our reason to evaluate more carefully what our emotions have decided to do. However, if we focus on our feelings of hurt, thinking of how we have been wronged or simply how we feel instead of focusing on our evaluation of what is the best thing to do, the time-out ends and our emotions escalate. In this case, we have missed the window or closed it, so to speak.

Focusing on a better response (the best thing to do), or on an evaluation of the situation, or on a more appropriate emotion is what we should concentrate on if we want to keep our emotions at a comparatively low level. As soon as our focus wanders back onto our feelings they will begin to escalate, because whatever we focus on is magnified and takes up more real estate in our minds, creating what we feel is an escalation of our emotions.

To successfully use reason to evaluate our emotions we need:

- Speed to grasp the opportunity
- A determined focus that keeps our thoughts on the discovery of the best thing to do
- A time-out to focus on thinking

Each temperament uses the window of opportunity differently. The SPs become adept at using it to figure out their next best move. The SJs must discipline themselves to ponder the right or the wrong of their emotions. The NTs will naturally use it since deciding what is reasonable and makes most sense is what they do usually without much thought. The NFs need this window most since their emotions are the most reactive and so strong that they must practice arresting them and learning to take time out to process.

The emotions of an NF are usually caused by hurt, and they have little ability to ward off most of the hurts. The hurt is often mixed with a sense of injustice, so the situation becomes complex. This means more time is needed to think. NFs must learn to take a time-out as quickly as possible.

The Window Always Decides Something

Our emotions are most vulnerable to being changed or voted down immediately after we are conscious of them. At this juncture we always make a judgment whether to change our feelings or not. Mostly it is made by default: we just allow them to have their way.

- If the window closes without our taking action we have made a decision by default.

- If we decide to change our emotional response but don't effectively make the change, we have still made a response — a failed response.
- If we let our focus wander back onto our emotions, nursing their judgment, they will escalate. A decision to change something has to be made if we want to control our emotions.

As humans, we can't act without making some sort of decision, either automatically, programmed, or deliberated. The way we are designed to function is biased toward finding and making a decision whatever that decision happens to be. This is part of our intelligent design. Choose we do, and choose we must.

It was a learning curve for Mark. Mark was 22 and he thought of himself as an intelligent, rational creature. He, therefore, accepted the advice that if he wanted to be master of his emotions when he was tempted to totally lose control, he would have to learn to conquer all the little emotional challenges and master them first. Plenty of opportunity was at hand. He and Amy had been dating and, in getting to know her, he had noticed how different they were. She thought and felt the opposite way to him, or so he thought, and there were many chances to arrest his urge to correct her or try to make her think like he did. Swallowing hard and keeping his mouth closed was one decision he knew he could make.

She was protective to the extreme. Her emotions would harden her verbal responses whenever she felt he was about to do something that could be a danger or an embarrassment to him. He had been tempted to assert his freedom and independence. "I can handle myself," he would threaten with detectable annoyance. She didn't get the message in his retorts and he wondered how such a beautiful girl could be so controlling, or was the word stubborn. Of course, beauty and control are often found together in the female ISFJ.

So, he watched for all these little opportunities to practice taking the window of opportunity to think of the best response, mastering his closed mouth most of the time. At first he simply made no response. No response was a decision and a response. He told himself, "Whenever she tries to control me, I will do what she says but not say anything." He found he could do that. Then he began to pause longer and construct a response that would not cause a heated exchange like, "Thanks, I've got it in control," which also let her know he was capable in such circumstances and in command of himself.

He liked the self-control he felt. He noticed that his more challenging emotions were now much more easily managed. What was an imperfection in Amy had become the occasion for perfecting his own self-management. One day he would face a tougher test when emotions were running high, but for now he was his own successful master.

Something is always decided by decision or default for all of us, and we can make ourselves master of our emotions when we intentionally use the little occasions to practice.

Gaining Social Control

The way we are made is also biased toward our having the opportunity to exercise social control. We are social beings and social beings must act responsibly or social encounters can be disastrous. If we are to act responsibly in the face of the emotions of others as well as our own, we still need to control our actions and decisions before it is too late. Stopping to reason with ourselves can help us control the social encounter, not just ourselves. Not to take control is to give the control away, and most of the time that means giving the control away to others. Do we want others to control the situation and our lives? The window of opportunity is for the purpose of exercising our own personal control over ourselves and influencing our social circumstances as well.

Using our reason we can *decide* to choose a more rational course, or *change the emotion* to an opposite emotion (more about this under "Replacement"), or *act* in a way that will benefit others or us. The window of opportunity is not only a chance to change the way we think. It is about thinking right, feeling right, and acting right in social engagements.

When using the window of opportunity, we also need to understand that we cannot change other people, only ourselves. Most of our emotions, if we have been hurt in some way, will be centered on how we feel toward others and what they should or should not be doing. It is easy to fall into the trap of concentrating on what others should be doing and not on what we should be doing. When we do, their wrongs, not ours, take prime place in our emotions and can easily become the thing we think about most, giving priority to our emotions and not to our own reason.

Mary had been having a hard day at the "home office." Children were her responsibility in the home office and they had driven her to the edge of insanity. Constant whining was the last phase of their skilled strategy to break mom down and she was mentally, emotionally, and physically exhausted and ready for the fall.

As a result of all the disturbances to its peace, the house was not picked up: doing that was a full time job for Mary because she had lost control of the kids and, to an observer, they were running the house. In her utter fatigue, she waited with cautious hope for her husband to come home and rescue her. Yes, she knew she needed a better methodology of handling her children, but what worked with one did not work with the others. She was open to being helped and taught, but the pressing need was some immediate support.

The moment arrived. He stepped through the door with a smile on his face that faded quicker than a receding wave. There she stood defenseless and at the end of her wits. She had no energy left to combat his non-understanding of her plight.

"What a mess!" he blurted out with rising anger as he surveyed the condition of the home, "Can't you control the kids?" he roared as he took in the chaotic scene of kids wildly "tearing up the place" as he put it, adding for good measure how he was "ashamed of her."

She initially wilted before his blast, but her emotions, reacting to her hostile world, surged with an energy that stiffened her will and bolstered her tired spirit. She exploded at him; yes, right there in front of the children. With white hot anger she lashed back, momentarily stunning her husband and the kids with a verbal broadside. A nervous silence followed. She rushed into the other room and wept while she tried to think. He had effectively forsaken her, embarrassed her, and demolished her only hope of support. Alone in her hurt and anger, she couldn't think of what was best to do; she just ached with the pain that comes from being humiliated to the point of losing all sense of self-worth.

This was when the wrongs of her husband took front and center place in her mind and she could think of nothing but how he had hurt, humiliated, destroyed, embarrassed, and deserted her. All her emotions were negative, even vindictive and revengeful and multiplying by the second. She hated him. She knew she hated him.

She shook off the hand that was gingerly placed on her shoulder and stormed out into the garage, slamming the door behind her as if to say, "Don't even try to follow me." Her emotions were rising to fever pitch fast. Thoughts of leaving and never returning were hammering at her mind and winning support from her feelings.

As sometimes happens, her damaging emotions had overstepped themselves and their power had gone too far. A thought of leaving the children with their unfair, inconsiderate, sorry father sobered her a little and she began to think more clearly. She could not change her husband or even whatever the children were thinking. He had to mop up his own mess, the children would have to ... she couldn't think of that yet.

She could only change one thing, if she could bring herself to do it — herself. What was just and fair faded as her reason, thought a little late, at last surfaced. Thoughts of what was needed to be done now began to grow in her mind, followed by emotions that supported getting control of herself. It was time for supper. Wiping away her tears, she returned — not in triumph, but struggling to put on a calm exterior and to get something on the table for the children. Her reason had calmed her somewhat, and getting back to the tasks at hand helped too. A tightly closed mouth and a business-like attitude, as though she was again in charge, seemed to strengthen her.

She stepped back into the deathly quiet house. All eyes were on her and she shunned their gazes. She was at last beginning the task of influencing others by changing herself, although she never thought of it that way. Quietly, in almost a tense whisper (whispers can be threatening), she told the children to clean up the house. They obeyed without a word. Her husband slunk away into his office with his tail between his legs and with a mind spinning from his own panic.

She had taken control of her situation by doing only one thing — letting her reason change her emotions — and magically the people in her life had changed too. The house was fast regaining order and the family was learning a lesson, although she would not have wished to teach them this way. People learn lessons and social changes occur when we change ourselves.

Although this is an extreme, it illustrates the need when overcome with emotions of any sort to reach down deep inside for reason's calm voice and do what we know is best. In this case, reason helped her change herself, and in changing what she could and not trying to change what she couldn't (the others), she brought a semblance of peace to the warfront.

It is quite unreasonable to let what someone else has done control and mold our thoughts. We are giving others control of our lives when we do. Perhaps we can help arrest our anger or our feelings of hurt by asking "do we really want to have them control our lives? Do we want to hand over to them the influence that makes us, in effect, their slaves?" Do we not want to do what we can and follow the lead of reasonable emotions that empower us to rise above our circumstances and gain social intelligence?

The only way we can retain influence in the situation is to make changes to how we think, feel, and act. The sooner we do this when we are emotionally hyperactive, the better. Our chances at arresting our emotions is always greater at the start than later when they have had the chance to stir us more deeply.

We can also see that the window of opportunity is for finding solutions, not for ruminating over social problems. Intelligence of any sort is for making wise or right decisions, not for nursing our hurt. Finding solutions is the goal of evaluating, analyzing, and rationalizing. Logic helps us think systematically, and going over the benefits of the alternative choices, if we can, is a great use of the window of opportunity.

Why People Find Reason Alone Problematic

Using our reason alone is not a panacea. It is not cod liver oil for the emotions. A remedy for emotional control is found in reason, true, but also in the replacement of damaging emotions with other more beneficial emotions, such as willpower (sheer willpower is driven by emotion), determination, and appropriate actions. In Mary's story, reason was not the only player. It was the instigator of emotional change but was backed up with a supporting cast of powerful emotions and some well-chosen actions to round out the characters.

Here are some of the positive emotions that vied for being the ones to replace her initial hurt and anger, plus all the negative emotions that were developing fast as a result:

- The anger of fight that stiffened her will and fought off her complete emotional demolition (not all anger is negative)
- The anger of defense as she lashed out in response to her husband's insensitive and cruel anger

- Disengagement from her husband to find relief as she fled to the garage
- The freedom from further hurt that flight could achieve (reason countered this one)
- The personal sense of dignity that drove her to regain her composure
- The urge to meet her children's needs
- Taking firm control of the situation (determination) without revengeful emotions taking control and causing further damage.

Here are some of the actions she chose:

- Leave the scene of her embarrassment
- Allow a natural venting of tears
- Leave again for the garage when she was not ready to compose herself
- Return to take control
- Return to immerse her attention in making dinner.

Mary needed the help of these positive emotions and helpful actions. Just to do what made sense to her would not have helped without the help of other emotions and well-chosen actions.

Reason doesn't work well for some because their emotions can be too forceful to be overcome with reason alone. They can see the logic or the rationality of a course of action but not find the motivation or ability to do it. Our dominant emotions quickly build a resistance against being suppressed. They must be met with a more effective force.

For other people, they find rationalizations that are more interested in defending their negative, damaging feelings — the ones they don't want to let go — rather than finding a positive solution. When our rationalizations work against the goal of emotional intelligence, success is further away. We are all in charge of our own reasons and can do with them what we will. Reason serves whatever we fashion it to serve. This kind of rationalizing in defense of our negative emotions can certainly backfire.

Reason is also not an ethical power that always acts in the interests of what is right or in terms of emotional intelligence. Reason can be confused as to what is best or deceived into believing what it assumes is best. People can be frustrated, disappointed, can second guess themselves, and even punish themselves, finding willing reasons to do any of these things.

Another problem for some is that strict, unbending reason does not consider the feelings and the wishes implicit in some goals (especially feelings) that it thinks are unrelated or irrelevant. Reason can be harsh and its harshness can irritate those who are more sensitive. Reason can also be too cold to pour into an over-heated emotional skillet.

Reason is only as good as its assumptions, and those who put so much trust in reason often forget this. Reason or logic is a tool that helps us to think rightly, but if our presuppositions are false, all the logic in the world won't help. What the best emotional reaction is depends on the correctness and completeness of the information we have.

Each temperament uses reason in different ways: the SP to be tactical, the SJ to be logistical, the NT to be strategic, and the NF to be diplomatic, as David Keirsey has so insightfully stated. Each may come to different conclusions given the same information.

So when it comes to reason solving our emotional problems, we can be in a heap of hurt or, on the other hand, accurately directed to the best solution. Reason, like emotion, can be good or bad, helpful or hurtful. Our entanglement with our emotions is the cause of our troubles, and emotional intelligence is clearly not a simple matter of resorting to reason. Emotions must change.

The Reason for Reason

We need a check on our emotions, since emotions are a first impression phenomenon most of the time. They make sudden judgments and offer insight into what they detect is important. They protect first and adjust their judgments slowly and only after some persuasive force.

Reason is successful in making us intelligently emotional much of the time. How we think and what we think makes us who we are. It is thinking about our actions and reactions reasonably that makes us rational beings. Reason slows us down and forces us to think through matters deliberately and methodically, and our emotions need the application of this brake.

Reason also brings structure to our thoughts and we often sort out what is a better way of responding when our thoughts are orderly. Of course, some people do not use their reason in an orderly fashion because they have not learned to think in a logical or structured fashion.

Reason can and does, at times, cool down the excessive heat of our emotions and this is one of its more dependable assets. Calmness is a bona fide benefit. Cool and calm is how the NT wants to be all the time, but for the NF, cool and calm all the time is living without passion and that is unthinkable. The result is the NT crowns reason and the NF insists on a life of passion to give it ultimate meaning. Both are right.

Reason is most effective before the peak of emotional heat is reached and after the heat has dissipated. In the middle of the struggle, reason loses most of its ability to influence us because of the strength of our emotions.

Second Method — Right Actions

An ounce of action is worth a ton of theory.
~ Friedrich Engles

Simply doing the right thing seems to most people to be an obvious path to emotional intelligence. If we do the right thing, we typically believe we have acted intelligently. Even if our feelings and actions are in opposition to each other, doing the right thing makes us appear to others as composed — emotionally intelligent. Most of the instructions that we are given in lists of "Things to Do to Be Emotionally Intelligent" (an example is in *Emotional Intelligence 2.0* by Bradberry and Greaves) settle for urging us, with a deceptive simplicity, to just do the right thing. That's all there is to it, they seem to say.

Then why, we might ask, do people not do the right thing? They want to be emotionally intelligent, don't they? Is it because it's not always that simple? Is it because they lack the education and the reasoning ability to see what is right and proper in a given situation? Perhaps it's because they have never been taught how to act appropriately. Could it be that their culture is confused about what is appropriate and inappropriate, accepting right as wrong and wrong as right? Or do they live with the notion that we should just express our passions, regardless of what they are and whether they cause ourselves and others pain or not. "It's his problem, not mine," we often hear as a justification for unintelligent behavior.

Rather, I want to suggest that people may find it hard to do the right thing because their emotions get in the way of doing the right thing. Their emotions have other agendas and they often think of their emotions as obstacles too difficult to surmount. Some even feel their emotions can't be managed, that they are a wild untamable force of nature better left alone and simply excused when they prove to be uncontrollable.

"I have a temper," Jacob told me. "It's just me. That's the way I am." There was a crispness and harshness in his tone. "You can't teach an old dog like me new tricks. I do my best." It sounded a little like a plea for pity, but it was more a defense that says "I can't, therefore I am not to be held responsible." His anger had made his kids retreat from him whenever he returned home from a business trip. And when he left again, they would raise their hands and shout, "Yeah!"

I knew his family didn't want to live any longer under his constant rationalizing of his angry outbursts. What family would keep excusing an uncontrolled temper? "Have you tried to do the considerate thing and be patient with others," I asked him. He didn't respond or flinch. I wanted to say, "Do you like to be thought of as a weak, helpless individual that can't seem to take responsibility for himself. Do you want your kids, who are scared of your anger, to grow up and despise you because of it?" I felt the urge to slip that piece of ammo into the breach and fire, but fortunately I didn't succumb to this primitive reaction.

His face was red, he was fidgeting with nervousness, so I decided to use another means of attack — silence. I waited. The silence was becoming hostile to his evasive thoughts. He finally blurted out, "No one has shown me how!" He had lived for decades with anger toward his world for not helping him. It was not his fault, he wanted to maintain. This inner tension between what he was and what he wanted to be at last had surfaced for us to address it. The path to recovery had begun.

Humans don't live happily when they are a house divided against themselves. We are made to function harmoniously and with a consistency that makes us feel we have true personal integrity. Therefore, we must learn to do the right thing but also learn to think and chose the right emotion to accompany our actions, a combination that makes doing the right thing possible. It's our emotions we must address when struggling to choose the right action. Therefore, we have to learn methods of controlling our emotions.

Always acting according to the way we feel about things makes life too easy. "Feel it and do it" is a popular policy, but what if the feeling is wrong? When in teenage years the emotional system is trying to sort out intelligence and unintelligence, we are prone to worship the idea that if it feels good, do it. That policy avoids all need for emotional control. The soft road is then more easily chosen instead of the hard road.

Have you ever noticed adults acting emotionally immature and just letting their emotions have full reign? Is that where the teenagers get this insidious model, I wonder? Here is the fact: if we don't learn emotional intelligence as teens, we find it much more difficult as adults and often don't want to face the struggle. True?

Delayed gratification is an excellent method to force the control of our emotions by forcing self-disciplinary actions. Changing our actions changes our feelings. Delayed gratification is also a form of the most unpopular discipline of self-denial. But why should I deny myself anything, we ask? Because when we do, we learn to become our own masters, and when we don't, we give up the control of our lives to our emotions, whatever they happen to be in the moment. We become the proud (or ashamed) designers of our lives.

Incidentally, at times, some animals show a well-developed self-denial and the skill of delayed gratification. As human animals, let's motivate ourselves with the thought that surely we should not sink below the intelligence of the "lesser" animals. We all know that life without some self-denial is bound for trouble. Don't try it on the freeway!

Our emotions are often expressed outwardly by our actions, and all is well if our emotions are intelligent. If, however, our reason condemns our actions, we have destructively found ways of rationalizing our actions and feelings so that we believe we are acting consistently even when we are not. It's a sure way to fool ourselves. We call it rationalizing because the word rational sounds intelligent and we fail to notice the negative import of the word.

We rationalize our behavior when we use irrational reasons and arguments in defense of our position and even when we do or don't notice their unreasonableness. We are wonderful creatures, but we are on a journey of learning how to live intelligently. Have you noticed that even education does not make us immune to irrational defense?

Rationalization is a tool we use to avoid the trouble of having to honestly examine our actions and bring our misdeeds and thoughts to the judgment of reason and truth. Rationalization is often obvious irrational thinking. We must have a purpose, surely. We do. We rationalize our ill-chosen thoughts to preserve a kind of false feeling of goodness, rightness, and personal integrity, but we particularly rationalize our ill-chosen actions because they are our published thoughts and, since others have seen them, we must try to defend or correct the way we are seen.

Perhaps we need to define "actions" since we often do not recognize that all of our actions are indeed actions. Doing the right thing can be as simple as a change in facial expression, a kind deed, or a well-chosen word. Actions cover all physical expressions from speech (we forget this is one of our most potent actions) to any physical movement. We can also act by doing or saying nothing at all (we tend to forget these non-actions are actions too).

Any of these actions can and will influence our thoughts and feelings. We feel and think something whenever we act. Actions that are good or bad, right or wrong, any degree of approval or disapproval, are the materials with which we build our self-esteem, our reputation, and our character. We define ourselves.

Actions Influence Both Reason and Emotion

Because reasons, actions, and emotions all interact, we need to take a closer look at the ways they affect each other and alter us. Reason, emotions, and actions should provide a united front against unwanted or damaging emotions that are trying to capture our wills. We have been designed with the ability to handle our emotions, but we need all three in cooperation and the understanding of how to do it.

The relationship between emotions, reason, and actions is that of cause and effect. But it is a cause and effect that is multidirectional. Our thoughts (reason) can cause us to feel and act a certain way; our feelings can directly affect our thoughts and actions, and our actions can influence our emotions and reason. Sound complicated? It is a complicated system, but to operate this purpose-driven system isn't so complicated. Do one and it influences the other two to follow suit. Emotions, reason, and actions also interact with each other and affect each other in any order and in any combination, and usually all three areas are affected at once. We don't even have to activate them in a set order.

Feedback occurs from all three sources. We are equipped with receptors that read all that is going on in our minds, emotions, and actions. When we act, for example, this feedback changes to some degree what we think and feel. It also influences the timing of when we reason and feel. Because of this feedback, we are constantly learning to act in a more beneficial manner. It is our choice whether we learn or not, of course. The feedback happens anyway.

All three functions — reason, emotion, and our actions — stand in judgment of each other. Our actions are judged by our reason and our emotions and, likewise, our reason and emotions judge our actions. Perhaps we are best to think of the interplay of our actions, thoughts, and feelings as feedback mechanisms, checking on each other to keep us well informed. When they give a bad report, we feel guilty or ashamed or incompetent. When they give a good report, we feel happy, harmonious, and integrated. This is, as I have said, our built-in process of continuing education and our opportunities for constant growth. When we act intelligently we are more likely to act that way again, and we even feel better about ourselves.

Do you ever notice these feelings that are trying to direct us, like guilt, embarrassment, contentment or a feeling of positive reinforcement? These teachers and examiners that are built into our systems have our best interests in mind. Perhaps you, like me, have noticed how we tend, at times, to squelch some or all of these voices that are giving us valuable feedback. A growing awareness of all feedback is like paying attention to the teacher. Growth means change and we are being prodded to a better, more appropriate action.

An emotion or thought hasn't lived until it is expressed. Actions are our thoughts and feelings in their final form. It makes sense that if we change the final form, it will have some effect on the initial steps, emotion and thought. If we change our actions, we therefore change our emotions and make it easier to change them the next time. As I have pointed out, this is the principle nearly all ethical and religious systems advocate for us to use to change our lives, and it works. Change the action and our emotions and mental attitudes change too.

Changing our actions is sometimes the easiest thing to do when we are emotionally overwhelmed. If we can't catch the window of opportunity and think of the best thing to do, we can try directing our attention to changing our actions.

Elizabeth always had trouble controlling her emotions by simply thinking of the best thing to do, catching that window of opportunity. The extended family was coming for the annual Christmas family gathering and neither she nor her husband was looking forward to it. Her mother was always obsessively demanding, the mother hen who cackled with controlling confidence. Before the gathering even happened, everyone was laying their plans to avoid being in her presence while she was laying plans to engage each of them so she would feel wanted and important. Emotions were warring with emotions.

Her sister did not help any because she always felt impelled to whine and complain about all the events of the year, casting a depressive atmosphere on the season. Christmas is never more effectively sabotaged than it is by a negative spirit — remember Scrooge?

Her father, who was debilitated and in constant need of care, was always cool and critical of all that was done for him. Since they were all gathering at Elizabeth's place, the visiting family members felt it was her turn to care for her father and mother as well as taking care of all the daily details so that they could enjoy a break from responsibilities. It was a set up for a family disintegration.

Elizabeth had a family of her own to take care of. She had a husband, of course, but he got along well with his brother-in-law, and each day the two of them cowardly grabbed the chance to take off into the mountains to fish, while making sure they returned to the battle ground as late as seemed respectable. All her thoughts about this coming nightmare quickly turned negative and draining. She hated the thought of Christmas with the family.

But this time she learned how right actions could change her emotions. She made a list, assigned tasks to all, including her husband and brother-in-law, and arranged a night at the movies, a picnic in the park, and turns to go shopping and see the Christmas lights which included her in the enjoyment of everything the others had an opportunity to enjoy. Her actions had been called into service to lighten her negative spirit. Actions can do wonders for our emotions when well-planned and executed. Elizabeth even found herself laughing, a previously unheard sound at family Christmas events.

Don't forget to employ right and loving actions as a tool to achieve emotional intelligence because they can be the easiest path to regaining intelligent emotions. Only loving feelings give birth to loving actions, and only hateful feelings give birth to hateful actions. This relationship must be understood and owned by all.

Is Acting Intelligently All There Is to Emotional Intelligence?

It is emotionally intelligent to act right, but is that all that is needed? Some think so, as I have said. However, when we act right we can still fail to change the fermenting emotions inside of us, and they remain to await another time to make their appearance and disrupt our lives. For example, hate that is not dealt with will not heal itself. It can remain active in our minds for years.

I remember Dr. Henry Brandt, a psychologist, telling this story of the inadequacies of actions. A client of his was greatly disturbed at his neighbor for cutting down the trees the client had planted along the boundary of their properties. They had grown tall and obstructed the neighbor's view. The neighbor cut them off neatly at fence post height while the client was away. Unfortunately, the client had not planted the trees on his side of the boundary line but on the boundary line, making them joint ownership.

The client was furious and had lost his treasured privacy. He fumed daily as he left for work, when he returned, and at all other times that his busy mind gave him space to ponder the situation. Henry advised him to visit the neighbor and discuss the matter, air his feelings, and seek some kind of understanding while also changing his feelings toward the neighbor. If he didn't do this, Henry told him, his angry emotions would eat away at his peace and his neighbor would continue to control his life.

He thought about it, but decided that a vacation in the Caribbean would be a better solution. It was taking action, all right, but paying no attention to the needed changes in his reasoning and emotions. Besides, it was much more enjoyable than a visit to the hated neighbor where he might lose his temper and make matters worse.

The Caribbean island was paradise and, distracted by its beauty, he forgot about his neighbor for the moment. He planned a meal at an idyllic restaurant that overhung the emerald green ocean, a perfect setting to banish his cares. Ordering the best steak, he waited for it to arrive. However, his thoughts drifted back to the severed trees, the demonic neighbor, and the fermenting anger he had nursed all these weeks. His emotional pains returned with a vengeance. The steak arrived, attractively displayed and sizzling, and he recalled later in Henry's office how it tasted like fatty cardboard. He was a slave to his anger and a captive to his neighbor's actions. Something more was needed. What was it that Henry had told him to do?

Action solves the immediate needs, but the emotions still have to be effectively dealt with or they will keep burning away at our peace and our self-respect.

Authentic emotional intelligence is not just acting, or even acting correctly — such as using politically correct language or being acceptably polite — but thinking and feeling intelligently too. Therefore, we will now face the major challenge with developing intelligent emotions. Let's understand step three.

Third Method — Replacement

Replacement will finally release us from the hurt of our emotions. If we have not replaced a negative emotion with a positive one, we know nothing has really changed.

Reason is involved in this step too. It makes sense that if we replace a damaging emotion with an intelligent one, we have changed our attitude, mood, feelings, hurt, and whatever was turning our lives in the wrong direction. Because of this, our analytical minds may even advocate this step as the most important of all. So, to be sure we achieve emotional control, all the steps — our reason, actions, and replaced emotions — should be interacting with each other and supporting each other.

An intelligent emotion is, in essence, having the right emotion motivating us from the inside, in the right way, and to the right degree in each circumstance. Accomplishing this in the most efficient way is the path to being intelligently emotional.

It may seem a simple matter to say we need to choose the right emotion. But we know our emotions and how they have exerted their power over us and controlled us time and again. We can even grow to fearf their power over us. Watch a child of two years of age trying to control her emotions and it should be evident that we start life with this difficult challenge. Then watch an adult of eighty sink into a mood or display his anger inappropriately and the task appears insurmountable, or at least we understand the challenge never leaves us. Victory in choosing the right emotion comes one battle at a time — tougher for some than others — and it is never perfected in this life. Because the meaning we experience in life is in our emotions, replacing damaging emotions with healthy emotions creates a healthy meaning to our lives.

There are those who have hidden or suppressed their emotions — some for a lifetime — and appear to be in control of them when the truth is that they, too, have not conquered the incessant battle of the emotions, just buried their emotions out of sight or avoided engaging them in combat. They become like a mortician: impervious to tears and grief, stoic behind their professional smile. Suppression is not the only, nor the best, way of controlling our feelings.

Replacing a troublesome emotion does not mean hiding it behind a facade. It means choosing the most beneficial emotion and appropriately controlling its display. Allowing one's sorrow and concern to mold one's actions and even moisten one's eyes a little makes for a more empathetic and authentic funeral director. So also, expressing fear in our courage, nervousness in our hope, and hurt in our anger rings of integrity and makes us feel more real and authentic. Replacement is finding the right emotion and using it to appropriately mold our behavior.

We must face the reality of emotions in our lives and live in the richness of their meaning, seeking only to manage their emotional wealth.   Hiding them is not managing them. Breaking them in and taming their powers should be our goal.

Doing anything with our emotions is not easy.   Each step — reason, action, and replacement — is to be carved out of solid resistance.   Ugly emotions, such as revenge, anger, bitterness, jealousy, selfishness, and hate (truly the dark side of our natures) do not give up easily and can weaken our wills with their perverse persistence.

An ancient Jewish story goes like this. Jacob had swindled his elder twin brother out of his birthright and deceived his ailing father, whose eyesight and senses were fading, into giving him the all-important blessing that a father gave to the older son before he died.

When Esau discovered that he had been cheated out of the blessing and the birthright, he was furious. The story informs us that Esau held a grudge against his brother, Jacob, and then goes on to further explain how he felt. Esau, it says, was "consoling himself with the thought of killing Jacob."

Comforting ourselves with the thought of revenge is not a rare emotion. It consumes people even today and leads to wrong actions, all of which are on the dark side of life. There is only one real solution to this: replacing the ugly emotion with a stronger, healthy emotion that will compete successfully for dominance in our minds.

Here is the reason why replacing one emotion with another is ultimate emotional intelligence:

- When someone has hurt me, if I only change the way I think about them or the way I act toward them, my anger can still remain and eat away at me. If an emotion of revenge still beats in my mind after I have acted civilly, have I intelligently dealt with my emotions? Hardly. No real success has been achieved until I have changed the emotion.

- Emotions that remain to eat away at me may explode again over some other injustice. My mind has only changed its appearances. I have reasoned my way to a more appropriate behavior, but my mind is still owned by the damaging emotion.

- If I decide to act in a civil and even forgiving manner toward this person who stole from me, is that emotional intelligence? Again, hardly. In this case, I have acted with intelligence but have not rooted out the cause of my hurt, and my emotions remain unintelligent.

- If I decide to change the way I think, then also act in a forgiving manner, and then change the way I feel by adopting another emotion of, let's say, pity or love for my enemy, I now have effectively changed the way I feel. No damaging emotion remains to eat away at me and destroy the happiness of my life. My emotions are healed and my life is not cluttered up with negative baggage. Is this true emotional intelligence? Yes!

So the goal of all emotional intelligence is replacing damaging emotions with constructive ones.

Replacement in Its Most Positive Form

"Oh, 'tis love that makes the world go round."
~ Lewis Carroll, *Alice in Wonderland*

Fate, Time, Occasion, Chance, and Change? To these all things are subject but eternal Love.
~ Percy Bysshe Shelley

This step of replacing one emotion with another has been written about for two millenniums in its most well-known form. It has been advocated as the supreme "how to" by Jesus who made it the number one goal of all emotional intelligence. To quote him, "Love your enemies, do good to those who hate you, bless those who curse you, pray for those who mistreat you...do to others as you would have them do to you...then your reward will be great." Other ethical systems have mentioned the same goal in their quest for cohabitation without war and conflict. So, step three is the goal of all emotional control or intelligence.

Jesus is simply saying to replace your hate with love and kindness; this is the ultimate goal and challenge of intelligent emotions. Note, he is implying that we replace a damaging emotion with its opposite (hate for our enemies replaced with love), and then he tells us how to do it: use kind actions (blessing, praying, and doing good) to support and encourage a change in our feelings and complete our emotional intelligence.

Replacing one emotion with another is a brilliant insight into how we are made. Without replacing our damaging emotions with non-damaging emotions we cannot train ourselves to be intelligently emotional. It's one thing to be emotionally intelligent and make emotionally intelligent choices. It's quite another thing to entertain intelligent emotions and have them fashion our lives.

We have a filter that helps keep unacceptable thoughts and feelings from ruminating in our minds — our reticular activating system. It is made up of the values and choices that we have approved and believe in, and when it is designed to help us choose intelligent emotions, we have a built-in device that makes replacing a damaging emotion with a heathy one much easier. Our values and beliefs change our lives. We want that built-in help that our reticular activating system (RAS, our filter) can give us. Become intelligently emotional by training your RAS to value love over hate in the face of an enemy. It can be done, as many — from Jesus to Gandhi to Mother Teresa and many others in all lands — have demonstrated in their lives.

Just because it is hard is no reason to deny its validity. Positively affirm the beliefs that you want to guide and direct your life and nurture them. This is the way to develop an RAS that will help you replace hate with love. Apply this to all the values you know will make you the best you can be.

In the face of failure and ridicule during his run for president of the United States, Abraham Lincoln kept the emotion of confidence alive with hope and persistence, two values and beliefs he held dear. It was against all the odds that he believed. But notice, believing has to be driven by persistent emotions or our most cherished beliefs will blow away on the winds of adverse circumstances. He kept his valued emotions aimed at his goal. So must we, if we want to replicate his success.

If a butterfly can flap its wings in China and set molecules of air in motion that move other molecules until the increasing disturbance reaches the United States and causes a hurricane (called the butterfly effect), surely repeatedly replacing one emotion with another can create a pattern of control and intelligence in our mental systems that will set us up for the more likely achievement of intelligently emotional behavior. It's true that we are made to be able to achieve this most of the time. Most people simply don't try, have never heard of this possibility, or give up after a few feeble attempts. Some don't want to put in the effort to build solid heathy beliefs.

Our temperament is not made of weaknesses. We can't hide behind the claim that we have weaknesses that make it hard for us to choose a healthy emotion. Weaknesses are self-made and, therefore, can be self-changed. Our temperament is made up of strengths, all positive and beneficial, shaping us wonderfully if we develop them and use them (see my book, *INNERKINETICS*). Emotional intelligence, as we will see in chapters 8-11, is found in developing our strengths. So, don't say "I can't become intelligently emotional." Set your mind and heart on being what you were designed to be and believe with tenacity in the possibility of this life-changing goal.

Replacing a damaging emotion with a healing emotion, such as love, leads to the ultimate control of our emotions. All three steps — reason, action and replacement — are used when we do this. Let's rehearse the steps again seeing them from replacement's point of view:

- First, reason is engaged to change our thinking. When we are hurt by our enemies we normally think of self protection, revenge, a tooth for a tooth, walling people off from our lives and imposing whatever restrictions we can on ever seeing them again. We have to change this way of thinking for a more rational one or we will never achieve the step of replacement. Replacement calls for a change of mind, a rational mind built on healthy premises.

- Second, our actions are involved. We can't keep acting according to the demands of hate since that escalates hate and precludes the possibility of love. The actions we choose must be harmonious with love, not hate. Hate is the opposite of love and actions of hate are not love. Kind actions can come to mind, not bitter payback and ugly revenge.

- Third, hate must be replaced by love, and only then can we claim in the fullest sense to be intelligently emotional because our emotions are at last intelligent in the fullest sense. This third step begins with a choice.

Replacement Is a Choice

How you react emotionally is a choice in any situation.
~ Judith Orloff

Happiness is not something you postpone for the future;
it is something you design for the present.
~ Jim Rohn

Replacement, this third step, is a choice and a very demanding one. Unfortunately most people don't find themselves jumping at the choice of replacing hate with love. We even argue with ourselves against such a "foolish" decision. How can it be smart? Won't we open ourselves up to further abuse?

You might also think enemies deserve to be hated and they earn our revenge. "It is impossible to love your enemies," Ryan told me. "If I love my enemy, he no longer is my enemy," he stated what I thought was a refreshing insight, and then he surprised me with the claim, "I want him as my enemy; I want to destroy him for what he has done to me."

You can, no doubt, think of many more "reasons" to hate your enemies, can't you? As a result of all this reasoning in favor of hate, we find replacing hate with love rather awkward to even suggest. The pure form of this resistance to reacting with love is seen in the child who wants to strike back when struck. It is almost instinctive and is not, you may observe, always an effort at self-defense, rather an unvarnished attempt to harm.

Ask why it is that we create "no tolerance" rules for physical violence, yet we are complacent about nursing inner violence? If we teach our children not to hit others when they are angry, why not teach them how to replace the angry feeling with a more civilized one?

Who is being unintelligent? The one who continues to harbor an emotion that is slowly destroying them from the inside and will make their lives less happy and fulfilling, or the one who favors a radical change, a revolutionary way, living life to its maximum positive rewards, championing love?

Choice is a basic feature of the way our human systems function. We can choose to do almost anything. We love our freedom to choose. Yet when we are faced with the responsibility of choosing a kind and loving emotion or having to make a choice against our feelings of revenge and hatred, we try to weasel out of the responsibility to choose. We say things like we really don't have a choice, and we rationalize the unintelligent choice as the only possible choice. Aristotle's claim that we are rational creatures is being mocked by so-called rational beings when we do this. We surely can't defend such obvious irrational behavior that is inspired by negative emotions.

Love is supreme and, if we act with fairness and self-sacrificing love, there is no other demand or rule needed. Into the bargain, we achieve all the goals of emotional intelligence. Love is the perfect solution in a world of hate — not revenge and not payback. "Love your enemy."

Defense of ourselves and others does not require that we hate. Even the popular call to tolerance doesn't trump the superiority of love. Love is to be the aim. Without it we are an obtrusive hurtful noise in a society that needs harmony badly. Let's teach ourselves and our children the superiority of love that can be the most excellent and intelligent emotion.

Own Your Emotions

Our emotions are ours, not the other person's. Does it sound strange to say that? When we are hurt, for example, we don't think that way; we want the other person to own our emotion and do something about it. After all, hurt is an emotion that feels the disturbance that another person has inflicted on us. Why should we own the hurt?

But it is ours, not theirs. The hurt is inside of us; it is what we are feeling. Probably they don't even know we are hurt, or at least they may not know why. We are the only ones who can do something about our own feelings. That fact of how we are made to function will never change.

However, it doesn't appear this way to us when we are hurt. All we can think of is that we are hurt and it is someone else who has caused us to hurt. As long as we look at it that way, we will be caught up in the tornado of blame and revenge, pointing the finger at others. Both the blame and revenge can be of the silent, passive variety, inflicting wound for wound while also nursing and feeding our feelings of hurt.

The statement to "love our enemies" implies that we have been, and are, hurt and that we are to do something about our own feelings. It says nothing about addressing the actions or intent of our enemy or even thinking about them. It suggests we don't think about them.

Thinking of what the other person should do will not change our feelings. It will only increase their intensity and speed their journey down the same damaging road that they are already racing down. Reasons will pile on reasons in our brain for how we have been victimized, and we will take on the mindset of an injured person. That mindset will do nothing to heal our own hurt emotions.

Owning our own hurt means we can do something about it and that is always the best place to be: namely, in control of the next move. Let's think of our emotions in the terms of a game. I want the ball in my hands, not in the other person's hands. If it is in their hand, they have the next move and I don't know what that move might be. At this moment in the game they are in control. I am forced to play defense. In fact, I cannot play offense — that opportunity has been taken away from me. Is that the best place to be in a game or a life? I don't think so. I'd rather play offense any day.

So I don't want to be playing defense with my life; I want to have the ball in my hands. To have my life in the hands of the one who hurt me would be frightening. I don't want them controlling the next move in my life. So, I must make the next move and control my life. I must do something about my own feelings and catch the window of opportunity, use reason or take some action to change my feelings. This is what I need to focus on. Start by praying for those who despitefully use you. Do something and your feelings of hurt will begin to change. Keep the ball in your hands! Claim responsibility for feeling hurt.

Love and Its Actions Can Lead the Way

Focusing on love (or on whatever emotion is healing and helpful) when hate consumes us may not be easy, but in order for it to be easier it must partner with appropriate positive

209

actions. The forced loving action is a key to changing our emotions, so let's explore its purpose further.

I say "forced" since we usually have to force actions that are opposite of a negative, damaging emotion that has captured our minds. Loving actions can help lead the way to successful replacement of a damaging emotion, but we must act, not just think about it.

Remember, acting lovingly when hurt by our enemy robs the hate in our heart of its energy, weakening it and paving the way for another emotion to take over. Whatever gains our focus or attention is where the energy of the mind and brain is concentrated. If we focus on love, hate loses its vitality and cannot continue to grow and dominate the mind.

This fight we face for love to dominate in our minds rather than hate can be understood better when we remember that love cannot exist together with hate over the same object, in the same mind, at the same time. The mind cannot, at the same time, be both positive and negative. Therefore, we either oscillate back and forth from love to hate and hate to love, creating what we call a love-hate relationship, or one emotion must give way to the other.

This being the case, love, which is the greater force if we persist, will oust hate. Also, a positive frame of mind resists a negative, intrusive force like hate and sets up a barrier against it. We are not only designed to operate positively but are dominated by whatever emotion we choose to focus on. Therefore, let's focus on love and act lovingly, and love will be given the opportunity to take over the mind.

Just focusing on love doesn't make it easier, nor does it promise an immediate removal of our feelings of hate. It's only the way we begin the process of replacing one emotion with another. A struggle will almost always ensue. If we struggle, our perseverance will crown love the victor and the miracle of a fresh mind happens. We must stay the course and it is hard work at times, but keep flapping those wings (remember the butterfly effect) and changes take place in the neuronal pathways of our brain, making it easier and easier to repeat choosing an intelligent emotion in the future.

This penetrating insight into human nature answers the question, "How should we then live?" by pointing to love as the greatest asset or tool in our human emotional makeup. This is because love is more than an emotion — it is also a state of mind and an action. Producing a feeling of love toward someone is not love in full flower because it has not gone through the process of maturation.

Love depends on being given the chance to be born by our actions into the world and continue its work of affecting and transforming us and others. It matures when it becomes an action and becomes our mental state. Without this birth it sours inside us. Look at it this way: without becoming an action, love is stillborn.

To love someone and never express that love outwardly is to fail as a lover. That tells us love depends on being expressed to be love. So there is one emotion, love, that sums up all positive emotions and can replace all damaging emotions. All three steps to intelligent emotions — reason, action and replacement of negative emotions — are involved in true love. We function with emotional intelligence every time we use love intelligently, and we become intelligently emotional when it becomes our chosen lifestyle.

Cleansing the Mind

It is the experience of many that replacement not only is effective as a management tool but most efficiently cleanses the mind of negative passions. We have reasoned that each emotion can morph into another and yet another. Hate can morph into countless feelings and we can easily become confused over what we are really feeling and thinking. The more emotions that are involved in the takeover of our mind, the more entrenched they become. Love cleanses the mind of hate and all of its hurtful entourage.

Replacing the hate as soon as we are aware of it helps us halt the multiplication of other negative feelings that make the battle so much harder. Once love is in place, it also morphs into other emotions, strengthening its hold on our minds and behavior. Some commercial cleansers not only get rid of all the bad bacteria but leave a film behind that makes it more difficult for the unwanted bacteria to return and take hold again. An intelligent emotion acts similarly, cleansing and then protecting the mind against further negative impurities.

Focusing on love surely does calm the emotions of hate. Focusing on any positive strength of our temperament can do the same and eventually, if we keep our focus on an intelligent emotion, it will replace all negative inhabitants of the mind.

A Welcome Discovery for the "Fs"

For the Fs, this emphasis on love is a welcome discovery. Remember, their emotions must be consulted in any decision, and the task of redirecting their emotions from hate to love or fear to trust is more achievable because they are already very aware of how they feel and are troubled by it.

It is also positively refreshing for them to realize that they have deep resources of emotion and a practiced familiarity with how they affect their lives. A positive emotion, like love, leaves no residual feelings of guilt either. If love did have negative side effects, beside the possibility of being rejected, it might reasonably make them shy away from loving. Rejection is not necessarily a negative. The way we perceive it is what counts.

Love lifts our feelings of self worth and brightens our future with glimmers of hope, paying us good dividends while it lasts. It is better to love than not to love. For the NF, love can be particularly enticing and they return to it again and again even if their love has been spurned. Love and harmony is clean, fresh air to them.

It also makes sense to the reason of the F to choose a cleansing and positive emotion like love, which can also open up new possibilities for a relationship and preserve its true value. There is logic in emotions, a logic at times more effective than the logic of reason, and this is seen clearly when it comes to relationships. Love, more than reason, enriches a relationship. Even if not seemingly reasonable, love can win against immense obstacles and make the reasons that oppose it seem ignorant.

For the Ts, they may well choose the power of reason to quell the surges of emotion because, when they make decisions, they favor reason and seldom seriously consult their feelings. They are very familiar with the use of reason. So, if the change from hate to love or fear to trust makes sense to them, they may well quickly choose love. Having intelligent emotions insists on changing our emotions, not just our minds or our actions.

Reason Versus Replacement

Here is a comparison of "reason" and "replacement," emphasizing that reason alone is not enough: (compare this list with the list at the beginning of the chapter.)

- Both reason and replacement change the focus of the mind.
- Both calm the mind.
- Replacing one emotion with another (replacement) directly changes the state of the limbic system and, therefore, dispenses with the unwanted emotion effectively. Reason has only an indirect effect on changing our emotions.
- Emotions carry within them their own reasons. Love and hate have their reasons. One drains the power from the other and changes the nature of the mind.
- Sometimes there is no clear reason not to hate. Emotions can be changed without a clear reason. We can simply decide we don't want to feel a certain way.

- Reason sees only half of the world's realities, meaning it sees more dominantly what logic sees and not as strongly what emotion or love feels.
- Reason is slow; emotion is lightning fast.
- Both reason and replacement are not always to be trusted. Both must be evaluated. The reason or the emotion that replaces another must be the right one.
- The superior power of the positive makes both positive reasons and emotions able to effect a beneficial change.
- We really do not know what is the most advanced function of the brain; it all depends on what factors we use to measure what we call advanced. So reason, as our society accepts, is not necessarily the most advanced mental function.
- Great minds are great thinkers, but also great feelers.
- Imagination is enriched by emotion, not depleted by it.
- Emotions have the greater power over us and, therefore, can produce the most dramatic change.

To become intelligently emotional we need reason, actions, and replacement, all three. If they are firmly established as our default mechanism when we are challenged, we are well equipped to become intelligently emotional.

7 - The Intelligently Emotional Lifestyle

If human beings are perceived in potentials instead of problems, as possessing strengths instead of weaknesses, as unlimited rather than dull and unresponsive, then they thrive and grow to their capabilities.
~ Barbara Bush

Concentrate on your strengths instead of your weakness ... on your powers instead of your problems.
~ Paul J. Meyer

Build your strengths. They are what make you great.
~ Ray W. Lincoln

How do we live an intelligently emotional lifestyle? Briefly stated: by living in our strengths and intelligently using the positive emotions that drive them.

Our strengths are driven and empowered by emotions and in the intelligent operation of our strengths we have the secret to the prevention of emotional breakdown and the key to developing a lifestyle of emotional strength and wisdom. This is the life!

Sabotaged by Weaknesses

We often fall into our weaknesses without planning to do so. Why? Since we fail so often, is it because we are made to fail or is it because we just can't avoid it?

Cars fail with consistency when they run out of gas, their tires lose pressure, water has mixed with the gasoline, their computer chips are damaged by extreme temperatures, or the oil level falls below the engine's requirements. They were never designed to run without gas or enough oil. Living in contradiction to our design ("living in our weaknesses" we will call it) causes us to lose control of our emotions. It even causes us to misjudge the right or wrong use of our emotions, causing another form of emotional unintelligence we might call self-deception. Failure should not lead to the belief that we are meant to fail.

Even though we fail often, we are meant to live in our strengths and feel their power energizing our lives. Falling into our weaknesses causes doubts, fear, guilt, and damage to our confidence. We become victims of our negative emotions and beliefs. If we don't recover and focus on our strengths we will spiral into defeatism.

We Repair Easily When We Fail

Man never made any material as resilient as the human spirit.
~ Bern Williams

Fortunately, we are made to be resilient and to repair easily and quickly. When we fall into our weaknesses and become emotionally destructive, we can quickly return to our strengths and using a positive, healthy emotion, experience the healing of our spirits as the weakness disappears and we return to live as we are designed to live. Living in our strengths is simply a matter of using them intelligently.

216

The human spirit can repair faster than the human body unless we remain in our weaknesses and nurture our woes. Some people gain a distorted pleasure from regurgitating their feelings of self-pity. The human spirit, however, returns to health immediately when we leave our weaknesses and return to the image in which we are made — our strengths. Emotional health lives in the proper use of these strengths and the emotions that drive them.

But what about the emotional damage of, say, childhood abuse? Does that repair instantly? No, but I would argue that as the abused person returns to use their strengths, they feel an immediate uplift in their spirit and the path to health is on its way. Time is an essential ingredient in the emotional healing process when we are wounded, but time alone won't help if we wallow in pity or self-destructive emotions. There is a need for personal cooperation if we are to heal from any wound, physical or emotional. We must participate in the requirements of health and healing to repair damaged emotions. Use of our strengths is a basic requirement for being healthy and emotionally intelligent.

If you are a parent and are worried about the emotional damage you may have done to your child, please remember, a child is perhaps even more resilient than adults and with love and care they will repair quickly. Focus on helping them develop their strengths and they will bounce back to being who they are designed to be. Paranoia about doing harm to their children can easily develop into a debilitating fear and doubt for parents. It's not a place of emotional strength or leadership. Both parent and child must live in their strengths and when they do, their weaknesses disappear.

Do Weaknesses Really Disappear?

Whatever we focus on, or pay attention to, is where the energy of our minds and our emotions is centered. If we focus on an unwarranted fear or hate, these emotions will generate energy in us, and as we have observed, the more we focus on them, the more intense and energetic they become. Their energy is negative and by that I mean it is destructive. We develop toxic energy and its effects are felt in all we do.

When we switch our focus to our strengths, the energy center also changes. We begin to feel the lift our strengths produce in us and their positive energy. Feelings change because the attention center has changed. Isn't that great news?

Healthy energy is generated when our center of attention changes from our weaknesses to our strengths and the negative emotions, robbed of their energy, begin to wilt and fade. If the change is fully made, the weakness and its negative emotions disappear from our consciousness together with their toxic activity. We need to teach our children to change their focus when they are living in their weaknesses, and when they feel the change from negative to positive energy, they are in the process of learning to be emotionally intelligent. The process of recovery is the same for mature adults.

Why Are Our Weaknesses Unintelligent?

Can't our weaknesses be intelligent? For example, isn't dislike normal to humans and at times an intelligent act? The feeling of dislike produced by biting into a rotten apple may save us from a digestive disorder: is that not an intelligent emotion? Isn't it smart to dislike some things and isn't dislike a negative feeling in most people's judgment?

First, let's sort out the assumptions in this argument. It is assuming that all dislikes are the same and all dislike is normal and all dislike is negative. That simply isn't true. Dislike of lutefisk may be regarded by Norwegians as a cultural weakness but by others as a sign of intelligence. Dislike of being taken advantage of is not negative. Dislike is an emotion that can be positive or negative. So why are our weaknesses unintelligent?

Since weaknesses for our purposes must be defined as anything that damages ourselves or others and our relationship to others (all others, including friends or God), they are negative and are not intelligent.

Doing damage to others or ourselves is surely not emotionally intelligent. We do ourselves no favor when we live under the influences of our weaknesses and their emotions. As we have said, living under the influence of our weaknesses inevitably means living under the influences of their emotions. We can't separate the two. Our weaknesses are driven by unintelligent emotions. Whenever we overuse, don't use, or misuse our strengths, the emotions that drive us to do so are not intelligently working for our good. Therefore, for our purposes, leaving behind the healthy use of our strengths and living in our weaknesses is not being intelligently emotional.

The Cause of Most of Our Emotional Distress

Emotional distress is caused by failing to live in our strengths. Go in a direction that does not satisfy and fulfill you and you create negative emotional pressures that will drain your spirit dry.

Imagine a wife whose strengths include a gift for creative writing, busy at home, looking after the kids all day, every day for years, feeling empty and unfulfilled without time to do what she loves and finds rewarding. She becomes irritable and finally angry and unmotivated in even the simplest of duties. When she makes time to begin writing again she feels her emotional health returning. Living in our assets creates emotional strength and health. She must do this.

Everything about living in our weaknesses is emotional trouble. Most people are angry or irritable, moody or sad, because they are not using their strengths as they were designed to be used. This is the cause of most emotional distress.

Can We Be Emotionally Unintelligent When We Use Our Strengths Correctly?

No, because the emotions that our strengths generate are positive and uplifting, helping — not damaging to others and ourselves — and, therefore, they are intelligent. Everything about the emotions that drive the use of our strengths is designed so that we function intelligently. They are intelligent emotions.

Our emotions make a judgment about what is good for us and when we live in our strengths, we are following their best judgments and generating the healthy payback of feelings that enrich us. These feelings are the way our emotions tell us we are living as designed, fulfilled. Our emotional system functions as our guide when we follow the strengths of our temperament and malfunctions when we don't. Reason will concur.

We may, however, be perceived as unintelligent if we do not react according to the expectations of others. That has nothing to do with our intelligence but with their perception of us, which may or may not be biased by their ideologies or thoughts. Of course, we need to take into account the feelings, thoughts, and behavior of others, and this we will also do when we live in our strengths.

Are We Responsible for the Misuse of Our Strengths?

Blessed are the pure in heart
~ Matthew 5:8
(The heart was seen in ancient times as the seat of the emotions.)

The answer would appear to be "yes." But it isn't as simple as that. If emotions can take us by surprise, as we discussed in a previous chapter, then are they not the responsible creators of our weaknesses and aren't we simply the victims of their desires? Emotions can happen so fast that we don't have time to think. Also, some of our emotions are automatic responses: for example, the emotion of fear under fearful circumstances. We just feel them and only after the fact do we have the opportunity to think of what we should do.

However, we are the ones who decide if we are going to continue in our weakness and negativity. From the moment our window of opportunity opens, responsibility begins. We live in our weaknesses only if we choose to do so. Therefore, we are responsible not for the initial surge of our automatic emotions that happen too fast for us to be able to think, but for the decision to continue to focus on them or not.

Of course, if the initial emotion is unintelligent, its purpose is to create weakness in us. It has selected the path for us to tread and we must decide if we want to walk it or not. The unintelligent pressure or urge inside of us is not in our best interests and we are responsible not to fall to such unintelligent emotions.

The Ultimate — Living in Our Strengths Is Being Intelligently Emotional

Nothing is impossible. The word itself says "I'm possible!"
~ Audrey Hepburn

The first thing to do when our emotions are taking us for a ride that we don't appreciate is to focus on our strengths. Choose a strength, preferably the opposite of the negative emotion we want to get rid of, and focus on it while avoiding its overuse, nonuse, and misuse. Avoiding the wrong use of our strengths is not difficult or too complicated. We can soon train ourselves in the right and considerate use of our strengths.

Using a strength means choosing any action that is generated by that strength: a word, deed or, in some cases, even just a smile, and we will feel the lift back into our strengths. Actions are a method to keep us intelligently emotional.

Will choosing to act in line with our strengths once keep us from falling back into our weakness? Of course not. We must continue to live and act in our strength if we want to avoid falling back into our weakness. Living in our strengths or weaknesses is a moment-by-moment experience. It helps, of course, to develop the habitual use of our strengths so that we can more easily reap the benefits of a positive, healthy lifestyle. Habitual actions can be a great benefit in the fight to remain intelligently emotional.

Here's another help. Be happy all the time — we have reason to. If you feel you don't have reason to be happy, then change your beliefs about what is happening to you or how you are perceiving your world. Being happily related to whatever is occurring makes it easier to do what is emotionally intelligent. Positive attitudes also develop when we are living in our strengths, and that results in positive emotions and actions.

Thirteen Pointers to the Intelligent Use of Our Strengths

Before we list our pointers, let's again make sure we are on the same page and understanding words in the same way. I am using the word *strengths* in a special way as the name for the urges and drives that are inherent in our temperament. You will find a listing of these strengths in the Appendix, "Lists of Strengths in Each Temperament." Our strengths are the urges or drives we have in common with other people of the same temperament, although we may have them in different intensities and operate them differently.

I am not using the word strengths to refer to talents or skill, which are often called strengths. People often are led to think of strengths that way. *Talents* are the gifts that the strengths inside us fuel and support. *Skills* are a learned ability. A person who is an NF temperament may be a talented violinist, for example. The NF strength of passion will fuel this talent and stamp it with a very expressive, passionate character, but the talent the person has developed in playing the violin is not to be understood as a strength of the temperament. Anyone of any temperament can play a violin well. Nor is being a skilled accountant a strength of a temperament. It is something anyone can learn but not all will enjoy. So think of the basic urges and drives of your temperament that fuel or drive your preferences as your strengths, and for our purpose here, don't think of talents or skills as strengths.

Surefire emotional intelligence requires the understanding of both our strengths and the emotions that motivate them. Follow these suggestions to intelligent emotional living.

1. Become aware of your temperament's strengths and the characteristic way you use them in your daily life. You can't make use of what you don't know or of what you are not aware. If understanding and memorizing all your strengths seems too much initially, go to the alternative approach in our second pointer.

2. As an alternative: Become aware of just one of your strengths and then study how you use it to begin with, the one you most wish to develop and fully understand. Make a decision to do this. Also, study how you should be using it, making adjustments until you are using it in a healthy manner. Then choose a second strength and do the same with it.

3. Once you are aware of the strengths of your temperament and how you use them, intentionally focus on them as you go about living your life. Your aim is to center your life around your temperament's strengths so you can develop them to their maximum. (Don't make the mistake of focusing on your weaknesses. They are not what will make you great. What you focus on is what you maximize.) The key is intense, intentional focus.

4. See yourself in an honest, positive light. You have been designed wonderfully for a wonderful purpose and you must believe that. That doesn't mean you won't make mistakes or make wrong choices, even do bad things at times. However, if you brood on these failings you will build a negative perception of yourself and this will be a cause of much emotional trauma and emotional ignorance. To walk the path of surefire emotional intelligence, you must think well of yourself while being aware of adjustments you need to make as you become better and better.

5. Learn to recognize when you are **not using** your strengths. If you have memorized the main strengths of your temperament, with some practice this won't be too hard. If you are concentrating on one strength, think of how and why you are not using it. You should be flagged by feelings of emptiness and dissatisfaction or a sense of having no current direction in your life. Being aware of the times you don't use a strength sets the stage for a positive remaking of your life.

6. Learn to recognize when you are **misusing** your strengths. Remember, if your use of your strengths is causing damage to yourself or others, or even if it is inappropriate in a given circumstance, it is a misuse. Also ask yourself: am I using my strength in the best way possible?

7. Learn to recognize when you are **overusing** your strengths. Overuse is also damaging to others and yourself. It strains relationships. An overuse can be very damaging.

8. Always focus on your strengths with a positive attitude. This is not the same as keeping a positive attitude to life. You must optimistically and with positive, good intentions, focus on your strengths to develop them. Believe you can develop them to their maximum. Don't limit yourself with limiting beliefs. Your faith in how you have been made and in your attaining dramatic results is critical to motivation and, therefore, to success.

9. Your plans for the use and development of your strengths should be realistic only in the sense that the next step is achievable. The end goal may be way beyond your current reach, but the next step should be only a small stretch. Those who don't pay attention to this principle often fail because they de-motivate themselves with expecting or attempting too much too soon.

10. When you live in your weaknesses, you fall victim to negative emotions. Therefore, to remain in firm control of your emotions, you must strive to keep all your thinking and acting positive. That way, you keep away from negative emotions that drive hurtful urges. A positive emotion on which you focus is also a controlled and growing emotion. That is the goal of being intelligently emotional. Emotions, like thoughts, can become more familiar and easier to intentionally use if you surround them with affirmations.

11. Repeating positive emotions builds strength into your emotional intelligence. This is because when you focus on a positive emotion you have increasing control over it. It takes up increasingly more space in your mind and this drives out damaging emotions, making the intelligent use of your strengths easier.

12. Worry (a negative and damaging emotion) finds it impossible to live in a mind that is focused on using and developing its strengths. Drive worry out by focusing on developing your strengths and their emotional energies. For example, to develop optimism, focus on the energy of a positive outlook.

13. Finally, you cannot live in your strengths without choosing to do so. Being intelligently emotional begins with making the right choice. The right choice puts you on the right road to success and there is nothing better than being on the right road if you want to arrive at your chosen destination.

Temperament, IQ, EQ, and Our Strengths

It has been suggested by Howard Gardner in *Cracking Open the IQ Box* that IQ (intelligence quotient) is responsible for about twenty percent of the success factors in life. EQ (emotional quotient) and other factors like social environment, opportunity, and plain luck make up the rest, he says. What about temperament? It also plays a large part and is involved in EQ. Living in our strengths and not our weaknesses is the key to functioning with EQ and maintaining a lifestyle consistent with intelligent emotions.

When we think of EQ, we are thinking of multiple emotions. For example: Motivation is an EQ factor, so is determination when faced with opposition and persistent frustrations. Other EQ factors include hope, faith, self-control over the negative forces of disappointment, delay of gratification, control of blame, and management of anger. We could also add the positive use of the emotions that drive our strengths. All of these play a large part in our success or failure and are part of being intelligently emotional. If we live in our strengths, we will develop intelligent emotions.

It is a well known fact that the Fs, and particularly the NF, can stunt their own growth and development by allowing themselves to be hijacked by their emotions, lost in self-condemnation and sick from disharmony and hurt. Their emotions then drain any positive motivation of power. They also lose the refreshment of hope, and negativity can sap their optimism.

SFJs, on the other hand, can be tormented by worry and anxiety. So, our temperament will provide us with different EQ challenges. However, if one temperament has a greater challenge to control themselves emotionally, that is not an excuse to use as a rationalization for their failures since that same temperament has so much more to gain from achieving emotional control.

For the Ts, being insensitive, trying to suppress emotions, building their confidence on reason alone, and developing a feeling of superiority over others (because Ts seem to control their emotions so well) can limit their personal growth and their usefulness. Limiting the operation of emotion in their lives so that it damages themselves and their relationships is a well-known mark of unintelligent behavior among Ts. Both Ts and Fs walk the tightrope of emotional challenge.

It is not too much of a stretch to say that being intelligently emotional determines the value of the life we will live and controls our destiny. Academic intelligence does not prepare us for the trials and tensions of frustration or the disappointments and despair of negative circumstances. EQ, however, makes a promise that if we learn its secrets we will manage our lives with wisdom and success.

Temperament — our strengths — gives us the best user-friendly path to attaining EQ. Living in our strengths and not our weaknesses is the only way to achieve surefire intelligence in our emotional lives.

We will now take each temperament and its strengths and show how each can be developed using intelligent emotions and not overused, not used, or misused emotions. As you read, many examples will, no doubt, come to your mind of all these positive and negative usages of your strengths. I will supply some examples. Don't aim at avoiding the wrong use of your strengths — rather focus on maximizing your strengths.

Proceed to read about each temperament or turn to the temperament that interests you.

8 - Intelligently Emotional SP Strengths

How to Use This Chapter

1. If this is your temperament please focus on the intelligent use of your strengths, not on the nonuse, overuse, or misuse. Remember the principle that whatever you focus on magnifies and becomes an energy center. We want the energy of positive emotions to be produced in our strengths and not the energy of negative emotions to be generated in our weaknesses.

2. If this temperament is not yours, perhaps it is your child's, spouse's or friend's. Try to understand their emotions and the reasons why they feel the way they do, and heed their cry to understand them in their struggles.

3. Appreciate the emotional content and its intelligence in each strength. No strength is unintelligent. You may have associated a particular strength with a misuse that bugs you or you may feel it is wrong, so try to sort out and understand the judgments of your own emotions.   If you are of a different temperament, to understand will be difficult for you but essential for your appreciation of the person of this temperament and their use of emotions in their temperament.

4. Enter into and learn the intelligence and unintelligence of all people's emotions. Their intelligence may be opposite of the intelligence of your own emotions. To you that may seem impossible, but emotions depend on the source from which they come, the purpose for which they are intended, and the appropriateness of their use to be labeled intelligent or unintelligent. For personal growth, parenting,

and simply the appreciation of others and how they are made, this will be a most rewarding journey of discovery.

5. If you are reading to understand and then parent your child more intelligently, please recall your child's actions that remind you of what you are reading and focus on the emotions that fire those actions and strengths. Your understanding of your child's emotional drives that arise from the intelligent or unintelligent use of their strengths will help you be a super parent.

The SP

Living in the Present Moment

Your present circumstances don't determine where you can go; they merely determine where you start.
~ Nido Qubein

Focusing on the present keeps negative emotions from lingering and stops us from ruminating over the past or the potential troubles of the future, which could cripple us. The present keeps the spirit fresh and bright. Each moment is new. As troubles and challenges arrive, they are quickly replaced with the interests of the next moment and emotional control is managed with greater ease when this is the natural way to live and enjoy life. This is the way an SP is designed to live and must live if they are to find happiness.

Living in the present moment also keeps taking the focus away from the troubles of the past and helps the SP forget them. The worries of the future are forgotten, too, in the thrill of the present and the SP stays focused and expectant. Living in the present sets the stage for an optimism that is emotionally intelligent and that goes a long way to providing a bright and healthy foundation to life.

All of the SP's emotions are affected by this orientation to time. It can result in producing negative emotions if it is used to avoid the lessons of the past and the hopes and promises of the future, so it is a strength to be developed. Don't lose sight of it. Focus on using this strength to encourage freedom from destructive emotional bondage to the past and crippling fear of the future.

231

KEY THOUGHT/ACTION: Capture the brilliance of an optimistic view of the present moment. Live in its light.

Nonuse:
Whenever the SP does not live in the present and squeeze the joy out of it, they can easily lose their optimism and become depressed. Negative emotions develop, robbing them of control. Nonuse of any strength is unintelligent!

Overuse:
The ever-changing present can be a place to hide from the pains of life. When we constantly hide from pain in the excitement of the present, this strength creates a weakness that will surely catch up with us. Emotions are then not controlled, just swept out of sight. This is also a misuse of the strength. Learn the mistake of hiding in the present.

Misuse:
Living in the present can be a means of escaping the guilt of previous behavior that should be faced and rectified. Damages done to others also need to be reconciled, not forgotten. Whenever the SP lives in the present to escape the responsibilities of the past they damage themselves further and the guilty feelings create a kind of residual pain with which we are all familiar. Another negative emotion, upset with themselves, is then formed and fed. Learn to deal with guilt and don't leave your past in an untidy mess — baggage you will carry with you to create future pain.

Brave, Bold, Daring

Courage is a dominating feeling that leaves no room for other feelings. If courage and fear try to live together in our minds at the same time, one has to dominate and drive out the other. There is only room for one. We think one thought at a time and feel one emotion at a time. Courage keeps us focused and keeps other emotions and thoughts subservient to its high demands.

Courage in the SP is emotional intelligence as long as it is willing to swallow a dose of wisdom. What constitutes foolish bravery is understood differently by the brave and the timid. Therefore, the argument as to what is wise and what is not goes on interminably, fueled by fear or courage. We must all discover the parameters of wisdom for ourselves based on our tolerance for risk and our abilities.

Fear can be emotionally unintelligent and most often is. Bravery helps the timid overcome fear and develop a more intelligent emotion. Courage is also a strong factor in creating confidence. Courage is a truly intelligent emotion.

KEY THOUGHT/ACTION: Develop your courage to melt the ice of fear.

Nonuse:
A nonuse of courage opens the door wide to fear. Fear is a feeling the SP hates. Unlike some people, they find no warmth in it. A loss of emotional control is inevitable in the negative atmosphere of fear. Its unpleasant feeling and potential pain forces the SP to avoid it. When it is present in an SP, the SP trembles. Fear also develops other fears and its general non-intelligence as an emotion is seen in the fact that it creates a fear of fears. Some fears are intelligent, so we must distinguish between negative and positive fears.

Overuse:
We can be too brave and daring. To cultivate a brash boldness that amounts to foolhardiness is also not beyond the bold heart of the SP. Learning where bravery ends and foolishness begins is emotional intelligence for the SP. Because of the dangers inherent in overuse, an understanding of the limits of bravery generated by knowledge and experience brings a more sage-like attitude.

Misuse:
An overuse of this strength is also a misuse and being brave in a cause that disregards the rights of others is a misuse. Harming and hurting others lacks intelligence because it is an

act of disrespect and aggression. However, for the SP, overuse together with misuse is the real threat to their emotional intelligence.

Spontaneous, Impulsive

Impulse can catch the moment of opportunity and provide excitement. The spontaneous SP is adept at finding an alternative to boredom that is emotionally rewarding. Many a sad moment has been averted by a spontaneous change for the good and the SP knows this well, in this case displaying intelligence.

When rightly used, spontaneity leads to emotional intelligence by making a better choice and instantly executing it. Impulse depends on speedy emotional reactions more than the slow process of analytical reasoning and therefore can be executed with speed. When a fast reaction is needed, spontaneity can be sagacious. The emotions of each strength can be a factor in the making of good judgments and spontaneity should not be overlooked by those who are more cautious and timid.

KEY THOUGHT/ACTION: Intelligent spontaneity spells freshness.

Nonuse:
For the SP temperament, failure to use this strength can rob them of joy, the opportunity for action, variety, and a sense of fulfillment — all of these and more. The SP also uses impulse to break the sameness of routine, keeping their emotions fresh and vibrant. When life becomes monotonous, the darkness of depression waits for them. Take spontaneity away from an SP and we have lost the nature of the SP. Encourage their spontaneity.

Overuse:
Too many new starts in life can lead to change for change's sake in the SP. The SP can then be accused of being an

emotional butterfly. Even for the SP who loves change and gains much refreshment from it, instability knocks at their door when there is too much change.

The SP who accepts every job offer to satisfy an impulsive urge for constant variety will rob himself of direction and purpose in life, not to mention a reliable reputation, while at the same time creating an emotional weakness. Overuse of impulse can not only make fools of us but can weaken our resolve and determination.

Misuse:
Bad choices as well as good choices hammer on the door of opportunity for the SP. Seizing all opportunities without first making a wise judgment can be the downfall of the SP.

Values should educate our emotions to help us avoid bad choices. Building them into our beliefs will also create a sense of personal integrity. The SP must create a healthy value system to inform their decisions quickly and wisely. Lost integrity from foolish moves will eat away at any positive emotion.

Effective, Tactical, Aggressive

Effective:
We cannot be really intelligent with our emotions if we don't use them effectively and, therefore, the strength of effectiveness in the SP lends its aid to making emotions intelligent. The SP can be very discerning in the use of emotions. Certainly they can detect the slightest change in expressions and forecast the observable intentions of others quite accurately, giving them what appears to be a sharp intuition.

But emotional astuteness is more than the effective use of our emotions: it is also the right, helpful use of emotions. When the SP is using their emotional alertness and speedy detection of another individual's reactions, they can distinguish themselves in the minds of others by the quick impact they make. Their emotional acuity and effectiveness is due to more than this one strength, however.

Tactical:

Tactical judgments are the kind of initial, first impression judgments that emotions make. When we see danger, our emotions immediately make a tactical decision to fight, flee, or get prepared for some other action. The tactic is in choosing an immediate action and the goal is safety and preparedness for the next move.

A tactical mind also selects the best emotion to be expressed at the best level of intensity and in the best way for the achievement of a specific goal. It is creating order and arranging responses in a purposeful way. Sounds complicated and it is, but SPs become expert tactical minds with practice.

Aggressive:

Emotions don't sit around, passively waiting for permission to declare themselves or empower us. They aggressively take control of us. Sometimes we wish they wouldn't. They waste no time and act with a boldness that can surprise others and us.

Immediate action is not necessarily the wisest choice, but we are presented with our emotion's decisions without waste of time and we, not our emotions, must take responsibility for whatever we end up doing. Waste no time, miss no opportunity, and never leave the owner of the emotions without emotional guidance: this is their brief. The brief fits the purposes of the SP.

If we are going to change our emotions we need to act aggressively and replace them quickly with another emotion for the best result. So, aggression can qualify as an intelligent emotion.

KEY THOUGHT/ACTION: Only the right emotion, with the right purpose expressed appropriately, breathes intelligence into effectiveness, tactical success, and aggressive behavior. Focus on making these right choices.

Nonuse:
Nonuse simply negates effectiveness, tactical insight, and aggressive behavior. A lack of these things will depress and anger the SP. Self-image, if depressed like this in an SP, can cause a "don't care" attitude and complete de-motivation if severe enough. Watch for this and start using the strength to avoid depression.

Overuse:
Trying to be too effective forces an over-concentration on one goal to the exclusion of all that the present moment offers. Only if the goal is amply satisfying will the SP stay with the goal and not be distracted. Therefore, relationships as well as projects must be kept fresh and exciting to keep their continued interest at a high pitch. In a relationship, an SP will supply this as long as competition from another SP in the relationship does not become too serious. In any case, a focus that is too narrow loses contact with other important goals in any relationship .

Aggressiveness can be overdone easily and with damaging results. It can breed anger, hate, and their families of hurtful, hostile feelings. Violence is often the child of aggression. When an emotion grips us, aggressiveness can know no limit and escalates fast. Speedy control of aggressive emotions and wise decisions is where the intelligence lies. Even positive emotions such as love need to be managed or they, too, can control us, forcing unwise decisions.

When the intellectual spirit of the culture is to express yourself without concern for long-proven values and to create new values based on personal desires, wisdom is out of vogue. Yet wisdom is intelligence in its highest form. We are emotional creatures, but the presence of reason and rationality as a control measure for managing our emotions suggests this free spirit without accountability is unintelligent. We function best when our emotions are responsible to standards outside of our own little world — objective not subjective standards. Values that care for all people and the welfare of our planet, for example, lead in the direction of wisdom.

Misuse:
Criminal actions need to be effective, tactical, and aggressive or the criminal fails or is caught. These strengths are valued by both good and evil goals, meaning the SPs goal and purpose determines their intelligence or lack thereof.

Emotional intelligence cannot be defined as the skillful use of emotions for our own interests without concern for others. It is the opposite. It is also not the use of damaging emotions but the use of helpful emotions. When relating to all the other people in our world, morals, for example, are essential values, encouraging universally beneficial emotional control.

Teaching the right use of our emotions is the same as teaching right choices. The word "right" in this context has a meaning other than choosing in favor or our selfish desires and always for other than harmful aggression. Even though aggression has been effective in changing our world, it does not mean it is right or intelligent. Again, the purpose for which it is used dictates its ethical status.

Easily Excited or Aroused

Arousal is the name of the game for most of the SP's emotions. To excite and be excited is their nature. There is a drive and a passion in their emotions whether they are headed for good or harm. The SP expresses emotion at full throttle in a sudden burst of feeling. It is not likely to be long-lasting, which is good if the emotion is harmful. If the emotion is a helpful emotion that needs to last, the SP must struggle with making it a constant feature of their lives.

Being easily aroused is a double-edged sword. Wisdom and discernment is needed in the expression of excitable emotions. Wisdom only comes from learning and that means the practice of wisdom.

KEY THOUGHT/ACTION: While traveling at full throttle, steer in a wise direction.

Nonuse:
Excitement is fundamental to the optimism of the SP. Without it, there is a loss of motivation and boredom sets in that frustrates and saddens them. Squelching their longing for excitement solves nothing and results in rebellion or anger. Nonuse is emotional suicide for them.

Overuse:
The overuse of excitement destabilizes them. They become hyper and can lose control of their emotions. Easy arousal does not suggest restraints and they must be built in.

To appreciate the contrast, consider the SJ whose emphasis on caution displays plenty of restraint. Boundaries to limit the upper level of excitement, if flexible, provide a safety factor and introduce the discipline of control that the SP will accept. Optimism, too, must be kept in control.

Misuse:
Perhaps misuse is less of an issue. Excitement can be a destructive emotion when we are excited over something that damages others or us. As in all cases of misuse, the purpose over which we are excited can change intelligence to unintelligence.

Wants to Make an Impact on Others

Emotion is designed to make an impact. If it makes no impact on us and others it fails in its purpose. This strength in the SP displays the purposeful heartbeat of emotion; don't despise it. Perhaps you are noticing that the use of the strengths of the SP are natural expressions of optimistic emotions.

Because the SP is optimistic and driven to find excitement, emotion is always near the surface and emotion initiates the impulsive desire to make a big impression. Optimism and impulse combine in this strength. This is why the SP child can be emotionally volatile. However, they are surpassed by the NF in the race for the title of Volatility Champions. No temperament, however, can match the SP's urges to make a huge impact wherever they go.

The benefit or curse of this strength, like so many others, lies in the purpose for which it is used. An emotion drives us and wisdom says we need to be aware of the direction in which we are being urged to go.

KEY THOUGHT/ACTION: In wanting to make an impact, emotion provides the power.

Nonuse:
Not so damaging is the loss of the ability to make an impact. However, because it is a strength in the SP they will always seek to make an impact in one way or another. Sometimes it is dramatic and at other times it is a well-disguised tactical move to impress that is not so noticeable.

Emotional wisdom occurs when it is controlled and used to benefit others as well as themselves. Experience, knowledge, and good judgment live at the heart of wisdom and making an impact benefits most when all three are driving forces. Increasing these three qualities improves the chance of beneficial emotions driving the strength.

Overuse:
Wanting to make an impact is an attempt to get attention and perhaps boost the self-image. Overuse can lead to an over-stimulated self-image, resulting in a fixation on oneself that is not appreciated and irritating to others — a rank pride in some cases. No one likes an egotist who is inflated beyond realistic truthfulness. Too much attention-getting is indicative that all is not healthy in the human spirit.

Misuse:
Misuse can range from disturbing a class or teasing a sibling to committing a crime just to impress one's peers. The urge in us for feeling important has no ethical direction and actions that hurt others simply to get noticed can roll off the assembly line of the SP endlessly and without conscience in extreme cases. SPs are the performers in life and performers are not much good if they are not noticed, so anything is used to impress where ethical values are not in play to condition the action.

Lighthearted, Playful, Tolerant

Both the lightheartedness that is characteristic of the SP, and seriousness that marks an SJ, are intelligent emotions. They are, as always, subject to overuse. Lightheartedness and playfulness contribute greatly to the SP's ability to remain positive in the face of negative happenings and it therefore encourages their optimism. SPs need to keep this lightheartedness actively contributing joy to their lives. Without joy, we dry up — a condition no SP will welcome.

Tolerance often arises out of the urge not to take each other too seriously. SPs can allow a lot of leeway in behavior and belief. Many do not take their own beliefs too seriously. Intolerance to them reeks of control and judgmental decisions as well, which are two things the SP detests. Therefore, tolerance is a lighthearted emotion.

The line between tolerance and the wise expression of personal convictions is best negotiated with love, not with an eye on tolerance or intolerance. Even a dispute about what is tolerance and intolerance can quickly become a loveless, accusatory tussle. Tolerance has value when it seeks equality and freedom of expression, encouraging the full flower of love. Intolerance can quickly degenerate into tolerance for the things it approves.

KEY THOUGHT/ACTION: When lightheartedness fuels optimism and optimism drives lightheartedness, happiness is not far away.

Nonuse:
Who would want the SP not to relish their playful emotions and lightheartedness? It thrills them and us. They will typically fight for the freedom to express this strength.

Nonuse is rare and usually indicates that something is wrong in their lives. The nonuse of tolerance is so unlike the SP that it indicates the same. Expect lightheartedness and tolerance from SPs and be concerned if you don't see it.

Overuse:
Where is the limit to playfulness? "It is enjoyment, and who wants to be short-changed on that," says the SP. While the SJ is the workaholic, the SP is the "play-a-holic," to coin a word. "Play first — life is so uncertain" could be the SP's motto. Overuse of these emotions is desired. The boundary between use and overuse is where overuse clashes with responsibility. Responsibility has the ring of a cracked bell to the SP. They understand its importance but are pulled emotionally in the direction of play, or at least a life without all unnecessary tension.

Misuse:
"Even play can be abused" is a statement an SP will accept, but with reluctance. It is the abuse of the privilege and freedom to play that characterizes most misuse of this strength. Once again, the issue of discernment must come to the SP's attention or they will play at inappropriate times.

Ultimate Optimist

I have made the point in the previous chapter that the core emotion of the SP is optimism and I have defended its wisdom and healthy impact on all our lives. Optimism breeds joy. Joy is a basic need. We must see it as a food, nutritionally enriching humans. Pessimism, the opposite of optimism, harbors the dark shadows of depression and gives safe haven to all the negative emotions that reject an uplifting view of life and its difficulties.

KEY THOUGHT/ACTION: The optimist looks up; the pessimist looks down. Which direction pleases most?

Nonuse:
How can the SP be a pessimist? It takes a great deal of effort to suppress the natural lift their spirit's feel. Therefore, nonuse is found only in the saddened soul that borders on depression or is deep in its grasp. Don't expect to see nonuse in the hopeful, happy, healthy SP.

Overuse:
Overuse is common and any SP will ask, "Can you be too optimistic?" We can, but the SP asks, "If optimism is needed 95 percent of the time in the race of life, why worry about the 5 percent?" That's optimism! It is hard to draw a line and make the SP see the sense of trying to be less optimistic over the remaining 5 percent. Only when the yellow caution light has turned to red can they be persuaded to wait or tone down their optimism.

Misuse:
Misuse is overuse. Using optimism for damaging purposes is not common, but it can be part of a manipulative scheme. The apron strings between hope and optimism have never been severed and one depends on the other keeping optimism from misuse.

Action

Action can be saved from being misused by any wise emotion or corrupted by any negative one. Indirectly, our actions can support and feed positive emotions, showing us that the emotions behind an action can be intelligent. Being neutral however, actions can't be labeled intelligent or unintelligent until they take the side of help or hurt and the emotions that drive the actions become evident.

KEY THOUGHT/ACTION: Intelligent actions are fired by positive emotions.

Nonuse:
Without action, the SP will become sick in their spirits. And when blocked from the physical expression of their desires, they lose a sense of direction. Emotions that demand to be expressed dominate the SP. All kinds of aberrant behavior can result when expression is inhibited. This is a tragic loss for them. The path is to create the opportunities for expression with guidance in learning wise expression.

The action, of course, does not have to be exuberant such as in sports. It can be the action found in arts or crafts or even the composition of music. Physical action is a medication for the spirit just like joy, and it truly fulfills the SP.

Overuse:
Overuse of action usually takes care of itself. Tiredness calls for a halt and rest replenishes the loss. For the overactive child who disturbs a class with his antics, emotional unintelligence can also appear in a lack of concentration or a lack of sensitivity to the needs of others. Teach not just the limiting of action, but address the emotions behind it if you want success.

Misuse:
Actions are misused constantly in our world, and right behavior is a necessity that all people demand even though the interpretation of what is right varies greatly according to a person's beliefs. Misuse of action should be easy to identify if it harms us or others.

A Focus on the Physical Senses

A focus on the physical senses is not the same as action. It is the appreciation and development of physical actions as a core stimulus in the SP. A focus on the physical senses is obviously a central theme in the SP's life of actions. Sensing, touching, feeling, and all the thrills of physical dexterity are the essence of pleasure to them. The ballerina's graceful rhythms and the subtle turn of a head to express interest or distaste are art forms to the physically focused SP.   Emotion fills every move and is also produced by a well-expressed action, rewarding the actor with a generous lift to their spirits, particularly when the applause is thunderous. Because we are physical beings, the emotions behind this strength are largely intelligent.

Many messages are sent from the muscles to the brain, recording appreciation of the physical world's sensory pleasures, and the SP finds great satisfaction from this stimulation.   Judgments of these sensory messages as physical pleasure or pain fills the SP's day and therefore initiates intelligent responses along with the unintelligent.

KEY THOUGHT/ACTION: Let me feel the movement and I am in touch with the essence of life.

Nonuse:
When the focus wanders from the physical senses, which is rare, the SPs are not who they are made to be. All the emotions that encourage sadness and disappointment flood their minds, disturbing both their conscious and unconscious thoughts. We always need to be focused on being who we are and reaping the intelligence of our positive emotions. When that is not happening, the downside of life emerges to take control.

Overuse:
When we are focused on our physical senses, overuse is hard to define except when we must focus elsewhere. The focus on theories and abstract learning, which the SP finds

unnatural, can constantly be disturbed by the stimulation of physical senses. This makes concentration on such ethereal matters difficult for the SP.

The SP learns best while active or with hands-on lessons that make use of the physical senses. It is no surprise that they can memorize with ease when shooting hoops or jogging around the lake. Combine the use of their physical senses with the task of learning abstract data and principles, and success will come more easily.

Misuse:
Like all strengths and their emotions, misuse occurs when the purposes for which we use them are disturbing or damaging. Healthy goals for all our activities breed emotional intelligence and avoid senseless or damaging results.

Generous

Generosity, if aimed at helping others or at gaining a desired relationship, shows itself in kindness and sensibleness. Its opposite pole is meanness. If the emotion of prudence teams up with generosity, intelligent decisions can be made more easily. Generosity and kindness need another emotion to guide them. The SP is by nature both generous and impulsive, so they need to show care in rushing to their emotions for guidance.

KEY THOUGHT/ACTION: The emotions of the SP are themselves generous.

Nonuse:
If the SP is not generous it won't necessarily send him into a depression or cause him to suffer a loss of self-image. It is more an urge that pleases him and validates his good intentions with the use of a little drama in the process. So, there are no serious consequences if the SP is not generous.

Overuse:
Overuse can be an issue, particularly if the SP's repeated displays of generosity are used to impress someone with his admiration or honor and the resources for his generosity are running dry. The practical aspects of overuse must be a matter of concern, while the emotions can remain honorable. Prudence and judiciousness help keep the practical issues in check.

Misuse:
A misuse is usually an overuse or inappropriate display of generosity. We can, of course, be generous for purposes that harm others and damage ourselves. They are the misuse of the emotion because no guidance or understanding exists to avoid a misuse.

Dramatic

Drama is full of emotion. Both helpful and harmful emotions make use of theatrics to make a stronger impact. When trying to influence and persuade, a dramatic presentation can do wonders and the emotions behind the drama can be intelligent, making and empowering good decisions.

Drama can also be entertaining, giving joy to many while indulging in lightheartedness and humor. The emotions in drama can change people and alter the way we see the good and the evil in life. The SP is both dramatic and a lover of drama.

KEY THOUGHT/ACTION: A dramatic personality impresses many people. Use it wisely.

Nonuse:
The nonuse of dramatic displays will not do the SP much harm. A strength will be temporarily suppressed, but it is likely to resurface since it is tied to other strengths like making an impact, being effective, and responding to the physical senses.

Overuse:
When overuse is an issue and the emotions are clearly not under control or are being used to manipulate others, society will usually teach the individual by withdrawing from him or ostracizing him in some way. Overuse of drama as a tool to get our own way is a mark of immaturity.

Immaturity is caused by a lack of emotional intelligence. Emotions are responses to our world both outside of us and to the thoughts and feelings that sweep through our minds as well. Hasty acceptance of the first emotion that hits us or showing an inability to discern the right response constitutes a lack of understanding and wisdom which is at the heart of unintelligence. As we have noted before, first comes knowledge, then understanding of what we know, and only then wisdom appears to help us make the right choice. Immaturity is either a lack of knowledge or a shortage of understanding or an inability to force a right choice when we know we should.

Misuse:
When drama is the tool to get our own way or make the life of another miserable, such as when a child uses emotions forcefully to disrupt the household or get back at parents for their denials of the child's wishes, it is decidedly a misuse of this strength. The office can be full of drama as well as the home, and much anger stems from the dramatic attempt to get our own way even there.

Control of our emotions predates the need to behave more intelligently, but this is the hardest lesson to learn. Alternate methods for making others aware of our desires and the choice of alternate emotions to show consideration for others are the more judicious paths.

9 - Intelligently Emotional SJ Strengths

How to Use This Chapter

1. If this is your temperament please focus on the intelligent use of your strengths, not on the nonuse, overuse, or misuse. Remember the principle that whatever you focus on magnifies and becomes an energy center. We want the energy of positive emotions to be produced in our strengths and not the energy of negative emotions to be generated in our weaknesses.

2. If this temperament is not yours, perhaps it is your child's, spouse's or friend's. Try to understand their emotions and the reasons why they feel the way they do, and heed their cry to understand them in their struggles.

3. Appreciate the emotional content and its intelligence in each strength. No strength is unintelligent. You may have associated a particular strength with a misuse that bugs you or you may feel it is wrong, so try to sort out and understand the judgments of your own emotions. If you are of a different temperament, to understand will be difficult for you but essential for your appreciation of the person of this temperament and their use of emotions in their temperament.

4. Enter into and learn the intelligence and unintelligence of all people's emotions. Their intelligence may be opposite of the intelligence of your own emotions. To you that may seem impossible, but emotions depend on the source from which they come, the purpose for which they are intended, and the appropriateness of their use to be labeled intelligent or unintelligent. For personal growth, parenting,

and simply the appreciation of others and how they are made, this will be a most rewarding journey of discovery.

5. If you are reading to understand and then parent your child more intelligently, please recall your child's actions that remind you of what you are reading and focus on the emotions that fire those actions and strengths. Your understanding of your child's emotional drives that arise from the intelligent or unintelligent use of their strengths will help you be a super parent.

The SJ

Lives Tied to the Past

The past is a treasure trove of truths to be learned from experience and a wealth of memories to be cherished. People have not changed much in recorded history, so we can learn about ourselves from our past no matter how distant it is. Admittedly, culture and technology have changed but love, anger, fear, resentment, hope, and all the other emotions and emotive values that probe the hearts of people remain very familiar.

The past contains wisdom and emotional fuel that when we use it intelligently can keep us from emotional danger and extremes. The SJ is bent on doing this and, in the process, they feed on the emotions that focusing on the past can generate.

Happy memories medicate and lighten our moments of sadness. Wisdom also lies in the stories of human excellence. Stability in the storms of life is bolstered by the encouragement of those who lived like solid rocks with enduring power. This central strength of the SJ temperament, when positively used, is a great resource for our models of emotional intelligence.

KEY THOUGHT/ACTION: The past is our teacher and experience is the field-testing of ideas.

Nonuse:
Whenever an SJ fails to celebrate, remember, and encapsulate the lessons of the past, they fall apart in fear, worry, and anxiety. The past is their emotional anchor. Negative emotions rage in the SJ whose mind is focused on present concerns. The SJ must draw emotional strength from past lessons and promises.

Overuse:
We live in the present, not the past, so when the SJ who tries to live in and repeat their past ends up trying to make it the law of the present, change that is inevitable leaves them behind. They can become anxious and focused on their troubles rather than on constructive solutions and new ideas. Negative emotions of fear and worry inevitably create inner disturbances.

Misuse:
Anxiety causes us to run from the concerns of the present and the SJ has a tendency to flee to the past and hide in its comforting memories. Then they can try to insist that others hide with them. Consequently, they misuse the past and try to halt the tide of change.

Careful, Cautious, Concerned

To the SJ, caution is intelligence. Rash judgments and actions are scorned by caution. And when caution is in charge it tends to also disdain both risk and change, all of which add to the unshakable image of the SJ temperament. Not only the image but the emotions of the SJ can benefit from this rock solid persona.

However, concern can morph into worry without giving us any notification. Even though this danger waits to destroy the stable SJ, who is it that can do without at least some caution in the face of the uncertainty of life? It is intelligent to meet the unpredictability of each moment with time to reflect and then cautiously make good choices. Caution at times wisely forces a "time-out" to consider the next move in the game of life. All emotions find their best expression in the face of careful thought. Living in this strength brings a sense of sobriety to the SJ image.

KEY THOUGHT/ACTION: Cautious and concerned, the SJ walks with measured pace through life.

Nonuse:
When caution is not used, a feeling of anxiety rises to shake the foundations of the SJ. Carefulness is a way to avoid unwise steps and they know this well. Yet when negative emotions like fear prevail, they lose all care and, without thought, forge on, blindly persistent. It is a failure that can cost them dearly.

So for the SJ, use your caution, concern, and carefulness to avoid the meltdown that carelessness, a lack of concern, and the lack of caution creates. Cautious is an intelligent emotion when used wisely.

Overuse:
Whereas nonuse comes mainly from being overtaxed, worried or afraid of something, overuse is an almost expected use of caution for the SJ. It can become their addiction. Caution evokes emotions of safety and control and they are addictive to the SJ. Therefore, they can be guilty of too much of a good thing.

Rules and regulations are given more importance, beliefs are fossilized, and behaviors become routine when the SJ is overcautious. For change to enter this bolted castle over a mote and past wary guards requires the slackening of these cautious protective measures. Rejection of change all too often happens. The negative emotions of worry caused by overuse of caution are responsible.

Misuse:
People can be frustrated by caution when it is used as a tool to delay their aims or projects. It can be the tactic of the malicious and vengeful. Any strength can be misused and this one is no exception. A misuse of caution can be powered, for example, by angry, jealous emotions.

Thoughtful and Prepared

Being prepared can equip us to survive many expected and unexpected emotional traumas. We can pre-think what might happen and make as many preparations as we feel will keep us in control of ourselves and the situation. SJs are natural planners so little in the regular course of life hits them by surprise, and if it does, it is not likely to have that advantage again. Preparing for things calms a mind that is subject to worry.

Key to emotional control is preparing ourselves by thinking through the options we may face. This can even be enjoyable to the SJ — in fact, it will be a preferred path for all Js since they like to get a decision made and hate to wait in the cooling winds of limbo. They also strive to probe the future, hoping to rob it of its surprise attacks.

A practice of thoughtfulness also helps us recognize more quickly that we need to activate our rational mind when a negative emotion surges and when it must be evaluated before it escalates out of control. It also builds into our emotional systems safe models of behavior that increase our ability to control our emotions in the future. When living in this strength, an SJ can be resolute in the face of trouble. We all need to develop our use of forethought, if not all the way to the SJ's level.

KEY THOUGHT/ACTION: Be prepared or abdicate the role of self manager.

Nonuse:
Obviously, when not thoughtful and prepared the SJ can quickly spiral into worry and outright fear about the possible outcomes and lose control of their emotions, usually retreating inside themselves to silence or withdrawal. The once unshakable thinker and planner shatters into a thousand fragments and loses all their J backbone. SJs can be so emotionally immersed in concern and worry that they cannot function as they are designed to. Thoughtfulness returns them to feelings of control as they fashion the next step. The SJ does not want to move without the feeling that they at least have some input, hence nonuse is destructive to their mode of operation.

Overuse:
Can thoughtfulness be overused?   Yes, and it can delay seizing an opportunity.   Over-preparation stiffens life, losing creativity.   The harsh edges of an over-ordered life keep out joy and the pleasure of spontaneity.   Overuse can create its own negative emotions that take control of us.   Life cannot be totally arranged, ordered or made routine.   There is too much we have no control over.

Misuse:
Preparations can end up being an act of procrastination, a mechanism born maybe of the fear of facing an unwanted event.   It is easy to rationalize over-preparing for events.   It offers us the opportunity for hiding our fears behind the busyness of our lives.   Over-preparation then demands we follow its well-prepared path and the result can be a narrow mindedness that cramps our lives.   Spontaneous insights are lost too.   The misuse of over-preparedness mainly hurts ourselves but can be used as a tool to hurt others.

Responsible, Dependable, Solid Work Ethic

This strength makes the SJ indispensable to society. Responsibility creates dependability which, in turn, develops a solid work ethic.   The SJ feels an obligation to support and nurture society and this emotion characterizes the healthy ones among them and powers the strengths of responsibility.

We're all glad someone feels this way, of course.   The obligation they feel is an intelligent emotion because it focuses the SJ's thoughts and actions.   It cannot exist without a sense of care which is also their positive strength.   Positive actions abound wherever a responsible attitude exists.

No one likes work just for work's sake, but this intelligent attitude is that work, if it has to demand our time and sacrifice, is best approached positively.   Work must be done or goals are not achieved, so the emotions that surround a responsible work ethic are constructive and helpful in maintaining a positive work atmosphere both for the SJ and for the environment in which they work.

Dependability engenders trust. Trustworthiness lies at the root of all happy relationships and the SJ may even prefer trustworthiness to excitement in their relationships. Their friends are likely to be there for them if this trait is characteristic of their behavior. Although any temperament can exhibit this strength and enjoys its emotions, it is dominant in the SJ.

KEY THOUGHT/ACTION: If not responsible and reliable, then what? The thought is unnerving to the SJ.

Nonuse:
An SJ who is not thought of as a respectable, responsible citizen is unhappy. Their unhappiness is because they cannot envision a society that does not function reliably without responsible behavior and they must be a part of creating such a society. Why do all people not see this "obvious" need, they wonder. To them the need for responsibility is self-evident. Emotions in the face of irresponsibility often show little restraint.

In themselves, being irresponsible creates a sense of shame or hides behind a thin veneer of justification. Dependability is lost and a solid work ethic disappears too when they succumb to irresponsibility. All the emotions that either arise in the SJ or in others as a result of irresponsibility are damaging. Nonuse of these essential drives plunges them into weakness and inconsistent behavior.

Overuse:
Overuse can appear in the form of control or in trying to make other people into SJs. As in most of the SJ strengths, overuse enters the irritating territory where people feel they lose their freedom and are being ruled. Responsibility is defined differently and one person's standards for responsibility is another's restriction of personal expression.

Where the line is drawn is the argument and society, unless dictatorially governed, usually cannot agree.   Negative emotions flare at the imposition of standards even if standards are necessary for productivity.   It is often the emotions rather than objective facts that drive the definitions.   When this happens, the emotions on both sides of the argument turn negative and damage everyone.

Overuse of a solid work ethic can result in becoming a workaholic.   Then work becomes the priority and that distorts the meaning and purpose of life.

Misuse:
It's hard to imagine a misuse of responsibility or of a solid work ethic.   Overuse, which also can be a misuse, we have dealt with.   Judgment of others, which is more than simply holding people to the demands of a responsible work ethic, can result from a misuse of this strength.   Judgment condemns others and that spawns angry emotions and does much harm, of course.

Do What Is Right, Law Abiding

Life for the SJ is governed by a belief in the necessity of laws and regulations.   Only when something is malfunctioning in their lives are they a law unto themselves. Most SJs see their values in black and white, right and wrong. The need for laws arises out of protecting the right and restraining the wrong.

There is a well-defended wisdom in having laws to restrain our untamed urges and provide consistency in our society. Although it is only one side of the coin of social structure, intelligence is stamped all over the idea that laws apply to all and therefore create a degree of conformity in communities. The emotions that drive these ideals for the curbing of chaos are rewarding to the SJ.

Emotions need restraint at times and encouragement at other times. Fear of chaos, concern for the welfare of people, and the emotions that create feelings of security drive the law-abiding spirit of the SJ and educate the thinking behind this intelligent strength. SJs who follow this urge inside of them and use their emotions wisely, stabilize themselves and society.

KEY THOUGHT/ACTION: Feelings of guilt trail the SJ who neglects his true convictions and need to protect.

Nonuse:
Acting inconsistently to the urge to do what is right will soon produce a load of guilt. We can suppress guilty feelings and convince ourselves that we can do whatever we desire but not without consequences that eat away at our happiness.

Free will says do what you please, but choice by its nature gives direction to our lives, and that direction is determined by whatever we choose. Nonuse of this strength to do what is right will shape a rebellious character. The emotions that drive the SJ to act inconsistent to their temperament lack intelligence.

Overuse:
Seldom will you find someone who overuses this strength. The most legalistic SJ breaks road rules occasionally. The moral perfectionist is not perfect. Their demand on others can enter the realm of micromanagement and unrealism and that we could call an overuse of this strength. The driving emotions behind an overuse are variations of pride, elitism, conceit, and sometimes even self-interest.

Misuse:
Criticism of other people's behavior in order to embarrass or harm them earns the title of a misuse. Holding people to unrealistic or impossible standards is also a misuse, the motive sometimes making the matter clear. Nonuse and its careless emotions, not misuse or overuse of this strength, seems to be its worst offense.

Strong Need to Belong, Social, Respectable

We gain comfort and strength from others and their simple presence can impart a measure of control over our emotions. Society is treasured, especially among the SJs, for the unity it offers.   Other people in a group who are well-prepared and emotionally stable can shore up the faltering hopes of an emotionally distraught SJ.   Belonging to a community also offers the cloak of respectability. For emotional reasons, SJs may choose the community they live in with care.

A group of people with similar interests offers a sense of acceptance and approval — emotions SJs crave.   It warms and confirms the anxious ones among them while it adds a lift to the self-image of all the group's members.   Emotional support can be an intelligent feeling.

The common emotional needs of likeminded people produce a kind of mutual sympathetic dance that unify their interests and concerns.   Again, the routines and traditions of club membership alone can act to steady the nerves in times of emotional trauma.   People need people and none more so than the SJ who, when alone, can wither in the drying winds of fear, worry, and loneliness.

KEY THOUGHT/ACTION: Togetherness breeds confidence and confidence produces a healthy self-esteem.

Nonuse: Not to find the support of other like-minded people leads to the panic of loneliness and helplessness. The mental chaos of panic is a condition that strikes fear into an SJ's heart and dismisses all reason and hope.   Emotions then run rampant.   Something as seemingly harmless as having to belong to society can avoid the chaos of these feelings of inner disintegration.

Overuse: A club can become a crutch, an escape from true control of our emotions. An addiction of any sort hides a need and SJs need emotional strength born of their own self-willed mastery.   The support of others can be an unhealthy dependency. Overuse of the need to belong is injurious to personal growth.

Misuse: What does it look like to misuse this sense of belonging? It creates a person who is dependent on others when self-reliance and inner strength are their greatest need. We must discern when to use this strength and know when it is toxic to personal development.

Steady, Not Easily Shaken

Some people seem unmoved and unmovable. They appear to have a rocklike solidity that can weather any storm. Life is focused and simple for them and they both construct its routines and keep them in place with discipline. Several strengths feed into this one, and SJs usually appear as though they have life figured out and changes of any sort can be seen as unnecessary.

Staying the course through rough weather and fair and being able, as the British say, to keep a stiff upper lip in a world that is largely unknown and unpredictable requires intelligent emotions and a strong determination to guide them. The SJ sees an easily-shaken individual as frail, feebly avoiding life's challenges.

KEY THOUGHT/ACTION: "Steady ahead" is the nautical version of an SJ's image.

Nonuse:
The leaves of the quaking aspens that grow in the Colorado mountains, where sturdy pine and fir trees have given ground, shake nervously in the wind and remind me of an SJ who is not using this strength. All the emotions of fear that unnerve their resolute spirits result in a contagious disease of the human spirit. Nonuse of this strength is so non-SJ like.

Overuse:
To not be easily shaken is a benefit not easily overused. Can we be too steady? Maybe, since being steady as a rock is to be motionless. Progress and advance requires we move ahead and that means, to some degree, risk. Avoiding risk altogether will slow progress. Motionlessness produces fears of its own.

Misuse:
Being not easily shaken is only a misuse when it is used to hurt or harm others. Stubbornness is a form of misuse of this strength. Corruptive motives of any sort always create a misuse of a strength. Unless the SJ is unchanging for reasons harmful to others or themselves, this is a strength hard to misuse.

Trusts Authority

Authority has a role to play in society for the good of all, and trusting the leaders to do what they should in the interests of others should, in the SJ's world, encourage leaders to act with integrity. You must believe in the system or your lack of trust undermines it. Authority is a power given to leaders without which leadership is a mere symbol. So this emotion of trust in the SJ looks for a positive return on its investment.

If an authority fails to be trustworthy the trust placed in them is not thought of as wasted, rather it's time for a change of leader. Another emotion in the SJ will take over, namely a feeling of justice, accountability, and the leader gets what they deserve. Trust is not unintelligent unless it's overdone. It often motivates people in leadership to perform with integrity. Many an intelligent emotion is foiled, however, with overuse or misuse.

KEY THOUGHT/ACTION: Trust should encourage integrity in leadership.

Nonuse:

When authority is not trusted who do we trust to lead us? Everyone? But everyone has their own objectives and opinions and who has the authority to decide which recommendation to take? To unify a group we always need leadership, and when the SJ believes this and does not trust leadership they hurt the system they support.

Trust is the basis of all relationships and without it leadership, which in its turn must also earn the people's trust, loses the people's confidence and falters. Trust is a two-way street. Lacking trust in authority, a society injures itself, and leaders who fail to gain the trust of the people fail to gain support and become ineffective. Nonuse can be injurious to all.

Overuse:

Leadership is given a free ride when the emotions of the SJ trust without requiring accountability. When overdone, the emotion of trust leads the SJ to become complacent. Overuse of trust also weakens the integrity of trust itself and it becomes another emotion — less intelligent and with less muscle.

Misuse:

People in authority can misuse our trust in them and the supportive emotions our trust generates, of course, but we can misuse our trust in our leaders by exchanging the promise of trust for selfish ends. Trust, although such a seemingly harmless emotion, can and has been misused in the criminal world, for example. Often, the damage of a harmless emotion misused is not readily noticed — not until the damage is obvious.

What appears to be a harmless trust is in effect encouraging the corruption of leadership. The harmony we feel when trusting others is not necessarily an intelligent emotion either.

Supervisors, Managers, Systems, Routines

Control does not need defense as being an intelligent emotion. For a supervisor or manager, a lack of control engenders thoughts of mayhem. Control means having the ball in your own hand — managers want precisely that.

Systems and routines aim at maximizing the advantage of control. They bring order to the chances to influence and direct the course of events. Under the influence of order, the emotions of others can be restrained or utilized for a central purpose. However, what we must be aware of is how we exercise control and how much control we have. The desire for total control is in most cases not the emotion we will want to generate. The SJ believes in the essential nature of control, passionately believing in its effectiveness. The love of success, using systems and routines, motivates the detail-oriented SJ.

Anyone who has his own emotions under self-management is likely to succeed. Anyone who sensitively uses the authority and power of management when supervising others without overuse or misuse of their position earns the praise of others.

KEY THOUGHT/ACTION: Control is an intelligently emotional measure.

Nonuse:
When supervision or management is not in play, SJs fear the worst. Emotions of fear and concern and all the degrees of fear in-between emerge to play a dangerous offense in their minds.

Nonuse is unimaginable because of the felt warning of these emotions. And the SJ has a case. It is all too well-recorded that a lack of management and inadequate or nonexistent systems can be the root cause of failure in our own lives or in the work we undertake. Disastrous results spring from the shadows of nonuse.

Mentorship is a form of supervision and we can all benefit from it or, if we choose, experience the detrimental effects of walking the complex, tricky paths of life alone. Failure to swallow our feelings of pride and welcome the emotions of learning, encouragement, and guidance that mentoring offers will mark a lack of intelligence.

Overuse:
When we use management as a tool to control others rather than guide and direct them, it can become an abusive strength. Others will usually let us know when we have crossed this line by their complaints or by simply walking out on us. A disdain and disrespect of us follows. We have acted with a lack of prudence or, worse, with abject disregard for another person's rights and sense of dignity.

Misuse:
The list of possible abuses by power-hungry leaders would fill this book. Misuse of control is a malignant disease of the human emotions and one that in our society is usually followed closely with dire consequences enacted by angry victims. The lack of sound judgment and the feelings of attaining power over others further corrupts and distorts emotions that are otherwise noble and necessary.

Stoical

To not show one's feelings or to complain in the face of pain and discomfort is a valued stoic emotion and, in this sense, the SJ is usually very emotionally intelligent. Surely stoics are SJs. However, in forcing ourselves to be nonchalant about all things and nonreactive to pain, we remove the evils of emotional excess, or so the stoics felt. That's going too far for intelligent behavior to thrive. Emotional excess is not rectified by suppression of our emotions but by the proper control and exercise of them, and this the SJ can also do quite well when living in their strengths.

The SJ's seriousness and determination gives them the spirit to endure most discomforts and pains. Endurance without the drain of negative griping makes for an intelligence in the face of suffering that is hard to better.

The SJs are usually not stoics in a philosophical sense but in this more practical sense. The British, as I have mentioned, seek to keep a "stiff upper lip," which is their attempt at this same practical stoicism. Trust the SJ to say things like "tough it out" or "suck it up," expecting anyone to be able to do this with the same success they exhibit.

KEY THOUGHT/ACTION: A stoic attitude while under pain increases the chance of emotional control.

Nonuse:
When the SJ complains and whines, they lose their rock-like image. It also affects their feelings about themselves and encourages a low self-image, which is not at all helpful to the persistent, worry-prone SJ. SJs bear their burdens and can make the mistake of doing so all alone, but when they fall apart under the pressure and stress of adverse events, they seem no stronger than the weakest among us. Nonuse is a sad expression of the stable SJ.

Overuse:
Overuse appears when the SJ is misusing the strength by trying to exclude all emotion and feeling from their lives.

Misuse:
This misuse of a stoical attitude fails because we cannot live without emotion. Life only has meaning because of emotion. If this book has said anything, hopefully it has registered that. Imagine a wedding or funeral without any emotion — they would have no meaning to us. Even to try to be non-reactive to pain is not an intelligent control of our emotions since pain can serve the purpose of warning us of danger and probes us to appropriate action. Reacting to the emotions that pain signals can save us from loss.

As already noted, the attempt to remove emotions as though they are harmful to us, which is the position of some stoic philosophers, only leads to a life of barren, unfulfilling moments. Like misuse of any strength, the harm can give birth to damaging emotions that flood in to fill the void: too many to name. Casting out one demon only makes room for another.

Logistical in Work and Play

Everything in order, in the right sequence, and measured to achieve the right goal describes the essence of logistical intelligence found in the mind of the SJ. Order, like its counter emotion, spontaneity, is emotionally intelligent. The mind that is detail-oriented and follows sequence easily is no less intelligent than the global mind that leaps to pattern identification. In fact, the logistical mind is easier to "control" and keep focused as it moves with a determined steady pace down the narrow path from one detail to another.

Any mental activity that does not miss a step and follows the rhythm of orderliness creates emotions that calm and steady a person when stressed. Coordination of these steps, relating one thing to another logically, is perhaps one reason why the SJ's conversations proceed associatively, one idea leading to another. Aunt Mary's sprained ankle leads to talking about cousin Rex's strained and severely bruised knee and to Joe's bruises on his face, etc.

These emotions that orderliness and coordination create move seamlessly through both work and play in the life of the SJ.

KEY THOUGHT/ACTION: Intelligence of any kind loves order of some kind.

Nonuse:
Logistical intelligence betrays an orderly mind and just to think of not being orderly is frightening and detrimental to the SJ's

feelings of security. Nonuse is no option and emotions will lose all stability if this happens.

Overuse:
A logistical approach to everything does not allow for the creativity associated with impulse, spontaneity, and intuition. A sudden unrelated mental jump can lead to new creative associations. Also a total lack of impulsiveness makes for a dull, routine life that seldom creates happiness or the excitement of variety.

Misuse:
A misuse is similar. Only when step-by-step thinking is inappropriate to the task at hand would there be a misuse of this strength.

Communicates with Details

A concern for the details is not necessarily an emotion or skill that notices all the details. SJs are concerned with details, for certain, and hence have a better than average recall of them, but they can fail at representing the facts accurately like any of us because some details are hidden from them or have been lost to memory. Concern for the details results in a desire not to misuse them and this leads to a concern for communicating with the details. Woe to the speaker in a conversation who leaves out a detail in the presence of an SJ. The SJ will feel compelled to correct the "error."

Facts are made up of details, the individual elements of the piece of information. Communicating details accurately adds to the SJ's sense of security. If I have the facts right, meaning the details, I can feel secure in my conclusions and actions, figures the SJ. It is hard for them to feel secure any other way, such as with the use of hope or faith. That feeling of being right, secure, and certain are foundational emotions to the SJs temperament. Except in its misuse, how can we fault this intelligence?

KEY THOUGHT/ACTION: The facts please, as well as the details. Such communication is comforting.

Nonuse:
Caught at not accurately representing the facts, the SJ squirms uncomfortably and attempts a self-defense. They have been caught deficient where it really hurts. Their self-image suffers and if they doubt themselves, toxic emotions rush in and remove the all too precious feeling of security. Many negative emotions flood the mind of the SJ who does not communicate with details.

Overuse:
Sometimes, to listen to all the details of an adventure related by an SJ can be tiring. To them it is simply representing the facts fully and correctly. The damage of this overuse of communicating to others all the details that have impressed them is a minor fault, if a fault at all.

Misuse:
Misuse is also hard to imagine. Only if the goal is to communicate briefly, preserving the impact of brevity, could it be regarded as a misuse.

Good Samaritans, Helpmates

Helping is emotionally satisfying to the helper. But it is much more. To the SJ, it is a duty that they think all should feel toward society. Duty introduces yet another emotion. Being the social temperament, they work and play for the social good and feel the reward of this selfless caring. They must belong to society, as we have noted, and make a meaningful contribution. Therefore, everyone friend or stranger, in fact one who is simply a member of the human race, is to be cared for when in need.

Emotion supports this spirit of helpfulness with a surging sense of pride and integrity. Even if others don't help their fellow human beings, the SJ feels they should do their duty and be who they are.

KEY THOUGHT/ACTION: To be focused outward on others can lead to the steadying of our own emotions.

Nonuse:
Emotions of guilt can plague the SJ who does not help others. It makes them feel strange; we all do when we don't use our strengths.

Overuse:
This can be a problem. Helping others to the neglect of ourselves ultimately depletes our resources and we can no longer help. Neglect of ourselves opens the floodgates to all of the feelings that say we are being used and the reminders that others are not caring for us like we are caring for them. It is a depressive state and one that drains all joy from service.

Misuse:
Again, it is difficult to feel that this strength can be misused. Perhaps, only with the intent of using it to create opportunity to commit a crime or to deceive with intent to hurt.

Nondramatic, Concrete Speech

"Tell it how it is," that's the SJ cry. No flowery poetic speech for them. Plain language is more factual and please don't leave out the details. This non-dramatic, concrete speech represents reality to the SJ and makes them feel as though they are getting the truth without deceptive decoration.

The emotions that drive this strength encourage in the SJ feelings of ease, avoidance of mistakes, being right and keeping to their expectations of accurate communication. Plain speech is no guarantee of accuracy, but it makes the SJ feel as though truth has been attempted in a realistic manner.

KEY THOUGHT/ACTION: Plain speech, without embellishments or metaphors, communicates adequately for the SJ.

Nonuse:
They live by this strength! Attempts at flowery speech are disdained and a sign of being someone you are not. Emotions that crave exactness warn them against purposeful use of abstract, vague language.

Overuse:
Overuse is not an issue since plain factual speech should be the operating mode of the SJ.

Misuse:
How can we misuse plain, straightforward, unemotional speech? This statement seems to make great sense to the SJ and we will find some SJs disturbed if we don't communicate this way.

10 -Intelligently Emotional NT Strengths

How to Use This Chapter

1. If this is your temperament please focus on the intelligent use of your strengths, not on the nonuse, overuse, or misuse. Remember the principle that whatever you focus on magnifies and becomes an energy center. We want the energy of positive emotions to be produced in our strengths and not the energy of negative emotions to be generated in our weaknesses.

2. If this temperament is not yours, perhaps it is your child's, spouse's or friend's. Try to understand their emotions and the reasons why they feel the way they do, and heed their cry to understand them in their struggles.

3. Appreciate the emotional content and its intelligence in each strength. No strength is unintelligent. You may have associated a particular strength with a misuse that bugs you or you may feel it is wrong, so try to sort out and understand the judgments of your own emotions. If you are of a different temperament, to understand will be difficult for you but essential for your appreciation of the person of this temperament and their use of emotions in their temperament.

4. Enter into and learn the intelligence and unintelligence of all people's emotions. Their intelligence may be opposite of the intelligence of your own emotions. To you that may seem impossible, but emotions depend on the source from which they come, the purpose for which they are intended, and the appropriateness of their use to be labeled

intelligent or unintelligent. For personal growth, parenting, and simply the appreciation of others and how they are made, this will be a most rewarding journey of discovery.

5. If you are reading to understand and then parent your child more intelligently, please recall your child's actions that remind you of what you are reading and focus on the emotions that fire those actions and strengths. Your understanding of your child's emotional drives that arise from the intelligent or unintelligent use of their strengths will help you be a super parent.

The NT

If passion drives you, let reason hold the reins.
~ Benjamin Franklin

Time Is Relevant to the Task

When the NTs venture into their ingenious mode of creating something new, they have a feeling of satisfaction that feeds their spirit. When deeply troubled, the NT can find a refuge in becoming absorbed in a task that sparks his curiosity and ingenuity. He forgets about time and the troubling issues.

So strong is their focus that they feel only the call of reason which they follow without any sense of loss or the need to keep glancing at the clock. Logic drives them relentlessly if they are familiar with its principles and they feel all is right when they are immersed in its pursuit. Time is simply irrelevant.

For the NT, emotions must be kept under lock and key and an eye on the clock can certainly awaken emotion's powers within them. "Will I get through on time," is a disturbing question. The perception of the NT is that emotions destroy the clarity of the mind and a time constraint can do no less. Focus and rationality are their favored tools that rob time of its significance.

KEY THOUGHT/ACTION: Time can be the enemy of unwavering focus.

Nonuse:
An NT whose mind is not engrossed with some project or who is challenged by some threatening deadline is fair game for fears, doubts, and skepticism about himself, all aimed at destroying his own sense of worth. The NT's mind is his

favored retreat and when it is not available, he becomes easy targets of the hated emotional meltdown. When not controlled by the demands of the task, emotions begin to rule.

Overuse:
Locked away in their mental hideout, NTs can lose all earthly connections. Social life is neglected and the routines of life can also be dismissed. Blinders restrict their vision and seeing only what lies in the path of their focus can cause not only the loss of emotional control when disturbances occur but the deliberate attempt to bury the emotions that the intrusion of time has produced.

Not to acknowledge the place time has in their lives by overemphasizing its irrelevance and burying themselves in their projects is not always emotional intelligence: it can be a form of emotional immaturity. NTs live with the danger of underdeveloped emotions and any pressure, even that of an approaching deadline, can activate the dreaded emotions and they then may fail to control unexpected emotions with which they are not familiar. NTs must be aware of the relevance of time to life and treat its intrusions as a reality in their lives to avoid the eruption of unintelligent emotions.

Misuse:
Inconsideration for the time constraints of others while absorbed in their tasks can be a misuse of this strength. The little positive connections in life brought about by consideration and notes of gratitude can be neglected in favor of the "higher" goal of their project. (Child NTs will show an unwillingness to disengage from whatever is consuming their attention, such as a Lego project.) Emotional insensitivity and an ignorance of relationship skills can then plague them.

Strong Will, Determined

The NT's focus on a task is accompanied by a very determined will. It is the will to achieve, the will to remain fully focused for the duration of the task. The appeal of the task's goals feed the focus and the will. "Don't disturb me" is also to be interpreted as "Don't step in the path of my goals."

When the NTs make a judgment, they must be right or lose confidence in the accuracy of their intellectual abilities. They can be quite determined that they are right, and often they are. Whether right or not, arguing is one of their skills and in this also they are very determined and must not lose.

Argumentativeness fuels their reputation for being strong-willed. Everyone has a streak of stubbornness and the NTs cannot claim exemption — in fact, they can claim determination as their strength.

The intelligence in this strength comes from the way it supports their intense focus and strengthens their temperament's drives. Pride, confidence, a strong self-image, together with other feelings of earned superiority, make the NT veritably unmovable when entrenched in their convictions. It is a fine line between intelligent determination to succeed and the foolishness of thinking they are the only ones with a claim on success. The NTs who live in their strengths avoid such misguided stubbornness while remaining firmly focused.

KEY THOUGHT/ACTION: A strong will goes a long way to creating success.

Nonuse:
Nothing is more unlike an NT than a weak, wishy-washy will. It is willpower that sustains their intellectual drive. Nonuse of this motivating strength leaves them wilting in the heat of self-criticism. It is a pathetic sight to see a weak-willed NT.

Overuse:
We all know how relationships become battlegrounds when both partners are entrenched in their own opinions. An overuse of determination is nothing less than unintelligent stubbornness. There are few good words for the overuse of this strength. It can also create a mental block in any project.

Misuse:
Of course, a strong will can be misused. A person who has a strong will can hide the truth about something behind their dogmatism. A determined will can squelch criticism and the birth of a better idea. Where determination is distorted to some selfish or damaging purpose, of course, it corrupts.

Strategic, Theoretical Systems

Strategy is the product of forethought and planning. To distinguish it from the logistical planning of the SJ, it lays plans for contingencies and prepares us for the unexpected. It functions in the world of theory and depends on the building of reliable theoretical systems to enable it. Intelligence is written all over this mental exercise.

The emotions it produces are, to name a few, certainty, confidence, openness, achievement, and the warmth of greater control over the uncontrollable future. Astute thinking and the feeling of genius (for some) can make this strength very motivational. Recognition of a good strategy will heighten the emotions we have noted and introduce the NT to their true feelings of satisfaction.

KEY THOUGHT/ACTION: "What if" is a mental challenge that forces the mind to explore. Strategy is the structured result of such mental adventures.

Nonuse:
When NTs proceed without a strategy, they feel tentative and the feeling eats away at their confidence. If they build no theoretical system or follow none, they flounder and the inventiveness that belongs to them is stymied. Nonuse of these strengths shows itself in emotional hesitancy and a lack of confidence. Emotions that are not confident soon become attached to a fear. The NT hates mental cowardice.

Overuse:
Sometimes the NT can get lost in theory that is so unrelated to reality that work is of no pragmatic use. They may not recognize that it is of no earthly use. Not everything needs strategy and an overuse destroys the freedom to be impulsive and spontaneous, choosing at times to depart from strategy and follow intuition.

Misuse:
Misuse is confined to misplaced or damaging purposes that hurt others as well as the NT. Using strategy for selfish purposes is a struggle some young NTs find hard to overcome. Guilt is not far behind when our strengths are misused, and the NT will face the consequences of the wrongful use of a great strength.

Intense Curiosity

To have an intense urge to know or discover lies at the core of the NT's emotional makeup. Confidence is built when they discover and learn. Investigation, testing, and the scientific method appeals greatly to an NT. How would we increase our knowledge without curiosity? This strength is in all temperaments but is paramount in the NT and certain of the NFs. Not knowing creates a kind of mental pain.

The emotions that are fed by this strength are all intelligent. Because of these emotions, NTs are driven to be learners, builders, designers of theoretical systems, strategists, and architects of much more than just buildings. They are convinced of their usefulness and importance to society. The "N," which stands for intuition, stimulates enquiry, investigation, and insightful ideas because it is searching for new perceptions into the relationship of things. However, in the NT, their curiosity is mostly limited to rational and pragmatic purposes since emotion is not emphasized in the NT. In the NF, curiosity includes the world of the imagination and willingly invades the world of fantasy, not being limited by reason.

KEY THOUGHT/ACTION: Never let the unknown remain so.

Nonuse:
I can't imagine an NT who would not be intensely curious. As we develop, our curiosity increases and it never really ends for the NT. Life is one great act of discovery. Without this passion and drive they will feel unsatisfied with life and it most certainly will lead to a kind of depression with atypical behavior resulting.

Overuse:
The only issue with overuse is their abdicating other responsibilities and relationships in their life. By nature, curiosity is all-absorbing. Add to that the strong focus of an NT and it can seem unwittingly to be all there is in life. Our passions are experienced in the context of life and its necessities. Therefore, other people in the life of the NT can be neglected when their thirst to know takes over. The overuse of curiosity can also make others think they are not essential helpmates and individuals in their own right, negatively affecting the NT's relationships.

Misuse:
The misuse is usually the overuse of this strength. Sometimes this strength is used to investigate with the purpose of destroying someone and in that case, the intent and purpose is the misuse.

Questioning Skeptical

A number of the NT's strengths can be helpful in producing emotional control. Strategic thinking, independence, what makes sense, and being skeptical are all valuable tools to this end.

Here we face a much needed strength that, although it is prominent and indispensable in the NT temperament, it is present and helpful in all temperaments to some degree and makes emotional control reachable for all.   Remember, we said that emotions judge on first appearances and can be wrong. A healthy questioning of our emotions helps greatly in reestablishing emotional control.   The best time to question our feelings is after they have initially surged and before they settle into an established mood.

Questioning is a rational act and skepticism a rational attitude. They amount to, when correctly used, an examination of the rational base of our emotional responses and beliefs. Do we have good reason for this emotion?   Should we continue it? Would some other response be better? Emotional intelligence somehow always involves the rational mind at some point.

KEY THOUGHT/ACTION: Never let a question go unanswered.

Nonuse:
When the NT fails to use this strength, they become someone they are not, so fundamental to their makeup is this questioning.   Accepting at face value anything or anyone seems wrong to the NT. Therefore, nonuse is rare in them.

Overuse:
Overuse is common.   Nothing is taken on trust and, like doubting Thomas of biblical fame, evidence satisfactory to the NT is always needed if they are to believe anything. But faith and trust are the essence of relationships and the power behind much that life requires of us. As a result, overuse that says "I trust no one" can lead to damaging their relationships or at least minimizing the satisfaction an act of trust can engender and making them appear arrogant.   All the emotional benefits of trust and acceptance are then jettisoned.

Misuse:
A skeptical attitude can lead to intellectual pride that is an emotion some NTs seem to exude. This can quickly lead to a negative skeptical attitude, always putting people down and seldom lifting them up. Doubt, instead of being an evaluation with a positive purpose, can become a negative tool for tearing

down people's beliefs. When it does, it fosters destructive emotions and is far from emotional intelligence.

Even when skepticism is used, which will be insisted on by most NTs as an essential tool for arriving at the truth, its attack on other people's ideas creates a negative emotional climate, one that is resented by others.

Independent, Self-Reliant

Dependence can be pernicious when overdone, whereas independence in the mind of NTs is always a noble trait. However, the NT can have a problem when they carry their independence too far. Within prudent limits, independence sparks some very comforting emotions like feelings of freedom, expansiveness, escape, non-coercion, options, worthiness among their peers, and the ability to feel unbound by the restriction of rules and the demands of others.

"Live free or die," heralds the motto of the State of New Hampshire. Discovery, which is what the NT is about, needs no boundaries imposed on it. The SPs with their individualism might join the NT in the words of Patrick Henry, "I know not what course others may take; but as for me, give me liberty or give me death."

A feeling of independence bolsters the self-esteem of the NT and brings them great self satisfaction when they can feel they are truly independent. Everyone needs to be as self-reliant as possible and setting that goal is in itself a boost to the NT's self-esteem. While no temperament displays the opposite strength called dependence, the nearest is the strength of trusting others found in the NF, or the SJ's need to belong, and these, too, can be intelligent even if a tension exists with the idea of independence.

NTs will fight to maintain their independence. Try to take it away and you will find how tenaciously they cling to it and treasure it. It is a great strength and a worthy goal.

KEY THOUGHT/ACTION: Strive for self reliance.
Nonuse:
To not be independent is by definition to be reliant on others. That causes the NT to feel sad and useless. We can think of many situations where humans must be dependent on others, but it's the feeling the nonuse of this strength brings that the NT finds troubling, not the risk of self-reliance. Their drive to be independent must be encouraged or they will sink into gloom.

Overuse:
There are many occasions when all of us are dependent on others. Trying to eliminate all of these dependencies (an obvious overuse of independence) is futile and shows the lack of a realistic understanding of life. It is a sure pathway to failure. We are made as social, dependent beings. Any use of this strength must know the limits of total freedom and be wise in choosing self-imposed limits, especially when it comes to building a successful relationship. People like to feel needed. A lot of anger and disappointment can be avoided when we build a relationship on mutual need for each other.

Misuse:
Acting independent of someone when we are actually trying to reject them is a misuse of the strength: a cloak hiding our true designs. In that case, we are better served to tell the truth about our feelings in the spirit of love.

Acting independently when we need to work as a team is also a misuse. Strength, power, and the meeting of minds generated by a united effort is ignored when we are not team players. Anyone can imagine the emotional consequences of deception and isolation.

Calm, Cool, and Collected

That image of outward calm that is a hallmark of the NT makes them appear to be capable of exceptional emotional control.

When our bodily expressions are under control, it certainly looks like our emotions are also. If we add to this outward calm the ability to keep our mouths shut, we escape a myriad of other emotional traps. Slow to speak is an effective tool used to master ourselves. The NT is often slow to speak, allowing time for their thoughts to develop.

Being collected is having our wits about us, uninfluenced by pressures that can stir unwanted emotions. Being calm is not being devoid of emotion or unaffected by emotion. The absence of emotion only leads to unintelligence. We are emotional creatures, and being calm is all about welcoming and managing our emotions so that we are not ruffled. The NT wisely endeavors to keep a steady course somewhat like the stoics of ancient Greece but for different reasons. In this emotional calm, they discover a boost to their confidence.

Cool helps, too. Emotion is heat and a cool demeanor at least eliminates the appearance of being hotheaded. When not overused, this is another tool leading to emotional mastery.

KEY THOUGHT/ACTION: The unruffled demeanor keeps the opposition guessing.

Nonuse:
The image of intellectualism, independence, and rationality demands that the NT remain calm, cool, and collected. When they are not, they begin to dislike themselves and feel that they are actually losing control of their lives or of the environment, which they also wish to control or keep an eye on. In their own way, NTs can be control freaks but the control is aimed at self-management rather than the management of others. For the NT, their emotions are not intelligent when they are easily ruffled and unstable. To look like NTs, they must remain cool, calm, and collected.

Overuse:
When overused, this strength makes them look as though they are devoid of emotion. Emotion is needed for us to be truly human. A distinguishing factor of humanity is the way we

express our care for each other. Humanitarianism is dependent on empathy and love, both of which are full of emotional responses to people's needs. Our emotional engine is not built to run efficiently in cold temperatures, so as valuable as a cool appearance is to emotional control, it must not be overdone or we fail to function with sufficient warmth to interact well with others. The frigid emotional regions are inhospitable to humans.

Misuse:
Often the cool, calm spirit is used as a weapon to disturb or even anger others. The strength is then a tool for damaging others. NTs must find the medium for the correct use of this strength in order for it to remain a pure attempt at managing their own emotions and not controlling or avenging others. Passive aggressive behavior is all too easy for the NT.

Logical, Reasonable, Must Make Sense

This strength is the root of the NT claim to be rational and function with logic as more than a goal, as a prized characteristic of their lives as well. We cannot call reason unintelligent so this is ipso facto true.

However, logic is not always right, nor is it a certain path to truth. The premises on which the logic is built determine the truth, or not, of the logical conclusion. So, logic is not always sage-like or the infallible tool of geniuses. Those claims lie more with the sage and the use of astute imagination.

The emotional value of reason and logic is, of course, not to be gainsaid. Reason can react positively on emotions and can temper many a runaway feeling. Always seeking to make sense is the path that logic and reason seek to blaze, but the sense is structured by logic and fed by the information the logic processes. Reason feeds emotions of calm, correctness, consistency, completeness, and strength.

KEY THOUGHT/ACTION: Reason can make sense of our emotions and emotions sometimes make sense of reason.

Nonuse:
For an NT to forsake logic is tantamount to a bird forsaking the use of its wings. No longer can the NT find their way or soar to the heights of their ingenious potential. Emotionally, an unreasonable NT must resort to desperate rationalization or sink into a depressed mood since they have sold out one of their basic strengths.

Encourage all young NTs to hold firm to what makes sense, and do not try to rob them of their birthright lest they become emotionally weak or emotionally volatile. When we deny our characteristic strengths we can fall to the opposite extreme.

Overuse:
The overuse of logic and reason has at times wrongly tried to discredit emotion's wisdom and richness. Overuse of logic comes at a cost. Emotions are intelligent, as I have argued, and although not always right in their judgments, can point us to the wisest solution for our problems at times. Emotions can also identify faulty premises.

Since logic and reason are not always right, it seems to be a case of the kettle calling the pot black when logic is overused and touted as the savior of every argument. Emotion will not be so summarily dismissed. The cost to the NT is error which is a despised currency.

Misuse:
As always, we can misuse a strength when we use it for false or detrimental purposes. People can be hammered with logical arguments all aimed at destroying the opponent's confidence or self-image. Logic is also misused when it is called on to judge subjective issues such as intuitive gut feelings and caring empathy since they fall outside of the territory of logic. We cannot afford to misuse our strengths if we are bent on developing intelligent emotions.

Ingenious

Inventions are the result of ingenious minds. Ingenuity is cleverness and originality at work, and the NT is the champion of such endeavors. Intelligence is required in the emotions that drive the ingenious mind. Emotions are produced in the mind of the NT that create feelings of achievement, mental acuity, pride, usefulness, and finding a place among this world's ingenious giants.

Dangerous emotions such as pride can lead to a fall, and the NT must keep this intelligent strength within the bounds of acceptable humility. If not, what is a reasonable emotion becomes the cause of decay. Proud people can be ingenious but usually suffer in their interactions with people.

KEY THOUGHT/ACTION: The world praises ingenuity and God exemplifies it.

Nonuse:
To feel useless the NT needs only to lose the drive to be ingenious in his thinking and discoveries. Average is not a word that inspires the NT. They must succeed in making this world a better place by the use of this creative strength. Nonuse is devastating to their sense of worth.

Overuse:
Can you think of an overuse of ingenuity? A creative drive is always needed and the world can use more of this intelligent urge. These emotions that power a strong drive to be original, clever, and creative don't seem to want to give up and we don't want the NT to do so.

Misuse:
Many inventions have been used to wreak harm on our world and some are intrinsically damaging. When we have used ingenious creations to damage our world or others, we have shown our lack of intelligence in both the emotional and rational realm. We then resemble the NT in decay.

Effective, Efficient, Competent, Achieving

The NTs fail in their own estimation if not effective, efficient, competent and achieving. Again, a strong driving force beats within the heart of the NT. They tend at times to be over-zealous about these traits when we consider life is so much more. But the brilliant light of these traits guide the NT hourly, daily, yearly, and incessantly, for some over an entire lifetime. NTs are not the only achievers but, to them, a high self-image is only possible when they achieve with effectiveness and efficiency.

The SP is also an achiever, as are any of the temperaments. Why then is this singled out as a primary strength for the NT? Because it is a center around which the NT's emotions revolve. In contrast, the SP's drive for effectiveness centers on excitement and adventure, and for the SJ, around success in maintaining order and control, and for the NF, around sensitivity and its giftedness with all things people-related.

The emotions we have already met that thrive in the NT's makeup surface here also, as expected. While the NT usually seeks to downplay the importance of emotion in all these strengths, emotion still plays a strong role in motivating the NT regardless of their attitude toward it.

KEY THOUGHT/ACTION: Competence drives efficiency and effectiveness, which in turn paves the way to success.

Nonuse:
Intelligence shines in each of these strengths. The emotions they encourage are very motivating. The loss of all these components of success when the strength is not used will certainly be disastrous for the sense of personal importance an NT craves. Success will evade them.

Overuse:
We can be so bent on being effective that the need to be loving and empathetic is lost in this intelligent drive. For some

obsessed persons, overuse of this strength happens apparently without their notice. They focus on achieving and the world passes by with all its concerns. The day-to-day concerns can take their toll on the NT and in what they perceive as distractions they can, as a result, become ineffective and unfocused. The NT is not helped by giving undue attention to success. There must be a balance.

Misuse:
Misuse is the use of efficiency for negative or damaging purposes, namely to damage and hurt our world, other people or ourselves.

Abstract in Speech

Because the NT lives in the world of theory and the world of the "not yet," their speech is abstract by nature. Principles, ideas, and concepts fill the mind of the NT and lead to the creation of special technical languages among other things. Much of their abstract speech is technical jargon.

Whenever the NT's words are mysterious to others, it gives the NT a feeling of separation and perhaps even superiority, which can give rise to prideful emotions that lack intelligence. Abstract speech is intelligent when it is understood, when it opens up communication to more efficient ways of relating to others. Rewarding emotions arise out of the success of the communication, not out of feelings of superciliousness.

KEY THOUGHT/ACTION: Keep abstract speech intelligible.

Nonuse:
If limited to concrete language, the NT has no words to explore abstract ideas. Abstract and technical speech supports their searches so it is necessary to their success. For them not to use it is nigh impossible and would destroy their effectiveness.

Overuse:
Overuse is no problem within the circle of their understanding NT friends or cohorts. No one seems to complain when they understand the terms. However, for communication with people outside of their field of interest, problems can emerge.

Some people are turned off by NTs because they do not understand and keep asking for the NT to use plain language. NTs often can't speak plainly enough because they are immersed in their technical jargon and, therefore, don't talk about their technology in terms everyone understands.

To be seen as the "experts" releases comforting emotions for the NT, but being such experts sometimes does not let them participate in life and relationships with intimacy. Social skills often depend largely on how we can engage in a conversation about things everyone seems to enjoy. This can lead to a neurosis for the NT where they feel odd and not accepted, resulting in further withdrawal from people.

Misuse:
Except for trying to show off or appear superior, this strength is not often misused.

11 - Intelligently Emotional NF Strengths

How to Use This Chapter

1. If this is your temperament please focus on the intelligent use of your strengths, not on the nonuse, overuse, or misuse. Remember the principle that whatever you focus on magnifies and becomes an energy center. We want the energy of positive emotions to be produced in our strengths and not the energy of negative emotions to be generated in our weaknesses.

2. If this temperament is not yours, perhaps it is your child's, spouse's or friend's. Try to understand their emotions and the reasons why they feel the way they do, and heed their cry to understand them in their struggles.

3. Appreciate the emotional content and its intelligence in each strength. No strength is unintelligent. You may have associated a particular strength with a misuse that bugs you or you may feel it is wrong, so try to sort out and understand the judgments of your own emotions. If you are of a different temperament, to understand will be difficult for you but essential for your appreciation of the person of this temperament and their use of emotions in their temperament.

4. Enter into and learn the intelligence and unintelligence of all people's emotions. Their intelligence may be opposite of the intelligence of your own emotions. To you that may seem impossible, but emotions depend on the source from which they come, the purpose for which they are intended, and the appropriateness of their use to be labeled intelligent or unintelligent. For personal growth, parenting, and simply the appreciation of others and how they are made, this will be a most rewarding journey of discovery.

5. If you are reading to understand and then parent your child more intelligently, please recall your child's actions that remind you of what you are reading and focus on the emotions that fire those actions and strengths. Your understanding of your child's emotional drives that arise from the intelligent or unintelligent use of their strengths will help you be a super parent.

The NF

Meaning is found in our emotions and emotion in our meanings.
~ Unknown

Lives In and For the Future

If there is one temperament that keeps an eye wide-open to future possibilities, it is the NF.   They walk ahead into the future with all six senses alive and on alert, the sixth (intuition) being on high alert. What might be, should be, could be, and will be activates emotion in almost all the possible scenarios of their imaginative minds. Their inner world is constantly looking for the patterns that the facts of life and the hopes of the future reveal and suggest.

Emotional intelligence needs this vigilant future-watchdog-mindset to warn it of possible emotional dangers and to prepare ahead of time for the triggering of the NF's most powerful emotions.   Advance notice often supplied by their intuition is critical for them in preparing for emotional trauma. Keeping a watch on the future is their way of trying to maintain their inner peace.

NFs are elated or traumatized by future possibilities and they feed their positive emotions with an injection of hope whenever they can. "Without hope," one NF wrote, "the people perish," and even though this is true of all temperaments it is especially, and of necessity, true of the NF.   So, emotional intelligence that for the NF comes from scanning and preparing for the future, aims at discovering some hope to lift their spirits and feed their determination so they can weather any storm.

KEY THOUGHT/ACTION: Hope is a life-giving emotion for the NF.

Nonuse:
When focused on the past, NFs tend to find reasons for feeling guilty about what they could have done better and engaging in self denunciation. All hope vanishes and depression enters if the future does not shine in their minds. They also cannot be too focused on the present because it does not always hold all the meaning and significance they want.

Hope requires a perspective that the present in its fleeting nature does not offer. So, emotional control is found in finding hope and faith that the future presents and in an idealism about the future that the NF clings to. For the NF, an optimistic view of the future spells the possibility of emotional intelligence. Without this optimistic outlook they wilt.

Overuse:
The future is not always rosy. Searching the future for hope can lead to an excessive introspection. The unknown nature of the future can't sustain too thorough an examination without negative emotions of fear and doubt surfacing. Since all scrutiny of the past, present or future results in introspection for the NF, this introspection can be the initiator of troublesome thoughts and feelings.

It is a complex problem to be strong on possibilities like hope and faith while being strong on comparing yourself to everything you find when you have a low self-image. Emotional intelligence escapes them often in this mix. Yet NFs are the emotional experts and emotional intelligence says to the NF, "Keep all things positive, especially your future expectations, and don't get lost in the future."

Misuse:
Have you heard of the phrase, "so heavenly minded they are of no earthly use?" This is unfair when used of the NF, but if the future is where they live in a fantasy world, lacking touch with reality, they can find it hard to keep their feet on the ground. This is especially true of the NFs who have a P in their

profile. They can tend to misuse their imagination and fantasy by trying to escape the realities and demands of the present. With this avoidance of reality the NF can quickly become unintelligent.

Idealists, Dreamers

To dream of an idyllic perfection and make it an aim or a goal is not unintelligent. Exciting emotions are quickly generated when we dream of the ideal relationship, a perfect life or a fantastic future. Not only do the emotions of excitement emerge but refreshment to a weary or worrying soul is gained by such momentary mental escape. Hence, the NF daydreams or fantasizes for the refreshment it brings, often not telling the world of these secretive methods of recharging.

Dreaming, even day-dreaming, is not a disconnection from the realities of life, but a stop to refuel so they can face the present, having been remade and empowered. When they pull in to the refueling station of imagination and dreaming, helpful emotions fill their tank.

Dreaming has been given a bad rap by the earth-bound SPs and SJs and at times by the rationally focused NTs. It sounds so unreal. However, there is reason and logic in a practice that so effectively achieves its purpose. The mind of the NF is rational, as Plato in his selection of words that describe both the NT and the NF leads us to believe.

So, reconstruct your understanding of this NF strength and realize the sound premise on which it is built and the logical urge that leads to its successful application. Encourage the power of dreaming (imagining is its modus operandi) and the NF will thank you with their friendship.

KEY THOUGHT/ACTION: Idealism is imagination struggling to be reality.

Nonuse:
Because the NF depends on imagination to fuel a number of their strengths, to be less than idealistic would not make sense of how they are made to function. The ideal is the driving force in their passion and the goal of their perfectionist tendencies. Avoid it and the strengths of the NF lose their unity.

Regardless of idealism's possible misuse, not to use it would be worse than the dangers of an over-optimistic ideal. In this temperament, we should always keep in mind what motivates them to achieve: their idealism, which drives them to make their dreams come true. They should not be urged to forsake their dreams.

Overuse:
Overuse of an idealistic belief can cause much pain when it is not achieved. For the NF, expectations are dashed and the world is perceived as unfriendly or unfair. The NF with their idealism has attempted what others claim is foolish. Caution should warn them to examine the possibilities more carefully so as not to be foolish.

For example, holding too fast to the belief that your loved one is perfect, only to see her fall from grace because she is imperfect, invites hurt. The idealist garners little sympathy when their idealistic image falls and their pain begins. Danger indeed! But the NF can't be persuaded that the practice is all bad. Emotions of pleasure and relief feed their spirit when they idealize their world. These feelings that this idealistic imagination produces support their belief in the ideal. Overuse is a lesson hard for the NF to learn.

Misuse:
An idealistic dream can be used as an escape from reality, as a diversion or as a way to hopefully obtain sympathy, all of which are misuses of a great strength.

Imaginative

Reason and logic would be uncreative without imagination. A case can be made for reason and logic on their own to be unintelligent because they fail to consider all the facts — the facts of emotion. Again, emotions are facts. The NF brings to reason the richness of an imagination empowered by emotion that is necessary for a truly virile imagination. The universe is not big enough to contain their imaginings. They are not the only ones that use imagination, but they use it most.

Creativity is dependent on imagination and although the NF does not have sole claim to imagination, they certainly reach for its limits. Some would say reality is its proper limit, but if we limit imagination to what is already real, it cannot suggest new things and open up surprising possibilities.

Imagination without emotion to make it live, real and powerful in the mind, creates a mental desert. All the possible emotions are engaged when the NF imagines, and they all cause the NF to feel as though their mental wanderings are real life in all its colors and tantalizing senses.

KEY THOUGHT/ACTION: Imagination is the mind's new frontier.

Nonuse:
Life would be dead on arrival for the NF if they didn't use their imagination to spice it up with wonder and hope. Lifeless and cold indeed, and an open door for all the negative emotions that make an NF feel like less than nothing.

Overuse:
How can you overuse imagination? Granted it can be misused, but this is where all creativity resides. We need more, not less imagination. Even the world of fantasy is very rewarding, as the popularity of *Alice in Wonderland* still demonstrates generations later. Hidden in the weird portrayals of its characters is noble philosophy and we still benefit from its lessons written in the language of fantasy.

I would like to argue that the world is better for the imaginations of its great writers and the more we have of imaginative works, the more sensitive to the world of the unseen and not-yet-real we become. The more we are given opportunity to perceive our world through the colored glasses of beauty and mystery, the more we will value the wonders of our world and the power of the mind. Creativity benefits.

Misuse:
Imagination can be an escape when engagement with our world is the prime need. Imagination can become a disconnection with reality, a true head-in-the-clouds, a myth that lacks substance and leads people to unreality for less than noble purposes. Emotions are then tainted with questions and doubt.

Passionate, Enthusiastic, Value-Based Decisions, Eager to Learn

Passion and enthusiasm are a double-edged sword. First, the positive edge. They create positive emotions that enable the human spirit to accomplish the unbelievable and soar with wings above the negations of life. Without these, the NF feels inanimate, tentative, and without power. Passion makes any emotion stronger and the power of the NF's emotion is legendary. Put the two together and you get a ferment of the human spirit that tackles anything. Even danger is minimized by their potency. A passion for the positive can overpower negative emotions and keep them safely at bay. Skilled from the frequent use of enthusiasm, the NF develops considerable emotional intelligence from this strength.

Second, the other edge. Passion can be all-consuming and when it suddenly vanishes or is overcome by some negative doubt, the vacuum it leaves behind sucks all the hope and joy out of the NF's mental world. They are left with vanity (emptiness) as the ancient philosopher who wrote Ecclesiastes insisted, "Vanity, all is vanity." For the NF, when passion exits all emotional intelligence is lost.

An NF's passion extends to their values, affecting all their decisions. Values are built of rational and emotional judgments and, for the NF, they quickly become the essence of their lives. Values motivate them and shape them and they become personal values, deeply entrenched in their concepts of what is loving, right, and fair. Values are emotional hotspots for the NF, intelligent or otherwise, depending on the quality of the value they have adopted.

An eagerness to learn is also a passion-driven urge in the NF. They must know. Knowledge feeds their logic and aids the intelligence of emotions since it guides their judgments too. And the NF, particularly the Js, can't sleep if there is a lack of knowledge about a situation that concerns them. It is hard for them to wait until they do learn. This creates both intelligent emotions, such as a thirst for the satisfaction of knowledge, and unintelligent emotions, such as impatience. But learning is positive and the positive emotions make it a very intelligent emotion.

KEY THOUGHT/ACTION: Passion gives meaning to life.

Nonuse:
The nonuse of passion creates sad results. Life is nothing without passion, and all their emotions, even the negative ones (like the pain of having no emotion), are fired to white heat in the NF's fiery mind. Emotional intelligence for the passionate NF is keeping all emotions positive, while no emotions that they count essential can be absent.

Overuse:
The NF feels that no positive emotion can be overused. However, negative passions are often overused by the NF whenever they appear. Overuse of passion opens the door to loss of control and to selling out the emotions to an irrational emotional behavior, a thing no NF is wise to do. The way we are designed is to check emotion with reason before we sell ourselves to an idea or an urge.

Misuse:
Passion, when used for causes that damage others, even if in the mind of the NF the idea behind the passion is essential, brings about a loss of personal integrity and destroys the integrity in their passion.

Being passionate for destructive causes such as revengeful efforts certainly destroys their integrity. Their self-image also takes a blow if they hold themselves accountable for the wrongs. Purity of motive and purpose is emotional intelligence for the NF.

Trusting

To trust is to firmly and willingly believe in someone or something. Evidence is not needed, although it is welcome when it supports our trust. Some element of credulity, which may be undetected by the NF, causes them to believe in another person or idea at times almost instantly. Sometimes the trust is based on an accurate intuition. It also may be nothing but a trust in the goodness of humanity and therefore is extended generously to all. It also may be an optimism about people and things that drives their desire to trust. It may simply be the desire to please. Emotions, such as generosity, optimism, and the feeling that the NF would rather think good than bad about people, can intelligently spur their trust.

By some, this is seen as a definite weakness, laying oneself open to harm and ridicule. But the question the NF asks is, which is best: a trusting attitude or a doubting attitude? To them, trust opens up the possibility of a reciprocal reaction and the beginnings of a relationship.

We have to admit that the emotions trust produces are warm and helpful and this is perhaps what the NF, who is all about harmony and good feelings, treasures most. Which is best, a trusting attitude or a doubting attitude? You decide.

KEY THOUGHT/ACTION: Trusting others is beginning with positive possibilities.

Nonuse:
When the NF fails to trust others they feel judgmental and guilty of not treating the other person with warm respect. The feeling eats at them and they can only bear to be that way if they "toughen up" and develop a "don't care" attitude or are angry. They may be able to develop a reasonable facsimile of firmness if they try, but they will never truly mimic the toughness of the STJ. Only anger or fear makes the NF hard-nosed and resistant to another's pleas.

Overuse:
Perhaps we are all aware of the shortsightedness of the overuse of this strength. Too much trust may produce feelings of warm support for others, but emotions do not necessarily warn us of all the dangers. Only the results flag us. This often happens too late to realize the baneful effects and then we change course too late.

The line between a beneficial trust and one that leaves us open to abuse has to be learned. Teach yourself and your child how to be trusting of others first, since no relationships are possible without it. Second, teach them how to find a comfortable path to walk while not inappropriately trusting others and still being a welcoming person.

Misuse:
Misuse of a trusting attitude occurs when we show trust to others in order to deceive them. Setting a trap for their gullibility, for example, with the purpose of doing harm is designing to hurt. There is no intelligence in such actions.

Personal Growth, Meaning, Significance

This strength is obviously intelligent. Some people don't see the need for personal growth as much as the NF. NFs feel life is a journey, always trying to be the best you can be or at least to be better. Better means being significant and having personal meaning to themselves. Positive emotions fill them when they feel they are significant. They must feel it. Confidence and love of self-fulfillment are some of those uplifting feelings and they breed a host of others. These emotions build hope and the feelings of personal worth that enable their typically low self-image to rise.

The NF seeks to be meaningful not only to themselves but in the lives of others. For others to grow and find their potential or reach satisfying goals because of the NF's passion is deeply rewarding. It creates yet more of those encouraging feelings that spur the NF to even greater passion. Their self-image rises even more with the feeling of being all things to all people.

KEY THOUGHT/ACTION: To all NFs, a life of fulfilling meaning is their ardent prayer.

Nonuse:
From ages past people have always sought to know what the meaning of life is. It is more personal with the NF and a loss of personal meaning causes all their reasons for existing to implode. Life is not worth living without meaning. A nonuse of this strength can be the reason for feeling empty and dry. It can also lead to depression.

When they feel that they are not significant in the lives of others they judge they have not been successful. A restlessness follows and all emotions that normally give pleasure lose their luster too. Why live if personal meaning in life is not found? Others may not get this, but the NF knows it only too well.

Overuse:
Can meaning and purpose, significance and growth be overdone? The NF thinks not. When they have found fulfillment for themselves they are passionate to help the whole world find the same. The emotions that surround these strengths multiply with use and success.

Misuse:
Perhaps we could say that a misuse of these strengths occurs when they are forced on those who have no interest in them, content simply to live in the moment or be caught in repeating the past.   Seeing life in terms of materialistic goals sidelines personal growth too, and the NF in their passion may well try to forcefully convert such people.

Sensitive

Sensitive sounds like the opposite of emotional intelligence to some, but only if we are thinking of the damaging negative emotions that erupt defensively in the NF when they are sensitized by some event. Positive emotions that are sensitive to other people's needs as well as their own are helpful and intelligent.   These keep the inner life of the NF healthy.

The NF is known for ultra-sensitivity.   Their giftedness emerges when their emotional sensitivity interfaces with their imagination. The hidden world beyond reason is then opened to us all in their artistic expressions or intimate personal encounters.   Emotional intelligence for the NF is the use of positive emotions to enrich lives.

Love, hope, faith, gentleness, and goodness among other positive emotions, all aid and when they partner with self control, they make each emotion even more rewarding.   The more sensitive they are, the more rewarding their emotions are. Not just positive emotions but sensitive ones are what the NF is known for when they live in their strengths.

KEY THOUGHT/ACTION: Sensitivity opens doors between people.

Nonuse:
When the NFs lose sensitivity, they feel hard even to themselves.   When that happens they can become angry toward life and that dismisses all their assets. A non-sensitive NF is a failure to themselves and a disappointment to others.

Overuse:
When they are oversensitive they also become a threat to themselves and others. Too sensitive is defined as emotionally reactive to situations that don't warrant it. The NF will typically hate themselves for this inappropriate display and apologize profusely or sink into the mire of embarrassment.

This misjudgment can result in self abuse from self-denial to damaging themselves because they think they have been insensitive. They can whip themselves mercilessly for the mistake. Overuse of sensitivity is nearly always turned inward on themselves.

There is something dark about this punishing of ourselves for our failures. Why the NF does it is a mystery to others but not to them. They believe they have done wrong and the comforting words of others fall on their deafened ears.

Misuse:
Of course, the overuse is a misuse as well. The misuse is to blame themselves for being who they are and for letting a gift become a liability. Emotional intelligence sinks to its lowest in the temperament where it also finds its highest expression.

Intuitive, Insightful

Intuition can tell us messages that bear good or bad tidings. It is merely seeing things and receiving information that the five physical senses cannot detect. Reading those hidden senses can at times be unnerving. When our intuition reads the information that our five physical senses can't detect, it still makes judgments about what it sees and that creates feelings, some frightening, some calming and warming. Because intuitions make emotive judgments about what they see, they are acting with intelligence. We are left to interpret intuition's judgments and the emotions they create in us.

The most common form of intuition is insight. An intuitive person will have insights into another's feelings or condition.

These insights are also not without emotional responses. Insights can and do lead to ingenious and intelligent discoveries in both the physical world (usually the work of intuition in the NT) and in the world of personal interactions and meaning (the favored field of the NF).

Insight is a high level of mental functioning on which the NFs form their premises and build rational conclusions. Behind this intuition and insight may be the NF's sharpness at seeing the patterns that their global minds search out. Whatever the explanation for intuition happens to be, the emotions aroused by discovering something reward the mind and heart of the insightful NF.

KEY THOUGHT/ACTION: Insight is intelligence functioning at its best.

Nonuse:
Nonuse is a loss to the NF, creating a feeling of atrophy. Their human spirit shrivels and weakens much like a starved body and the feelings are not less dramatic. It feels like the true essence of who they are, people who can see meanings and peer behind the facts, is being buried. NFs are intuitive to the core. It is as natural as breathing to them and they don't even notice how often they rely on its messages. Take breathing away and we soon notice it — the same for the NF when intuition is eliminated.

An absence of insight or intuition creates a feeling of nonbeing and emptiness and a feeling of not being complete in some strange spiritual sense. Therefore, not to use intuition and its valuable insights is, indeed, to lose the meaning of who they are.

Overuse:
Only when the use of intuition is combined with an extra-intrusive sensitivity does it become a liability. The insights are then usually misjudgments, mistakes that cost the NF by resulting in their being read as paranoid or crazy. Overuse is in a real sense a misuse of a mysterious strength.

Misuse:
As is always the case, intuitive information can be used for harmful purposes and then becomes an evil in society. Because of the secretive and subjective nature of intuitive information it lends itself to abuse. Some, therefore, dismiss its usefulness altogether, and this is a shame since insight is an instrument we all value and need. Caution in its use is wisdom.

Emotional

If emotions are a strength in the NF, the question here is whether they are intelligent and we have already argued that they are. Intelligence belongs to all emotions, both good and bad, since they are judgments and judgments are decisions that require the use of intelligence. But as we know, not all our judgments are helpful or right.

Those that are helpful are doubly intelligent in the sense that they have made a judgment and made a positive and beneficial one as well. A positive emotion, helpful to us and others, makes life function wisely, although not always smoothly. Wisdom is an old-fashioned concept that has not outlived its usefulness in describing a worthwhile and satisfying life. The quality of our emotional judgments affect the intelligence of our emotions.

KEY THOUGHT/ACTION: Emotions determine the quality of our lives and to a large extent their wisdom.

Nonuse:
An NF will often hide emotions. Anger will be introjected and bottled up. The fear of embarrassment in a shy, reserved nature will make this tendency more common in the introverted NFs. The calm exterior does not suggest the tempest they are enduring on the inside. As a result, they can be mistakenly seen, at times, as unemotional.

"Not emotional" as a description of the NF is a contradiction in terms. They are the emotional temperament. They attempt to be unemotional at times, but they achieve giving that impression for short periods of time only. Born emotional, they must be emotional. Nonuse is hard to imagine in an NF.

Overuse:
Overuse is really a loss of control for the NF. When emotions are out of control they are in a state of overuse.

Emotions are such powerful elements of the human psyche that they can do untold damage when not managed appropriately. Control is the power to direct or restrain, the creation of a dam to stop unwanted overflow, or the redirection of emotions expressed with a wrong purpose to a new purpose. Therefore, control must be achieved or emotions can flood the mind's landscape, becoming overuse.

For the NF, one of life's prime lessons is to learn emotional control and only in control is intelligence found. Every time emotions appear in the NF they must be evaluated and their appropriateness addressed. Although the control of their emotions is challenging, it is where the NFs distinguish themselves.

Misuse:
Emotions can be misused, and are daily. We blindly follow them when we shouldn't. We use them for our own purposes, and we crush others with their power, all in our own selfish interests at times. A library of books could not contain all the possible misuses of emotions.

If the NF develops the strength of personal integrity and authenticity, becoming ethically responsible, they build a wall against the misuse of their emotions and create personal values that will guide them to success. For the NF, a firm set of values is an imperative in achieving intelligent emotions.

Empathetic, Caring

Empathetic emotions can make the empathizer experience the same emotions as the person they are caring about, even become sick with them. Emotions can arise quickly when empathy is not restrained or when it takes control of us. The fact that they can incapacitate the empathizer is what some people seem to focus on when criticizing this strength. However, it is a powerful strength driven by very healthy emotions when not allowed to dominate and incapacitate.

Empathy is driven by emotions that care and is intensified by the NF's sensitivity and emotional richness. So intense are the emotions that are generated in some people that they can become overpowering, resulting in the empathizer losing themselves in the other person's woes. The problem with this incapacitation is it renders the empathizer of no help to the one who needs them.

Care and love are seen in most of the animal world, but in humans they can reach their zenith. Because we see them in the animal world we realize that care for others is somehow an essential element for all creatures that have even a primitive self consciousness. The need for empathy can be seen in how social welfare and intimate bonding among individuals is encouraged by it. Empathy also plays an important role in battling the negative emotions of selfishness, division, strife, hatred, and violence.

Not only is this a necessary emotion to help stem the tide of humans destroying humans or humans suffering alone but in intensifying a love that drives the human heart to humanitarian goals. Empathetic people crave the feelings of love, care, empathy, and sacrifice for others, some even at the cost of their own lives.

Empathy is a product of love and caring and we all know the payback that these warm emotions produce. It is unique in care because it enters into the suffering of someone else, not just suffering for them or together with them.

KEY THOUGHT/ACTION: Empathy shares the pain of others and cements spirits as one.

Nonuse:
Sensitivity and emotional concern feed into empathy and therefore the nonuse of empathy would in part negate the usefulness of these emotions as well. The NF who understands that he has been made supersensitive would not think of not being empathetic. What appears as a nonuse of this strength in the NF is often an attempt at hiding the emotions that they feel will be too strong for them to handle.

However, anger or hurt will also cause the NF to be non-empathetic. They will withdraw from people who hurt them and then for a time they may very well be non-caring as well as distant. The solution is for them to dissolve the anger and hurt and then they will return to their loving, caring, empathetic selves.

Overuse:
When the NF overuses empathy, they become so engaged in the pain or hurt of others that they can damage their own emotional and physical health. It is hard for them to stop because the emotions of empathy are so strong and they keep getting pulled in by the logic that says "we must help people who are hurt and if we don't we will feel worse than we feel when we empathize with their pain."

Overuse is a problem for all oversensitive individuals. They must be made to see that damaging the caregiver will not lead to the best help for the one who suffers.

Misuse:
Aside from overuse, is there a misuse of empathy? Yes, the deceitful, blood succor who uses empathy to worm their way into someone's pocket book while posing as their loving caregiver is the scum of the care-giving world. The emotion of guilt is not felt by such people since they have probably long since numbed their conscience and drained their soul of human kindness.

Humanitarian

There is little difference between the SJ's "Good Samaritan" strength and the NF's humanitarian posture. Both have a concern for the individual and the world. NFs seem to report a dominant concern for human welfare and we could add for the preservation and welfare of the environment that supports the human race.

While all NFs tend to sympathize with humanitarian causes, the passion for this strength seems to vary considerably among NFs. Some will rate it as midway among their concerns or even less, and some rate it as a major issue. Humanitarian feelings can occur in any temperament and any person and are often fueled by personal experiences.

The emotions that drive the strength are positive and healthy, exercising love and care on a global or individual scale. When the passion is strong, it becomes a cause that they must defend, inspiring very committed crusaders. The emotions can then change, exhibiting more passion for the cause than for individuals.

KEY THOUGHT/ACTION: The passion for life is an expression of the NF's tender love.

Nonuse:
Some NFs, having become overwhelmed with personal concerns, are not observably humanitarian. Others have become jaded by the scams that operate in the name of human kindness. If the NF is not involved with humanitarian causes they are still, somewhere in their hearts, caring for someone deeply, and few are really devoid of the use of this strength. Nonuse does not carry inevitable emotional damage for them.

Overuse:
Many have devoted their lives to humanitarian issues and who can say they are misguided? The line that marks overuse is

drawn by values and the values that concern us most vary greatly with individuals. Each makes his own judgment and each must respect the opinion of others. We have overused it when devotion to some humanitarian cause ends in avoiding our individual responsibilities.

The emotions that drive the use and overuse of this strength can blind some NFs to other needs. The adjusting of values paves the way to creating a healthy balance.

Misuse:
Misuse of a humanitarian drive can occur when personal gain enters to rob the cause of its pure motives. These emotions of personal gain drive the scams.

Seekers of Harmony, Haters of Discord

All NFs are desperate seekers of harmony. Disharmony disturbs their ability to function smoothly and can often demotivate them completely. It is a cry for consensus, sympathy, fellow feelings, oneness, and more than anything, the absence of discord and strife. Gandhi, an NF if ever there was one, went without food for weeks to show his concern for the lack of harmony among his people. Paul of Tarsus (another NF) writes, "I beg you to all agree." A meaningful togetherness without bickering and strife sums up the aims of harmony. Due to the NF's high sensitivity, any disharmony not only gets a response from them but shakes them to the core and causes a steep rise of apprehension. Disharmony threatens all they stand for.

Harmony brings peaceful, pleasant feelings and, being sensitive to atmosphere and the slightest change in emotions, these feelings come as a warm kind breeze that soothes the NF's psyche. The inner world is so important they cannot neglect its cries. They thrive when it operates in a world of peace and love.

KEY THOUGHT/ACTION: Harmony is the inner condition that maximizes the chances of motivation for the NF.

Nonuse:
When discord is present the NF looks for the exit. They feel the pain of strife in a deep and personal way. The discord is personally felt and upsets their emotional equilibrium. This is true for all of us but so much more destructive of the NF's ability to function.

Nonuse also robs the NF not only of motivation but of the ability to continue with a task, demotivating them and, of course, fouling up their creative functions. This is enough of a disturbance, but discord also angers and hurts the NF. Emotions run rampant with discord hammering in their minds. Like the SJ who shatters under a sense of insecurity, the NF falls apart in the presence of discord.

Overuse:
Harmony is not everything. Overuse is a nervous loss of ability to manage the emotions that arise from discord. Sometimes discord can be the catalyst that leads to good things and creative events. So, the NF who caves in at all disharmony, overusing their desire for peace, may miss the opportunities and lessons that strife and disagreement can teach us.

NFs need harmony, but they must also learn to manage their emotions when disharmony hits, to live through the personal pain and solve the people issues by the use of creative people skills and the positive use of their emotions.

Misuse:
Any NF can feel the need of harmony so much that they elevate it to a status it does not deserve. Harmony is a great goal, but it is not the greatest goal. Love is a greater goal and so is goodness.

The cry for harmony can therefore be used to manipulate others, and with emotional strength the NF can be both effective and guilty of this. For their own productivity and health, the NF must learn the true value and place of harmony in a given situation and learn to manage discord and conflict. Your NF child will need a lot of help as they struggle to handle their emotions.

Kindhearted

> *The highest form of wisdom is kindness.*
> *~ The Talmud*

Love must be supported by kindness. Kindness is love in action. Although love goes so much further than kindness in its emotional achievements, kindness is essential to love. The emotions of kindness are similar to love. In the NF, because of hypersensitivity, opportunities for being kind are often found where others would not see them, and the feelings of a compelling need to do all they can to show kindness can take over the NF before they realize it. They may not detect it in themselves. Emotions are the speedsters of the brain, remember, and couple speed with over-familiarity at being kind, and the NF is on automatic mode.

There are times when the NF will not notice an opportunity to be kind. Their inner world can be engaged in some intense pursuit, muting the outer world's sounds and sights. It can be hard for the NF to break away from inflamed or even simply passionate thoughts, dreams, or plans. Hurt will quickly dispense with the urge to be kind. If lost in imagination they can be truly lost to the world for a time. There are many conditions that make this goodhearted emotion exit their consciousness.

There are also times when they won't consider being kind. Whenever angered and fighting to control their emotions, they can feel too emotionally overwhelmed to be who in their better moments they prefer to be. Kindness and anger can be opposites, and then they can't occupy the same mind-space at the same time.

Kindness evokes comforting emotions that result from friendliness, generosity, and considerateness, all of which lift the NF's sense of self-worth for a time, making them feel worthy of the attention of others. All emotions have their own payback.

KEY THOUGHT/ACTION: Sensitivity, empathy, and other emotions inspire kindness and call us to love.

Nonuse:
When disturbed and when they fall into their weaknesses, the NF temperament can be anything but kindhearted. They can hurt and lash out only to feel the pain of guilt and to apologize for their actions. An apology for actions can be more an apology for failing to be who they really want to be. The damage is great from falling into this weakness and can be a persistent cause of a low self-image.

Overuse:
Of course, we can be too kind when we give things or our time too liberally. We can enable those who need to stand on their own two feet. We can continue to hurt ourselves or make unhelpful decisions about the use of our time, etc. Kindness needs to be monitored with prudence and wisdom. Again, it is the strong emotions that draw the NF into unexamined kindness.

Misuse:
For selfish purposes, kindness can be used by the con artist and is an important emotion exploited by scams as well. Goodness can be mimicked and used for any destructive cause. It hurts to think of the mischief and the criminal acts that have been done under the guise of kindheartedness.

People Skills, Diplomatic

"A little honey will get you further than a critical statement," my father would say, (or you may prefer the American interpretation: "Honey catches more flies than vinegar") and the emotionally skillful handling of people beats clumsy, sour approaches any day. The emotional intelligence is obvious as is the social intelligence in this strength.

Emotions arising from the success found in motivating others, solving problems, handling conflict, making friends, quieting anger or dealing well with almost any human disturbance bolsters the feelings of the NF. They feel connected, useful, and meaningful to others. They seriously want to be all things to all people.

NFs practice the use of language when young and are well rewarded when they make it a lifelong study. The emotions inspired by learning, helping, being effective, and from the power the diplomat feels when successfully bringing people together is the NF's natural high. So much is achievable with people skills alone. The world of human interaction is open to the person who has honed the skills of proficient communication.

KEY THOUGHT/ACTION: Become a master of people skills if you would be significant in the lives of others.

Nonuse:
The nonuse of people skills and the harm it can do is well understood. It's what you say and how you say it that opens the way to people's hearts or slams the door violently in their face. People skills are a way of showing respect to others and of not charging into their delicate emotions, wreaking havoc and creating resistance and anger.

Instead of pointing out the myriads of ways we can do harm with less than adequate people skills, let's understand the pain it can cause to us and to others and praise the NF's list of strengths that make us recognize them as the natural diplomats of our race.

Overuse:
We can use this strength to do almost anything in the world of relationships Overuse is a misuse with few limits to the harm it can do.

Misuse:
Manipulation, deceit, selfish gain, and many other emotionally powered takeovers of people's minds stain the human experience and have done so for as long as humans have been around.   The misusers look for any vulnerability and exploit it. This is an ugly lack of goodness and a clear lack of intelligence if the definition of intelligence is what does not hurt others or ourselves.

Real, Authentic, Ethical

We have emphasized the inner character of the NF's life. Disturbances of the mind and personal values vigorously stir their emotions. To be less than real and authentic is unsettling to the NF, stirring strong feelings of guilt and unworthiness.

NFs require the stabilizing feeling of being authentic, which to them is more than just consistency of behavior, so they can feel good about themselves. Authentic is the feeling of being consistent, good, and ethical, even being right when it comes to moral issues or justice.   It is also knowing that our values and behavior agree.

For the NF, this inner authenticity builds a strong self-confidence, if not in themselves, in the rightness of whatever they hold dear. Emotionally, they are deeply rewarded by this sense of ethical reality and it makes them hold their heads high. This is a foundational strength that creates confidence.

KEY THOUGHT/ACTION: Authentic at the core means strength and confidence in the world.

Nonuse:
Because this is a foundational need for what has been called the spiritual temperament, any lack of it is devastating to emotional intelligence. In history, some NFs known to be devoid of all ethical values have become tyrants and monsters, powered by negative emotions that they have allowed to possess them. In order to function in their unethical ways they have convinced themselves that they are right. Sadly, at times we believe ourselves when we shouldn't.

Overuse:
The overuse of an ethical standard creates a holier-than-thou attitude and ends in the making of a Pharisee. Overuse is distasteful and unattractive, blinding the user to the reality about themselves. Emotional health is unknown in such an individual.

Misuse:
Misuse is again unbridled. Overuse is a misuse. Fortunately for most NFs, a low self-esteem keeps them from ill-founded claims of perfection. Being real, authentic, and ethical should be a measure founded in some objective standards to avoid self deceit. The emotional unintelligence goes without saying for the misuse of this important strength.

Romantic

As we might think, the word romantic comes to us from the French word *romanz*. In English it's a word with many shades of meaning. The idea of something being mysterious yet exciting can be romantic. The word is always related to love in some form such as an atmosphere that stirs our senses of beauty, or just a feeling of luxury, perhaps a sentimental memory or experience, something we idealize or an idealized sense of reality. All of these emotions are hidden in the word. Sunsets, writings, pieces of art, music, words, looks, almost anything appealing can be seen as romantic if it stimulates and awakens feelings of goodness and love.

The NF responds ardently to these feelings. They may or may not be referring to what we call romantic love when they call themselves romantic, but they are romantic because of their high sensitivity to beauty and appeal. They are truly romantic in their interpretation and expression of life.

Such feelings of appreciation can be developed but whether trained or not, they characterize the NF's view of the world. Like the French, the NF claims romance as an intelligent emotion, extremely satisfying.

KEY THOUGHT/ACTION: See the world through romantic eyes and you will always be alive and thankful.

Nonuse:
The nonuse of this strength is important or not depending on the person's evaluation of it. For those to whom it is revitalizing and a necessary stimulation for love to be awakened, a lack of it is quite depressing. When romance is not present, some NFs can be affected gravely, especially if it is absent for long periods of time. Emotions of worthlessness and emptiness can be evoked by a simple absence of romance.

Overuse:
The cry for romance is not the most important urge in life and therefore it can be overdone. It can, however, affect all waking thoughts and dominate the mind, making it an obsession of sorts. When the NF depends on it like an addict depends on their drugs or simply overuses it, their lives can be destabilized. Romance is the feeling of emotions stimulated by appeal together with the treasuring of those feelings, so it is easy to overuse such a pleasant craving.

Misuse:
Stories abound of men and women overusing romantic emotions to deceive others and create personal gain. The all-consuming nature of love makes people vulnerable to the

romantic abuser. When expectations vanish and love is lost, severe emotional trauma can result.

Introspective

Looking inside can be encouraging or disturbing. This strength is active on both the light and dark side of the mind. Therefore, it can be intelligent or unintelligent according to the results it produces and the judgments it makes.

Introspection such as we find in the Hebrew psalmists words, "Search me oh God and know my heart..." reminds us of our lack of inner knowledge, which encourages our prayer for help at understanding ourselves. Introspection is a journey of openness and candor into our thoughts, motives, intents, and desires. When positive it can be a revelation, a cleansing or a renewal of our understanding. It appreciates the good and notes anything that fails to meet with our approval.

Introspection also searches the meanings of guilt feelings and seeks to improve and cleanse the mind and heart from the emotional stains of our actions. In this pursuit introspection can produce beneficial results.

KEY THOUGHT/ACTION: "Know thyself," wrote the ancient Greeks, and they meant this for positive purposes and to affect positive results.

Nonuse:
We hide from ourselves to avoid the hurt of unwelcome discoveries and we refrain from too many internal visits. Too much introspection can hurt us and too little self inspection can do the same. A balance is healthy, so the NF should use the strength but only for positive purposes of health and healing.

Overuse:
Too concerned with self judgment and self examination, making every slight miscue a cause for severe disapproval, the NF can make this strength into an enemy of personal

growth when overused. More than perhaps any other strength, introspection can breed an atmosphere of hurt and self-degradation, continually lowering the NF's self-esteem.

A negative overuse of introspection can lead to depression and a self-condemnatory spirit, which infects the mind. It will destroy all that is good and loving in the NF.

Misuse:
Introspection should never be used for self condemnation. Whenever we discover our failings, it is for the purposes of forgiveness, cleansing, and learning. Mistakes offer a "self-taught university course" in self discovery and improvement, not self blame and disparagement. Emotions that condemn live on the dark side of the mind. Introspection, if not guarded, follows their every move.

Perfectionists, Must Do and Be Right

The strength named here as perfectionist is not to be confused with perfectionism. Perfectionism is an obsessive disease of the mind by which we are sincerely deceived. Then, is it intelligent to aim at perfection? Yes, because as limited creatures we are not perfect and fall short of perfection, but when we aim at it, we get much closer than when we aim at some lesser goal.

The aim is not the whole problem: it is what we do after we have missed the mark that also matters. Do we whip ourselves and condemn our efforts or do we accept our best attempt and seek to improve on it? What perfectionists do with failure forecasts the state of their self-esteem. As long as the perfectionist aims at perfection and accepts the results without self blame it is an intelligent exercise.

The emotions that follow the attempt are what point to the perfectionist's struggle to do right or to perfectionism. Crippling emotions point to perfectionism, while emotions that create a determination to do better or to simply walk away satisfied indicate helpful and hopefully motivating feelings. No one is a perfectionist in everything and the NF chooses his perfectionist tendencies. The message is to avoid perfectionism.

KEY THOUGHT/ACTION: Perfection is a great aim as long as we don't make it an unwavering demand.

Nonuse:
Not to call ourselves to the highest standard is to fail before we start. If we don't use this strength and develop the emotions that motivate it we will sell our life short. An easy target leaves us unchallenged and without the emotions that exhilarate us when we do better than we expected or hoped. Nonuse is living for the status quo and forfeiting the positive emotions that arriving near to perfection brings.

Overuse:
We all know the dangers of overuse. This strength is inherent with the possibility of defeat and too much defeat can hurt the sensitive spirit of the NF, particularly when they are negatively focused. No one said perfection must be achieved in one giant leap either. A series of small stretches lead us more effectively to the ultimate goal of perfection or so near to it that we thrill with the accomplishment. That way we can avoid the feelings of defeat and stay motivated.

Emotions of failure are potent triggers that can activate that consummate failure called giving up. The spirit of all the temperaments is resilient and wants another chance. While focused on the positive let's return and try again, but if the negative has hold of us, let's take a break from our efforts at achieving perfection.

Misuse:
The perfect is a worthy goal so any misuse will be for damaging purposes either to others or ourselves. Demanding that others be perfect is an obvious misuse of this strength. Demanding that we be perfect is the same misuse.

Abstract in Speech

Like the NT, the NF speaks of abstract things more than the SP and SJ. Their language is not as technical as the NT since their subject matter is more subjective and personal, unless like the NT they are engaged in technical matters.

NFs are known for their use of metaphors and superlatives, both of which invoke emotive words. Analogies that use concrete descriptions are used to illustrate what is subjective or abstract. Abstract ideas and concepts like love and mercy, justice and peace fill their minds and stir the NF's emotions deeply.

Because there are no concrete terms for values and for some beliefs we must compare them to concrete realities to make our meaning clear to all. Hence the language of metaphor and simile. It is like this or that. They also often personify ideas and give them the characteristics of people and even of God.

The intelligence of such a practice is in creating a way to mentally grasp, with emotional content, ideas and thoughts too ethereal or passionate for non-emotive words to convey.

KEY THOUGHT/ACTION: The abstract world needs abstract terms to unlock its relevance and meaning.

Nonuse:
The NF is lost when they can't employ abstract terms. The human is the most complex organism in the universe and concrete realities fail when speaking of a human's inner complexities and concepts. Nonuse is not likely in an NF.

Overuse:
Overuse can be a communication problem but the NF takes care of this by their frequent love and use of analogy and symbolism. Sometimes their poetic vein is overused and they appear to be flowery and out of touch with the realities of this

world's expectations. Say it plainly is what an NT or NF may hear at times as a mild criticism from the SP or SJ.

Misuse:
When not definitive enough abstract language can be misused because it falls short of communicating accurately. Emotions are stirred intelligently with accurate and emotive language.

Conclusion

Everyone wants to be intelligently emotional. The achievement is among the top achievements possible for us as humans and certainly necessary. We are imperfect beings and the pressures mounted by emotional urges are our most challenging experiences. Hence, make intelligent emotions and emotional intelligence your goal.

Use the last chapters as a check list. Don't focus on some grand distant goal of emotional excellence. That next step is all you need to be centered on, and the celebration of its accomplishment will fuel your energies for the one that follows.

Living in our strengths and perfecting them is the only path to a lifestyle of intelligent emotional behavior. Therefore, the attention you give to the final chapters of the book should not be neglected. The lifestyle that results will be a continual emotional high. Nothing surpasses the fulfilling feeling of being the master of your emotions while at the same time being what you are designed to be. As I have said in *INNERKINETICS,* follow your blueprint (the way you have been designed) if you want to be your best. You can also learn about your inner drives (your temperament) in-depth in the same book.

It is trite but true to say we only have one life to live. Let's live it with an intelligent understanding of ourselves and of our emotions. It's spring as I write and growth is in full swing. The weather changed the other night and a frost bit the young leaves of some trees, but I notice the trees are struggling, despite the setback, to sprout new leaves. Our lives must not bypass the struggles and excitement of the season of growth; a lifelong season for the development of our inner lives.

Appendices

Intelligently Emotional

Appendix One - The Temperament Key for Adults

Instructions

Both the Adult Temperament Key and Child Temperament Key used in InnerKinetics® have been developed using the principles of research into temperament that Myers-Briggs, Keirsey, and Harkey-Jourgensen have used for the development of their assessments. These principles, when used in assessments, have proved very reliable and can be depended upon. Any of the above named assessments of temperament are excellent guides to the discovery of how you are made on the inside.

As long as you carefully follow the instructions for the Temperament Key presented here, you should get excellent results.

This is a very positive assessment. We are looking for your strengths, not your weaknesses. There are no wrong answers since it is a self-evaluation. However, be as accurate as possible. Read these instructions carefully since a knowledgeable guide is not looking over your shoulder who you can't ask for help. It is imperative that you answer according to these instructions.

- Answer these questions according to your preferences (what you prefer), not according to what you think others would have you become.
- Answer each question individually. Don't try to be consistent.
- Aim to get through the key in about 15 minutes or less.
- Think carefully about each answer; but avoid over-thinking, which can lead to confusion. If you are over-thinking, ask yourself: "What am I the most?"
- Again, let me put it this way: You will see yourself as both (a) and (b) in some of the questions. Your answer should be

what you see yourself to <u>be</u> the <u>most</u>, or what you <u>prefer</u> the <u>most.</u>
- Your preferences are often different at home than at work. This can be due to the fact that at work certain things are required of you and, therefore, they have become your work preferences. You prefer to do it that way at work since that's what is good for you. If your work preferences differ from your home preferences, answer according to your home preferences.
- We want to know what really beats in your breast, what really satisfies, fulfills or pleases you the most.

The results should be accurate, but if you attend one of my seminars ask to be checked again. It's a service we provide. When you read the descriptions of the temperaments in Appendix II, you will determine whether they match your results in the Temperament Key. If they do not match the descriptions, then you answered with something else in mind, and you will need to switch to the temperament most like you.

This check on your answers is very helpful. The ones who are most likely to be confused about themselves are the NFs. They are the complicated temperament and have the greatest difficulties in understanding themselves for that understandable reason. Now, proceed with careful thought.

<u>Note:</u> You may also go to our website at www.raywlincoln.com/ RESOURCES where you will find a free, downloadable Adult Temperament Key.

ADULT TEMPERAMENT KEY

Check (A) or (B) for each question. Please answer ALL questions.

1. At social gatherings do you prefer to
   _____ A. Socialize with everyone
   _____ B. Stick to your friends

2. Are you more in touch with
   _____ A. The real world
   _____ B. The world inside your mind; the world of possibilities

3. Do you rely more on, or take more notice of
   _____ A. Your experiences
   _____ B. Your hunches or gut feelings

4. Are you (most of the time)
   _____ A. Cool, calm, and collected
   _____ B. Friendly and warm

5. When evaluating people do you tend to be
   _____ A. Impersonal and frank
   _____ B. Personal and considerate

6. Do you mostly feel a sense of
   _____ A. Urgency/upset if you are not on time
   _____ B. Relaxed about time.

7. When you see a mess do you
   _____ A. Have an urge to tidy it up
   _____ B. Feel reasonably comfortable living with it

8. Would you describe yourself as
   _____ A. Outgoing/demonstrative/easy to approach
   _____ B. Somewhat reserved/private

9. Which are you best at
   _____ A. Focusing on details
   _____ B. Catching the big picture, the connections, the patterns

10. Children should be
    _____ A. Made to be more responsible
    _____ B. Encouraged to exercise their imagination and make-
         believe more

11. When making decisions, are you more influenced by
_____ A. The facts or impersonal data
_____ B. Personal feelings

12. Do you feel more yourself when giving
_____ A. Honest criticism
_____ B. Support, approval, and encouragement

13. Do you work best
_____ A. Scheduled; to deadlines
_____ B. Unscheduled; no deadlines

14. For a vacation do you prefer to
_____ A. Plan ahead of time
_____ B. Choose as you go

15. When you are with others do you usually
_____ A. Initiate the conversation
_____ B. Listen and tend to be slow to speak

16. Most of the time, facts
_____ A. Should be taken at face value.
_____ B. Suggest ideas, possibilities, or principles.

17. Do you mostly feel
_____ A. In touch with the real world
_____ B. Somewhat removed, lost in thought

18. When in an argument or discussion do you care more about
_____ A. Defending your position and being right
_____ B. Finding harmony and agreement

19. With others do you tend to be
_____ A. Firm
_____ B. Gentle

20. Do you see yourself as
_____ A. Predictable
_____ B. Unpredictable

21. Do you mostly prefer to
_____ A. Get things done; come to closure
_____ B. Explore alternatives; keep options open

22. After two hours at a party are you
_____ A. More energized than when you arrived
_____ B. Losing your energy

23. Which best describes you
_____ A. Down to earth, practical
_____ B. Imaginative, an idea person

24. Which do you finally rely on more
_____ A. Common sense
_____ B. Your intuition/insights or your own analysis

25. In other people, which appeals to you most
_____ A. A strong will
_____ B. Warm emotions

26. Are you more controlled by
_____ A. Your head/thought
_____ B. Your heart/emotions

27. Are you typically
_____ A. Eager to get decisions made
_____ B. Not keen on making decisions

28. On the whole do you spend your money
_____ A. Cautiously
_____ B. Impulsively

29. When you have lost energy, do you find yourself mostly
_____ A. Seeking out people
_____ B. Seeking out solitude/a quiet corner

30. Do dreamers
_____ A. Annoy you somewhat
_____ B. Fascinate and interest you

31. Do you rely more
_____ A. On your five senses
_____ B. On your sixth sense/intuition

32. Are you more
_____ A. Tough-minded
_____ B. Tenderhearted

33. Would you more likely choose to be
_____ A. Truthful
_____ B. Tactful

34. Do you see yourself as more
_____ A. Serious and determined
_____ B. Relaxed and easygoing

35. Do you feel more comfortable when
_____ A. Things are decided
_____ B. Your options are still open

36. Would you say you mostly
_____ A. Show your feelings readily
_____ B. Are private about your feelings and keep them inside

37. Would you prefer
_____ A. To be in touch with reality
_____ B. To exercise a creative imagination

38. Is your way of thinking more
_____ A. Conventional
_____ B. Original and creative

39. What motivates you more
_____ A. Solid evidence
_____ B. An emotional appeal

40. Would you rather be known for
_____ A. Being a consistent thinker
_____ B. Having harmonious relationships

41. Do you tend to
_____ A. Value routines
_____ B. Dislike routines

42. Do you live more with
_____ A. A little sense of urgency
_____ B. A leisurely pace

43. Do you have
_____ A. Many friends and count them all your close friends
_____ B. Few friends, and only one or two that are deep friends

44. Do you place more emphasis on what you see
_____ A. With your physical eyes
_____ B. With your mind's eye

45. Are you
_____ A. Thick skinned; not hurt easily
_____ B. Thin skinned; hurt easily

46. When you are asked to create a "To Do" list, does it
_____ A. Seem like the right thing to do and do you feel it will be
           helpful
_____ B. Bug you and seem more like an unnecessary chore

47. Which word attracts you most or describes you best?
_____ A. Talkative
_____ B. Quiet

48. Which words attract you most or describe you best?
_____ A. Present realities
_____ B. Future hopes

49. Which word(s) attracts you most or describe(s) you best?
_____ A. Logic
_____ B. Loving heart

50. Which word attracts you most or describes you best?
_____ A. Plan
_____ B. Impulse

51. Which word attracts you most or describes you best?
_____ A. Party
_____ B. Home

52. Which word(s) attracts you most or describe(s) you best?
_____ A. Common sense
_____ B. Vision

53. Which word attracts you most or describes you best?
_____ A. Justice
_____ B. Mercy

54. Which word attracts you most or describes you best?
_____ A. Concerned
_____ B. Carefree

Intelligently Emotional

SCORE SHEET

Instructions:

1. *Place an ☒ in the appropriate column (A or B) to indicate the answer you chose for each numbered question. [Please note that the numbers run from left to right across the chart.]*
2. *Count the number of "As" in column #1 and write that number in box "c" (above the "E"). Count the number of "Bs" in column #1 and write that number in box "d" (above the "I").*
3. *Count the number of "As" in column #2 and write that number in box "e." Count the number of "Bs" in column #2 and write that number in box "f."*
4. *Count the number of "As" in column #3 and write that number box "g." Count the number of "Bs" in column #3 and write that number in box "h."*
5. *Add the number of "As" for columns 2 and 3 together and write the total in box "i." Add the number of "Bs" for columns 2 and 3 and write that number in box "j."*
6. *Repeat the steps in instructions 3-5 above for columns 4/5 and 6/7.*
7. *Which did you have more of, "Es" or "Is"? _____*
    Which did you have more of, "Ss" or "Ns"? _____
    Which did you have more of, "Ts" or "Fs"? _____
    Which did you have more of, "Js" or "Ps"? _____
8. *In the four letters you listed in Instruction #7, which two-letter combination below is present? Circle it!*

S and P   S and J   N and T   N and F

334

	1			2			3			4			5			6			7	
	A	**B**		**A**	**B**		**A**	**B**		**A**	**B**		**A**	**B**		**A**	**B**		**A**	**B**
1			2			3			4			5			6			7		
8			9			10			11			12			13			14		
15			16			17			18			19			20			21		
22			23			24			25			26			27			28		
29			30			31			32			33			34			35		
36			37			38			39			40			41			42		
43			44						45						46					
47			48						49						50					
51			52						53						54					
						g	h					m	n					s	t	
						e	f					k	l					q	r	
	c	d				i	j					o	p					u	v	
	E	I				S	N					T	F					J	P	

335

Follow These Steps to Finalize Your Temperament Identification

1. Read the descriptions of the temperaments that follow and select the temperament that is most like you. You may find that not all the aspects of a temperament truly reflect who you are. That's not uncommon. We are individuals and all are a little different, so what you are looking for is which of the four descriptions fits you best. Which is most like you?
2. You may find that you see a little of yourself in several or all of the temperaments. Don't worry. We all imitate others and therefore "borrow" strengths and characteristics from other temperaments for many reasons, not least to meet what others demand of us. What we need to know is which temperament we really are? As the research indicates we are one temperament, not a mixture of temperaments, and those glimpses of ourselves in other temperaments are simply our adopted strengths. Borrowed strengths or characteristics are just that, borrowed. Our own strengths are the ones that satisfy and fulfill us when we use them. We must know them.
3. Does the one that fits you best agree with your temperament key results? The two letters of the temperament you have chosen must occur in the four letters that your temperament key gave you. If they do, no further decision is needed.
4. If they don't, then you can go back and check your answers to the temperament key. Are they really what your preferences are and not what others have led you to believe you are or what you would like to be based on expectations others have given you? Make sure you answered the questions as instructed. A small number of people who take the temperament key may find it doesn't seem to ring true with who they perceive they are from reading the descriptions. If so, go with what you perceive is the temperament that fits you best.

The Four Temperaments

SP

They crave action, excitement, and stimulation, be it in sport, physical skills with the use of tools of all kinds, the performing arts, or even fine art. They are after a "good time" and only the introverted ones can happily sit still. SPs love freedom and act spontaneously; therefore, they do not take to authority with relish. Possessing a natural talent for all things physical, they can be the world's playmates. They are lovable, exciting, adventuresome, and brave risk-takers.

SPs are pleasant, tactical, and squeeze the last drop of excitement out of each moment. Adaptable, carefree, optimistic, individualistic, they crave self expression. Tolerance accompanies competitiveness and a generous spirit is usually seen in them.

Does this describe you best?

SJ

They are hard-working (many are workaholics) with a responsible work ethic, and they crave a feeling of security, which makes them somewhat cautious in their adventures. They coined the motto "Be prepared," and they like everything in order. Home, family, and responsibilities, all cast around rules and regulations. This makes them feel comfortable. They are the solid citizens and the backbone of society. They feel a sense of duty and feel drawn to be useful (helpmates). If someone does not do their duty it irks them.

Change can be unnerving and security is paramount if they are to be happy. They are more conservative than the SP and they like to feel in control of their world. They tend more to worry and pessimism rather than an optimistic attitude that all will be well. They must struggle to ensure all is well. Their nature is more serious and they are the guardians of society.

Does this describe you best?

NT

We could call this one the ingenious/technology temperament, although everyone craves the benefits of technology these days. They are curious and inventive, often finding their way into science and engineering occupations. NTs want to understand everything and build things. Often they are driven and compulsive, but display few people skills naturally. They are hard-working if what they are doing interests them. Feelings are not worn on the surface. NTs want to find new ways of doing things.

Facts, theories, strategies fill their minds and fuel their determination and focus. All things logical and only what makes sense guides them. They must feel independent, calm, cool, and intelligent. Scientific inquiry, mathematical, precision, and logical consistency in a skeptical mind describes them well. NTs are mindmates.

Does this describe you best?

NF

They care very deeply about people and their world and want to lead people to their potential and to feelings of wholeness. NFs are very passionate, tender, loving, soulmates who want to please. Their inner world is frustrated with struggles, and they are the influencers of society, often finding their way into higher education (as do the NTs) and into teaching, counseling, and personal growth. They champion causes that benefit society and provide for the betterment of humankind. They long to better themselves together with the aforementioned urge to help others be all that they can be. They are emotionally rich and complicated and are easily hurt with their emotions very near the surface.

NFs are influencers, empathetic, passionate, emotional, sensitive, introspective, and lovers of harmony among people. Mostly they are perfectionists, self demanding, idealists, imaginative, and visionaries living in the world of dreams both practical and fanciful. To these self-actualizers, life must have meaning and significance.

Does this describe you best?

If you are still puzzled or unsure of which temperament you are and which describes you best, then go to my book, *InnerKInetics*, and all should soon become clear.

Intelligently Emotional

Appendix Two - List of Strengths in Each Temperament

SP Strengths, Featuring Self Expression

Lives happily in the present moment

Brave, bold, daring

Spontaneous, impulsive

Effective, tactical, aggressive

Easily excited

Wants to make an impact

Lighthearted, playful, tolerant

Ultimate optimist

Action!

Focuses on the physical senses — graceful

Generous nature

Dramatic, concrete language

SJ Strengths, Featuring Rules and Regulations

Lives tied to the past

Careful, cautious, concerned

Thoughtful and prepared

Responsible, dependable, solid work ethic

Do what is right, law abiding

Strong need to belong, social, respectable

Steady, not easily shaken

Trusts authority

Supervisors, managers, systems , routines

Stoical

Logistical in work and play

Communicates with the details

Good Samaritans, helpmates

Non-dramatic, concrete speech

NT Strengths, Featuring Independence

Time is relevant to the task

Strong will, determined

Strategic, theoretical systems

Intense curiosity

Questioning, skeptical

Independent, self reliant

Calm, cool, collected

Logical, reasonable, must make sense

Ingenious

Efficient, effective, competent, achievers

Abstract in speech

NF Strengths, Featuring Idealism and Sensitivity

1. Strengths that Relate to Future Time

Lives in and for the future

Idealists, dreamers

Imaginative

Passionate, enthusiastic, value-based decisions, eager to learn

Trusting

Personal growth, meaning, significance

2. Strengths that Relate to Sensitivity

Sensitive

Intuitive, insightful

Emotional, from love to hate

Empathetic, caring

Humanitarian

Seekers of harmony, haters of discord

Kindhearted

People skills, diplomatic

Real and authentic, ethical

Romantic

Introspective

Perfectionists, must do and be right

Abstract in speech

Appendix Three - The Meaning of the Four Categories and the Eight Letters

Category One: E or I

The E-I category is where we are asked if our preferences lie with the E or the I.

This category determines whether we are Extroverts or Introverts. Extroverts recharge their inner energies best when they make connections with people or things outside of themselves.   Introverts recharge their inner energies in solitude and want for others to give them their space to recharge and not interrupt this process. They recharge from within themselves best. How we recharge best defines who is an extrovert and who is an introvert.

Category Two: S or N

The S-N category is trying to determine how we prefer to gather our information or data from the world around us and inside us. We are asked questions to determine whether we prefer the S or N method of information gathering.

The S stands for Sensing and the N stands for iNtuition.

The S method prefers the use of our five physical senses: sight, hearing, taste, touch, and smell. The Ss use their five senses predominately and primarily rely on the information gathered in this way. They live in the outer world contentedly.

The Ns prefer to use their intuition, gut feelings, and rely heavily on how they respond inwardly to what they see, hear, touch, taste, and smell or what they sense that the five senses can't pick up. This method depends more on the meanings, possibilities, and ideas that intuition tells them are there and matter, things often beyond the reach of their conscious minds. The inner world is consulted more than the outer world. The meaning of an event is more important than the event itself. They live primarily inside themselves.

Category Three: T or F

The T stands for Thinking and the F for Feeling. In this category we are determining whether we prefer to make decisions on the information we have gathered from our world outside or inside of ourselves predominantly, by a thinking process or a feeling process.

The thinker relies heavily on what they perceive as the facts. The feeler consults the facts as well but must also consult their feelings to see how they feel about what the facts are indicating they should do. The thinker is not likely to consider much how they feel when they make decisions and the feeler can't decide without thinking of how they feel or how others might feel.

Category Four: J or P

The J-P category has been unfortunately named. The J originally stood for Judgment and the P for Perceiving. The problem is the Ps judge just as much as the Js and the Js perceive as much as the Ps, making the words meaningless unless they are used in a technical sense, hidden from the reader. Therefore, let's think of the J and P as different **lifestyles**, which is what they really reflect. With this choice we are asked to decide which lifestyle we are most comfortable with in daily life.

The J lifestyle is all about coming to closure and living with a sense of urgency. They live with more stress in their demanding lifestyle than do the Ps. The P lifestyle is more laid back and they don't like to come to closure, showing more spontaneity and less urgency.

We have not often thought of ourselves in these ways but they reliably tell us what throbs in our temperament and drives our preferences. Thinking like this, outside the box of regular understanding, will help us find ourselves and discover the best tools for emotional management and living in intelligent emotions.

Intelligently Emotional

350

Intelligently Emotional

Selected Bibliography

Bradbury, Travis and Greaves Jean. *The Emotional Intelligence Quick Book*, Fireside 2005.

Goleman, Daniel. *Emotional Intelligence*, Bantam Books, 1997.

----------Social Intelligence, Bantam Books, 2007.

LeDoux, Joseph. *The Emotional Brain*, Simon and Schuster, 1996.

Lincoln, Ray W. *InnerKinetics*, Apex, 2010.

----------*The InnerKinetics of Type*, Apex, 2012.

Orloff, Judith. *Emotional Freedom*, Harmony Books, 2009.

About the Author

RAY W. LINCOLN

Ray W. Lincoln is the bestselling author of *I May Frustrate You, but **I'm a Keeper*** and is the founder of Ray W. Lincoln & Associates. Ray's is a professional life coach and an expert in human nature. His 40 plus years of experience in speaking, teaching, and counseling began in New Zealand and have carried him professionally to Australia and the United States. He speaks with energy and enthusiasm before large and small audiences.

It was not by accident that he became the international speaker and coach that he is today and acquired the ability to guide so many to a happier, healthier, more fulfilled life. Ray has studied extensively in the fields of Philosophy, Temperament Psychology, and Personology.

A member of the National Speakers Association, his expertise has been used as a lecturer and professor, teacher and keynote speaker, seminar presenter, counselor, and coach. He teaches and leads in staff trainings, university student retreats, and parents' educational classes, as well as other seminars and training events. He also trains and mentors teachers, executives , and other professionals — all with the goal of understanding our own temperaments and those of others.

Ray lives with his wife, Mary Jo, in Littleton, Colorado where they enjoy hiking, snowshoeing, fly fishing, and all the beauty the Rocky Mountains offer. Both are highly involved in their work (which they feel is the most important and most fulfilling work of their entire career lives), both filling the roles for which they were designed, as they travel to speak to groups and to present seminars and workshops throughout the US.

Our website, www.raywlincoln.com, is a great place to order additional copies of:

I May Frustrate You, But I'm a Keeper
INNERKINETICS
A Journey Through Fear to Confidence
Introduction to Faith and the Temperaments
The InnerKinetics of Type

We also have additional FREE resources to help you. On our website you can:

- Sign up for our FREE monthly newsletter, which entitles you to receive 15% off all purchases at www.innerkinetics.com, www.imakeeperkid.com , and www.raywlincoln.com.
- Find more helpful resources and information about our services.

OUR SERVICES INCLUDE

Professional Life Coaching
Educational Seminars and Training
Keynote Addresses
Educational Materials
Free Monthly Newsletter

www.ingramcontent.com/pod-product-compliance
Lightning Source LLC
Chambersburg PA
CBHW071344280326
41927CB00039B/1684